"Francis Schaeffer was an amazing man—intellectually brilliant and set on truth, emotionally intense, devoted to God and compassionate; like Jeremiah, perplexed by the world, not because he didn't understand it but because he did. As one of his editors, I came to know him well, but only after he emerged as a writer. For me Colin Duriez fills in the fascinating details of his early years. Yes, this was the man I knew—one who was surprised by God as his influence grew from his pastoring small churches to teaching thousands in auditoriums around the world, from conversations one on one or with a handful of students to intellectual sparring with elite secular scholars and pundits. Duriez knows his subject; Schaeffer, the Jeremiah of the twentieth century, walks and talks again in these pages."

—JAMES W. SIRE, author of *The Universe Next Door* and
A Little Primer on Humble Apologetics

"An excellent biography of this influential thinker, mingling personal memories and theological analysis. A must for Schaeffer's admirers and those wanting to develop his heritage today."

—ALISTER E. MCGRATH, Professor of Historical Theology,
Oxford University; Senior Research Fellow,
Harris Manchester College, Oxford

Other Books by Colin Duriez

LITERARY WORKS
The C. S. Lewis Encyclopedia
The Inklings Handbook (with David Porter)
Tolkien and the Lord of the Rings: A Guide to Middle-Earth
A Field Guide to Narnia
A Field Guide to Harry Potter
The Poetic Bible (compiler)

BIOGRAPHY
Tolkien and C. S. Lewis: The Gift of Friendship
The C. S. Lewis Chronicles

HISTORY
AD 33: The Year That Changed the World

FRANCIS SCHAEFFER

an Authentic Life

COLIN DURIEZ

CROSSWAY BOOKS
WHEATON, ILLINOIS

Library of Congress Cataloging-in-Publication Data

Duriez, Colin.
   Francis Schaeffer : an authentic life / Colin Duriez.
     p. cm.
   Includes bibliographical references and index.
   ISBN 978-1-58134-857-6 (hc)
   1. Schaeffer, Francis A. (Francis August). 2. Christian biography.
3. L'Abri (Organization)—Biography. I. Title.
BR1725.S355D87   2008
267'.13092—dc22   2007051431

SH		17	16	15	14	13	12	11	10	09	08
15	14	13	12	11	10	9	8	7	6	5	4	3	2	1

To
Christopher and Paulette Catherwood

CONTENTS

Preface   9

1   Beginnings (1912–1935)   15

2   Pastor and Denominationalist (1935–1945)   33

3   New Vistas (1945–1948)   59

4   Switzerland (1948–1950)   81

5   Crisis and Catalyst (1951–1954)   103

6   The Shelter (1955–1960)   127

7   The Pilgrimage to L'Abri (1960–1976)   153

8   The Last Battles (1977–1984)   181

Appendix   205
The Undivided Schaeffer: A Retrospective Interview with Francis Schaeffer,
September 30, 1980

Acknowledgments   223

Bibliography   225

Index   231

PREFACE

H is preferred medium was talk—conversation, whether with an individual or with a large group of people. He had the uncanny knack of addressing an individual personally, even if one was sitting with several hundred other people. His tapes, books, and films are best seen as embodiments of his conversation or table talk. The overwhelming impression of those who met him briefly or more extensively, particularly in connection with his homely yet expansive community at L'Abri in Switzerland, was his kindness, a word that constantly occurs in people's memories of him, whether Dutch, English, American, Irish, or other nationality.

His attire was quirky and memorable, dapper in knee-breeches and colorful tops, a goatee beard he wore later in life adding to his artistic, cultured appearance, far from the stereotype of the evangelical pastor. He was cool, knew about Bob Dylan, Jackson Pollock, Merce Cunningham, the older Wittgenstein, the younger Heidegger, and neo-orthodoxy and spoke of postmodernism in the sixties before it was clearly *post*. He bluntly challenged evangelical and fundamentalist pietism and later superspirituality as "neo-platonic." This challenge left at least one of his students, me, wondering at the time how it was "neo" as well as "platonic," but it had the desired effect of leading to a spiritual pilgrimage that was often painful.

Francis Schaeffer was a small man whose giant passion for truth, for reality, for God, and for the needs of people made him a key shaper of modern Christianity, larger than any label put on him. This biography portrays his formation and achievement, illuminating the complex person and his vivid teaching.

Having studied under Francis Schaeffer when young, interviewed him about the course of his life near the end of it, and heard many friends and others acknowledge their debt to him, I waited in vain for a comprehensive biography. I have therefore tried to meet this need. It is now nearly a quarter-century since his death, and it seems to me that his essential message is as topical and important as it was in his lifetime. He has some detractors, but for me, he always eludes their nets. I have attempted to give an affectionate, accurate, warts-and-all portrait of a fascinating and complex person whom people always remembered. To ensure a truthful and reasonably objective portrait, I have been guided by over 180,000 words of oral history concerning Francis Schaeffer. This oral history was gathered by the historian Christopher Catherwood, his wife (musicologist Paulette Catherwood), and myself. We carried out interviews in Switzerland, the Netherlands, England, Northern Ireland, and the USA, talking to a variety of people, including former L'Abri members, workers, helpers, students, as well as members of the immediate family.

I've also made use of PCA (Presbyterian Church of America) archive material, early writings of Francis Schaeffer, letters, biography and memoirs by Edith Schaeffer, writings of the novelist Frank Schaeffer, and assessments of the pastor-intellectual (including *Time* magazine and *De Spiegel*). I've put this into a continuous narrative so that the reader might get to know Francis Schaeffer, his vision and concerns, and the thrust of his teaching (the purpose of my book is, of course, biographical, not to give an analysis of Schaeffer's thought).

My hope is that my book may play a little part in drawing a new generation of readers to Schaeffer's crucial work and message—sadly, they can no longer have the benefit of the teacher in person. I emphasize *teacher*. Schaeffer was of the old school of teacher or master—charismatic, memorable, learned. Though he wasn't a scholar in the usually accepted sense, he pushed those who truly listened to explore more, to learn more, to be more prepared for living as a Christian and human being in today's post-Christian, media-rich, exciting, dangerous world. Like John Milton I believe the image of God is captured in a unique way in books, and though Schaeffer is dead, his mind and spirit are alive in his writings, even though they lack the elegance and style of a C. S. Lewis. His message can still leap from mind to mind, as it did at the time I remember as a student. Our world still cries out for his imaginative L'Abri ("The Shelter"), which can and should take many forms for differing needs.

A biography of Francis Schaeffer must account for his remarkable impact on people of many types—the intellectual, the humble laborer, the scientist, the artist, the doubting Christian, the questioning nonbeliever; man, woman, youth, and child; white, black, hairy, and smooth. After Francis Schaeffer's first visit to Europe, still suffering from the effects of war in 1947, a wall of parochialism in his life began to collapse—a process quickened by his friendship with the Dutchman Hans Rookmaaker and his own long-standing interest in and love for art. A biography of him (or a critique, for that matter) cannot itself be parochial in any sense, intellectual or regional. He was larger than any denominational or political context.

In this book I write about Francis Schaeffer's strengths and flaws, placing him in the context of his times, portraying the formation of his ideas and the genesis of his lectures, writings, seminars, and movies, as well as the complex person and his relationships. I portray the establishment and impact of the L'Abri community, and the deeper idea of a "shelter," as Schaeffer's most representative and abiding achievement, showing the development of this unique phenomenon and revealing its importance in the context of church and recent cultural history. The man himself is pictured as in essence undivided, rather than consisting of two or even three Schaeffers, though he went through sometimes anguished change and growth. Even his late and very emphatic association with the American church in the Reagan years was for him a development from the L'Abri work, not a capitulation to what he called the "middle-class church."

Though Francis Schaeffer is undivided, the distinct phases of his life are all portrayed here, each illuminating the other phases: his working-class childhood in Germantown, Pennsylvania; his intellectual and cultural awakening and student and seminary years; the ten years as a "separated" pastor in eastern and midwestern America; his early years in Europe working with his wife Edith for Children for Christ and speaking widely on the dangers of a new, deceptive liberalism as regards the Bible; the crisis in his faith resulting in a deep experience of the Holy Spirit; the birth and early struggles of L'Abri in Switzerland; the gradual opening up of a wider ministry through taped lectures, international speaking, books, and the formation of new L'Abri centers, first in England, then in other countries; and, at the end of his life, the dramatic, celebrity phase of the movies and large seminars, in which Schaeffer extended his cultural analysis to the sphere of politics, law, and government, putting his long-standing role as a compassionate controversialist into the spotlight, with all its distortions of view.

As I was completing this book, Frank Schaeffer's *Crazy for God* was published. This is a confessional memoir of his life. While it vividly and sometimes poignantly portrays Frank's own life and journey, it added little to what I had already documented about his father—as a biographer I knew his strengths and weaknesses. Many of those interviewed for this book spoke of them openly. What I must remark on is Frank's portrayal of his father as keeping up a façade of conviction about his faith, especially in his final years. This bears no relation to what was the case. Francis Schaeffer was always open about his personal struggles and failings—this was the secret of his strength as a pastor and as a counselor. He emphatically did not divorce his inner and public life. When I was a young student, on my first or second visit to his L'Abri community in Switzerland, I once joined him on the descent to the chalet-style chapel for his regular Saturday night discussion. Suddenly he confided, "Colin, I feel like I'm about to jump out of an airplane without a parachute."

In an unpublished letter to his close friend and peer Hans Rookmaaker, perhaps that same year, he confided that he was low after working hard on the manuscript of *The God Who Is There* with an editor: "I am so very much behind in every aspect of the work that I feel in a rather depressed mood which means of course that it is a difficult time. However, the Lord continues to open doors and we are thankful. . . . I would be glad if you would continue to pray for me personally because . . . this is a bit of a low period for me. However, I suppose I will be dug out in a couple of weeks and then I will feel better."[1]

As my book reveals, Francis Schaeffer in the twilight of his life was

---

[1]Unpublished letter to Hans Rookmaaker from Huémoz, February 1, 1967.

as convinced of the truth-claims of Christianity and the efficacy of what he called the finished work of Christ as he was after his struggles in the early 1950s and even immediately after his conversion in 1930. Indeed, his conviction continued to deepen into his closing years, allowing him no respite from his grief over the lost condition of human beings and still expanding his empathy for those whom he encountered. In his final film series, *Whatever Happened to the Human Race?* he included a powerful episode about the historical underpinnings of Christian conviction.

What is the essence of Francis Schaeffer? Is it his system of theology, his books, his political campaigning, the existence of L'Abri? Ironically, though he attacked first the "old" modernism, then the "new" modernism of existentialism, neo-orthodoxy, and even, in anticipation, postmodernism, he demonstrates what might be called an existential Christianity—living in the moment; embracing the reality of existence; seeing the underpinning certainty of Christian faith in the historical death and resurrection of Jesus Christ; and reckoning on the specific intervention of the Holy Spirit in conversion at a point in time in a person's life, after which he or she passes from death to life. Schaeffer might be dismissed as a scholar or even original thinker (though it can be argued he was both, but particularly the latter), but his realistic, existential Christianity is remarkable and perhaps unique for someone of his biblical orthodoxy in his generation and is the secret, perhaps, of his impact on many people of diverse backgrounds and nationalities.

A full list of acknowledgments appears toward the end of this book, but I must here especially express my thanks to Christopher and Paulette Catherwood, for their brilliant and enthusiastic help with the interviewing for this book; to Ted Griffin, for his wise and thorough editing; to others who added to this book in a very special way, including Lane Dennis, John and Prisca Sandri, Ranald and Susan Macaulay, and Udo and Deborah Middelmann. Though not well enough to give me more than a warm smile and greeting, Edith Schaeffer's published records of the family and L'Abri history, and unpublished Family Letters must have a special mention. While Christopher, Paulette, and I interviewed, we received kindness and hospitality of a Dutch, Swiss, English, Irish, and American variety. I particularly remember the kindness of Marleen and Albert Hengelaar and the inspiring memories of the late Anky Rookmaaker as she reached back in her mind to the war years; the events she recounted seemed as yesterday. It is a privilege even to share a little in others' lives.

Colin Duriez

CHAPTER ONE

BEGINNINGS

(1912–1935)

෨෨෨෨෨

Francis Schaeffer was the child of working-class parents of German ancestry. He was born on January 30, 1912, in Germantown, Pennsylvania, in the United States of America. On his mother's side his ancestry was English. In fact his great-grandfather, William Joyce of Nottingham, England, was the first of his immediate forebears to cross the Atlantic, in 1846. Joyce, a weaver by trade, made his way to the small town near Philadelphia where his descendant Francis Schaeffer would be born and settled there, taking up shoemaking. At this time Germantown was little more than its main avenue. Its name derives from the establishment of the town in 1683 by about two hundred immigrants from Germany's Rhine Valley. Later other nationalities were established there, such as a Polish community. When work declined because of mass industry, William changed his employment to mailman, walking twenty-five miles a day delivering the mail. He was a familiar figure in the neighborhood, known as "Uncle Billy," and was memorable for his forthright opinions on the state of the world and politics. His wife died at thirty-five, leaving him to care for their children.

One of his daughters, Mary, married Wallace Williamson in 1877. She was twenty-five, and he was twenty-six. Wallace died in the eleventh year of their marriage, leaving Mary with four daughters to bring up, including Bessie, Francis Schaeffer's future mother, who was eight when her father died. Mary survived by taking in washing and ironing, a process that necessitated her making her own soap. She also took her father into her home, where he lived until his death in his nineties. The hardship of Bessie's early life taught her to expect existence to be tough. She vowed she would "never be a slave to bringing up children" as

Mary had been. At the age of seventeen, in 1897, she achieved a diploma from the local grammar school. She had enough qualification with that diploma to teach in primary (elementary) school but instead remained at home helping her mother, even after her brothers and sisters left. The last years of the long life of this Germantown woman would be spent in a little village high in the Swiss Alps and would inspire a novel by her grandson, Frank Schaeffer, *Saving Grandma*.

Francis Schaeffer's paternal grandfather, "Franz" (Francis August Schaeffer II, named according to family tradition), and his wife, Carolina Wilhelmina Mueller, emigrated from Germany to America in 1869 to escape European wars with their attendant tribulations. Carolina was from the Black Forest area, and Franz possibly from the east, perhaps Berlin. Franz had fought in the Franco-Prussian war, being honored with an Iron Cross. As part of deliberately turning to a fresh life in the new world, Franz burned all his personal papers. Ten years after settling in Germantown, Franz was killed in an accident at work on the railroad in nearby Philadelphia. He left a three-year-old son, Francis August Schaeffer III. Carolina eventually remarried, to Franz's brother. The child, known as Frank, had only a basic education and, before he was eleven, joined many other children sorting coal to bolster the inadequate family income. Eventually he found work in one of the nearby mills. Still in his young teens, Frank slipped away from home to join the Navy. Each time he received his wages, most of it was mailed home to his mother. He learned to ride the rigging in all weathers before moving on to steam-powered ships. His experience at sea included serving during the Spanish-American War in 1898. His experience on the wild rigging taught him to brave heights and dangerous situations in the workplace.

Frank had had a Lutheran upbringing, and when he met Bessie Williamson she was a regular church attendee at a local Evangelical Free Church. Churchgoing was normal at that time, part of the social and community glue. Their courtship and engagement was dominated by a necessity both felt to prepare for a home together, acquiring furnishings, linens, and so on. They both wished to transcend the impoverishment and discomforts of their brief childhoods. They were both thorough and conscientious, and continued to be so in their marriage as their house on Pastoria Street was honed to their ways. Bessie was determined to have only one child, and that child turned out to be Francis August Schaeffer IV, the subject of this book. She was thirty-two years of age when she gave birth on Tuesday, January 30, 1912.

At the appropriate moment Bessie told her husband, "It's time to call the doctor." Frank disappeared into the night and quickly returned, riding in the doctor's buggy. In his excitement to get help, Frank had not noticed that the doctor was drunk. The physician was not too far gone, however, to tie a sheet to a foot post of Bessie's bed and tell her to pull on it with all her might while pushing. Bessie in later years told Edith Schaeffer, Francis's wife, "It was easy. I just pulled on the sheet and pushed, and the baby was there on the bed."[1] The inebriated doctor finished his tasks and managed to find his way back, but the following morning he entirely forgot the need to register the birth. Francis Schaeffer was not to realize until thirty-five years later that he had no birth certificate, when he prepared to go abroad for the first time.

As a child Fran, as he tended to be known to family and friends,[2] helped his father in his duties as a caretaker, which included carpentry. His home on Pastoria Street lacked the stimulation of books and intellectual interest in the conversations of his parents. There were no pets or picnics, and visits from play friends were rare. The young child would watch the horse-drawn delivery wagons and see the lamplighter kindling each gas lamp in the street at twilight. In winter there was the Mummers Parade, and in the summer a trip to Atlantic City. An old photograph shows a young boy dressed in a long, two-piece beach suit of wool, standing obediently on the edge of the surf as his picture is taken. A large obstacle to his development, which went unnoticed, was severe dyslexia. In later years many of his students at L'Abri noticed what seemed to them amusing mispronunciations: he spoke of Mary Quaint (instead of Quant), the film *Dr. Strange Glove* (instead of *Dr. Strangelove*), and Chairman Mayo (instead of Mao). His youngest daughter Deborah Middelmann remembers him frequently calling

---

[1] Edith Schaeffer, *The Tapestry* (Nashville: Word, 1981), 37.
[2] His mother, however, invariably called him Francis.

down to her for the spelling of simple words like *who* and *which*, even when she was as young as five or six.

Knowing him as a young adult, many would have predicted an ordinary working-class life for Francis Schaeffer: hard-working, conscientious, and orderly but nevertheless defined in its compass by his upbringing. Fran was never told that the school reported to his parents that in an intelligence test he had been found to have the second highest score recorded in twenty years. The parents, however, did at one time briefly consider sending him to a private school, Germantown Academy. Not surprisingly, Fran chose woodwork, technical drawing, electrical construction, and metalwork as his main subjects when he started high school. By the age of seventeen, young Schaeffer was working part-time on a fish wagon. He later admitted to having "barely made it" in high school.[3]

But this is to anticipate. A significant moment in Fran's education took place when he changed schools at the age of eleven. At Roosevelt Junior High School he had a teacher named Mrs. Lidie C. Bell, who was the first to "open doors" for him. Near the end of his life, Francis Schaeffer revealed in an interview: "Certain key people made a real difference in my thinking. It goes all the way back to my junior high school days when I had just one art teacher. I came from a family which was not interested in art at all. She opened the door for me to an interest in art."[4] From that point on, a fascination with art was a central thread running through his life. His annual visits to Atlantic City were also deeply significant to him. He had become a strong swimmer and remembered long after: "When I was a boy I went swimming from the old concrete ship which was beached off Cape May Point following the first World War. The ship's hull was tilted at a sharp angle. After I was inside for some time and then looked out through a door, the sea seemed to be at an angle and for a moment all the accepted facts of the external world seemed to go 'crazy.'"[5] As so often with his experiences, the event provided an analogy for human thinking about the world, shaped as this is by worldview and presupposition.

---

[3]Philip Yancey, *Open Windows* (Wheaton, IL: Crossway Books, 1982), 115.
[4]Ibid., 116.
[5]From a pamphlet written in the 1940s by Francis A. Schaeffer, *Sin Is Normal* (Walker, IA: Bible Presbyterian Press, n. d.).

At the time he entered junior high school Fran joined the Boy Scouts. As representative of his troop he took part in a speech contest. He kept the cup for the rest of his life: "Pyramid Club Four Minute Speech Contest Won by Francis A. Schaeffer, Troop 38, 1923." At this time he chose to attend the First Presbyterian Church of Germantown because of its link with the Scout troop. Belonging to the Scouts enriched his life at that time as he worked for merit badges and learned about woodland, camping, and trails. His father provided a membership for the YMCA, which was where he learned to swim and was able to do some gymnastics. Helping his father, Fran mastered many skills, such as building, laying floors, mending gutters, and plumbing. Some of the skills were employed renovating the new house at 6341 Ross Street, into which the family moved while Fran was in Germantown High School.

Fran made a significant discovery when he went to an electrical show at the City Auditorium. During the show there was a dramatic playing of Tchaikovsky's *1812 Overture*, complete with special effects. Hearing this piece of classical music was a new experience for Fran. Some days after this, he happened to turn on the radio just as this same overture was played. As he recognized it and listened intently, he fell in love with such music, a love that was to deepen, grow, and become a permanent part of his life.

According to his daughter Deborah, the core of Francis Schaeffer's life was there from the beginning: he was "a thinking person who was very honest about life." His inherent seriousness did not mean dullness. He enjoyed humor, for instance. From early days he was, in Deborah's words, "very serious about life, art, and music. . . . As a boy he loved hiking and going about the woods in Philadelphia." This intense demeanor was not out of keeping with his working-class background. Her father always reckoned, later in life, that there was a deep affinity between the working-class person and the intellectual. They shared an honesty in looking at life, whereas the middle classes often lived in a way that was divorced from reality. Fran remembered his own father as a deeply thinking person who asked what were in fact philosophical questions, even though he was not able to get past third grade because of family hardship.

The Saturday job on the fish wagon came to an end when Fran became disgusted at his boss's treatment of his horse. He found another job working for a meat market, then one descaling a steam boiler. Others followed, at which he always worked assiduously. A breakthrough came, with far-reaching consequences, when a Sunday school teacher got Fran a job helping a White Russian count, an émigré, to learn to read English. The count favored learning from a biography of the colorful Catherine the Great, who took many lovers. After a few weeks Fran informed him, "You are never going to learn English this way." With the count's agreement, Fran traveled into nearby Philadelphia and headed for its well-known bookstore, Leary's. He requested a reading book for a beginner in English. By mistake (a mistake he later took to be providential) he came away with the wrong book. This was one on Greek philosophy.

As he began reading the book out of curiosity, the effect was the same as when he heard the *1812 Overture* for the first time. As with classical music, a deep love for philosophy began. In later years he told Edith Schaeffer that he felt as if he had come home. From this time on, ideas were an abiding passion. His heartfelt concern for ideas was soon to shape everything he did in life. From reading about the peccadilloes of Catherine the Great, the count found himself learning English from an introductory text on philosophy. The same book marked a dramatic change in Fran's intellectual development. He devoured it, reading long into the night after his parents had gone to bed. Finding out about the Greek philosophers also led him to read Ovid, perhaps the *Metamorphosis*, a first-century writing that had an enormous impact on Western culture.

As he read he had a growing sense that he was gaining more questions but no answers. This awareness was reinforced when he realized that he experienced a similar situation in his church, which he later realized was influenced by theological liberalism—a modernist reinterpretation of the Bible, going back historically to the Enlightenment, which saw human reason as self-sufficient, in the sense of being the ultimate starting point in knowledge and interpretation of reality. What he was getting in his church was a constant questioning, but no answers to the issues of life. He became uneasy about his own agnosticism. He later disclosed that he reasoned, "I wonder whether, to be honest, I should just stop calling myself a Christian, and discard the Bible?"[6]

Churchgoing was quite normal at this time. He later observed: "The United States when I was young through the Twenties and Thirties showed basically a Christian consensus. It was, of course, poorly applied in certain areas, such as race or compassionate use of accumulated wealth."[7] Having tasted the thinking of the ancient Greeks, he thought it was only fair to read through the Bible, something he had never done. He ought to give it a last chance. So it was that, night by night, alongside his reading of Ovid he began reading the Bible from the beginning (as a book, he thought this was the way to do it). He began with Genesis: "In the beginning God created the heaven and the earth" and read to the very end: "The grace of our Lord Jesus Christ be with you all. Amen" (KJV). In his reading of the Bible he was surprised to find unfolding answers to the deep philosophical questions he had begun to ask. The dawning excitement would never leave him.

His son-in-law John Sandri vividly recalls how Francis Schaeffer would characterize the experience of reading the Bible through for the first time: "He came to the conclusion that basically the Bible answered in some way the questions the Greek philosophers were raising. That's the way he recounted it, as I remember. It really showed something about what conversion meant to him; that is, all the interconnection between the worldview of philosophy and the worldview of the Bible and bringing them together and seeing how the one takes care of the other, which otherwise would leave a lot of questions unresolved."[8]

After a six-month period of reading through the Bible (a habit he continued thoroughly throughout his life), he committed himself to Christ and the Christian faith. By September 3, 1930, he would be able to jot in his diary that "all truth is from the Bible."[9] Near the end of his life he recalled the events with deep emotion: "What rang the bell for me was the answers in Genesis, and that with these you had answers—real

[6]Quoted in Edith Schaeffer, *The Tapestry*, 51.
[7]Ibid., 127.
[8]Interview with Prisca and John Sandri, 2007.
[9]Christopher Catherwood, *Five Evangelical Leaders* (Ross-shire, Scotland: Christian Focus Publications, 2003), 112.

answers—and without these there were no answers either in philoso-
phies or in the religion I had heard preached."[10] Through reading the
Bible on his own, however, he at first thought he had discovered something no one else knew about, based on his experience of churchgoing,
which he believed represented Christianity.

In that period of isolation, Francis Schaeffer began to perceive the
world in a new way, a discovery that started to be reflected in his high-
school work. In English classes his writing improved substantially both
in content and style. Probably at this time he started writing poems, not
with great skill, but authentically responding to his changing perception
of things. He was popular at school. His yearbook records:

> F—friendly
>   R—restless
>   A—ambitious
>   N—nonchalant
> Fran is the well-known, talkative secretary of our class, a straight
> shoot'n youngster and an enthusiastic member of the Engineering
> Club.
>   Secretary of Class; Vocal Ensemble; Debating Club; Rifle Club.
> Mechanic Arts.

After graduating in June 1930 he looked for summer jobs, not easy
in the throes of the Great Depression. His father presented him with a
new Model A Ford as a graduation gift, and he began driving lessons.
His diary records his first trip to an art museum and many visits to a
city library to feed his new zest for reading. He saw movies and read the
poetry of Carl Sandburg. Then, in August, an event occurred that lifted
him out of his isolation.

In the heat of that month Fran felt depressed as he walked down
Germantown Avenue, the main street. He felt isolated and was also still
concerned with finding a summer job and was thinking about the engineering course he intended to take after the summer. As he walked he
heard the sound of a piano and hymn-singing. The sound was coming
from a tent pitched on an empty lot. He felt drawn in and opened the

---

[10]Edith Schaeffer, *The Tapestry*, 52.

flap. Inside a gospel meeting was in process, attended by a few people sitting on benches on either side of an aisle covered with sawdust. Fran sat down, and soon a lively sermon followed the enthusiastic gospel hymns. The man at the front spoke simply, telling of his freedom from a life of drugs and crime as a result of the gospel. As he outlined the gospel in his simple way, Fran suddenly realized that the speaker's belief coincided with his discoveries from reading the Bible. He was not alone. Fran moved quickly up what was dubbed at the time "the sawdust trail" in response to the invitation to the congregation to commit their lives. When the speaker asked, "Young man, what are you here for, salvation or reconsecration?" Fran was confused. As the evangelist turned away, Fran walked out of the tent in exultation. That night he jotted in his diary, "August 19, 1930—Tent Meeting, Anthony Zeoli—have decided to give my whole life to Christ unconditionally."[11]

Francis Schaeffer's father was particularly sure that his son should work with his hands. Though he had grown to be a somewhat small man—his height was five feet six inches[12]—he was strong and wiry and skilled in many tasks. Both his parents believed that church ministers were somewhat like parasites on society, not doing real work. This prejudice would become more important as Fran began to think the unthinkable—going into ministry himself. He knew that his father's threat to disown him if he took such a course was no idle one. But as yet his hopes and aspirations were confused by his newfound faith. In September 1930, therefore, Fran dutifully enrolled at the Drexel Institute as an engineering student. He soon was to sink deep into a dilemma, however, for he increasingly felt a distinct calling from God to be a pastor. Though his parents wanted him to be a craftsman like his father, well before the end of the year he was trying to persuade them that his life should dramatically change course. On December 16 he recorded in his diary, "Talked to dad alone, he said to go ahead and that mother would get over it." His father was a strong, tough man; the strength of his son's resolution resonated with him.

Throughout the late months of 1930 Fran was working by day and

---

[11]Edith Schaeffer, *The Tapestry*, 55.
[12]Ibid., 122.

studying by night at the Institute. In September he had managed, after standing in a long line, to get a job at RCA Victor for thirty-two cents an hour. The job only lasted about four weeks and demonstrated the unexpected qualities of Francis Schaeffer that constantly emerged throughout his life. At RCA Victor the work was organized in assembly lines. The work on the lines was accomplished by women, each of whom was responsible for an aspect of the production. On the vast factory floor, five men worked special presses, which fed amplifier parts to the assembly lines. (Fran himself was merely a "bus boy," involved in general maintenance.) Fran soon noticed the injustice of the system, relying as it did on the desperate shortage of work during the Depression. One of the "big bosses" would come onto the floor half an hour before work was due to end flourishing a handful of five-dollar bills. Fran remembered years afterward that the boss would yell, "If you guys at the presses will turn out more parts, double it in the next half hour, there'll be a fiver for each of you."[13] The presses would spurt, doubling the work for the women on the lines, dog-weary at the end of the day. But there was no reward for them. One day in early October one woman snapped. She rose to her feet shouting, "Strike, strike." Slowly others abandoned their frenzied work and joined in a chorus. Some encouraged reluctant women to rise by pulling them up by their hair. Suddenly Fran climbed onto a counter and yelled at the top of his voice (he had a piercing shout), "Strike, strike." Then almost all the remaining women stood up, abandoning their work. Fran was so angry at what was going on that he later realized that he could have followed his sense of indignation and become a labor organizer.

Out of work after the strike, Fran looked around for another daytime job. To his amazement he was offered one working with the father of a school friend, Sam Chestnut, delivering groceries, which took him through the next months. In those depressed times offers were simply not made for jobs. He felt increasingly that God was quietly but definitely leading him. It was the prelude to his momentous decision to become a Christian pastor. Back in September he had talked to a couple of people about studying at Hampden-Sydney College in Virginia, which had a

---

[13]Ibid., 58.

pre-ministerial course. One of those was Sam Osborne, Headmaster of Germantown Academy, who had studied there. Fran continued to seek advice and noted in his diary entry for December 10, 1930, "Prayed with Sam Chestnut today. Now my mind is fully made up, I shall give my life for God's service."[14]

In the new year, on his nineteenth birthday, January 30, he took an important step in implementing his decision. He switched from evening classes at Drexel Institute, with its emphasis on engineering, to evening study at Central High School, taking Latin and German and receiving extra instruction in the latter. Applying his considerable energy and ability to study hard after his day's labor, he achieved marks in the nineties for Latin and German. (Later, in seminary, he would master Greek and Hebrew.) This was an extraordinary achievement, given his poor results through much of high school and his dyslexia. At home, his parents made no mention of his intention to leave for college. His diary at the time records that he dated a student from nearby Beaver College, a prestigious institution for women in Glenside and Jenkintown,[15] but there evidently was no meeting of minds. By the summer of 1931 he was ready, academically at least, to enter pre-ministerial studies at Hampden-Sydney College. He had no idea, however, as to how he would pay his fees, which at the beginning of the 1930s were around six hundred dollars a year, a considerable amount in those days.

The long-anticipated day of leaving for Virginia dawned, and Francis Schaeffer got up before 5:30. When he had prepared for bed the night before, his father had instructed, "Get up in time to see me before I go to work. . . . 5.30."[16] He found his father beside the front door, waiting. Turning to look directly at his son he said, "I don't want a son who is a minister, and—I don't want you to go."[17] It was a decisive moment for both father and son. There was silence between the two in the early dawn light. Fran then said, "Pop, give me a few minutes to go down in the cellar and pray."[18] Descending, his thoughts in confusion, tears started. In the basement he prayed about the choice he must make. In

---

[14]Ibid.
[15]It was renamed Arcadia University in 2000. It is now coeducational.
[16]Edith Schaeffer, *The Tapestry*, 60.
[17]Ibid., 60.
[18]Ibid., 62.

his deep emotion he resorted in desperation to a kind of prayer that, in future days, he would advise many people not to make. Asking God to show him, he tossed a coin, saying that if the result was heads he would go, despite his father's wishes. Heads. Not content, he tossed again, declaring that if it was tails, he would leave for Hampden-Sydney. Tails. Still crying with emotion, he asked God to be patient and said that if the third toss was heads, he would go. There was no mistaking it. The coin landed affirmatively. He returned to his silently waiting father and said, "Dad, I've *got* to go."[19] After an intent glance at his son, his father walked through the doorway and pushed the door behind him hard to slam it. Just before the door banged, however, Fran heard his father say, "I'll pay for the first half year."[20] Years later, Fran's father came to share his faith, affirming his son's resolve.

Fran had carefully packed the day before, making use of a wooden crate his father had once brought home, coating it gray with some leftover paint. After packing clothes, books, Bible, and toiletries, he fastened the box's top down with four long screws. His clothes included his gray tweed knickers from high-school days, breeches he always found comfortable to wear. Years later he would take to wearing his hallmark Swiss breeches for the same reason, inspired by the example of his Swiss son-in-law, John Sandri.[21]

A few hours later Fran found himself at Hampden-Sydney College in Virginia, about sixty miles south-southwest of Richmond, near the small town of Farmville. A friend, Charlie Hoffman, had driven him down in his own Model A Ford and then took the car back to Germantown to await his return. The trip south took them through Maryland and into Virginia, the road taking them through Wilmington, Baltimore, Washington, D.C., and Richmond—a trip of around three hundred miles.

Hampden-Sydney is one of the oldest colleges in the United States, founded in 1775. It was in Francis Schaeffer's time, and remains, an all-men's liberal arts college. The Union Theological Seminary was established at the college, eventually relocating to Richmond. Its out-

---

[19]Ibid.
[20]Ibid.
[21]Interview with John and Prisca Sandri.

standing Federal-style architecture delighted the freshman, with its white columns, red bricks, and campus lawns fringed by extensive woods. He was not enthralled, however, at being allocated a room in Fourth Passage, Cushing Hall, notorious for the hard time given to pre-ministerial students in that dormitory.

Freshmen were soon initiated into what is now called hazing, being spanked with a stick or paddle for breaking petty and sometimes arbitrary rules made by older students, which might include sitting on a fence or not fetching something quickly enough according to the caprice of an upperclassman. Fran was beaten frequently by his roommate for the first few weeks until he snapped. Flouting the unofficial rules he turned on his tormentor, fighting him and finally pinning him down. Another student, the acknowledged leader of the pack in the Fourth Passage, observed the combat from the doorway. In his southern drawl he announced, "You're the biggest little man I've ever seen, Philly." That was the end of his hazing. The mainly southern students had dubbed Fran "Philly" since he was from Philadelphia. The divide was deepened by a contrast between Fran's working-class values of hard work and diligence and the lordly aristocratic attitudes of most of the students.

As he studied, preparing for later ministerial training, there were various indications of the unusual quality of Fran's character—the way in which he faced bullying, his service as president of the Student Christian Association, and his participation in a Sunday school for African-Americans in the vicinity.

The Student Christian Association had established prayer meetings in various dormitories, but the Fourth Passage was a notable exception. With great determination Fran set one up, persisting in asking fellow students along. The meeting was simple: Fran would read a section from the Bible, make one or two comments, and ask if anyone wished to pray. Two or three might pray, with Fran concluding in prayer. One student, exasperated at Fran's persistence in asking him to attend, threw a can of talcum powder at him, causing him to bleed above the eye. Undeterred by his bloody face, Fran asked him again to come. All right, said the student, if Fran would carry him. (He was six feet two inches to Fran's five foot six.) Fran took him in a fireman's hold and carried him, rather unsteadily, down a flight of unlighted stairs to the meeting on the floor below. (The bulbs had long ago been shot out by .22 rifles used by the students to shoot mice.) This was only one example of Fran's recruitment methods.

Another effective method was to broker a deal with students lumbering back after Saturday night's drinking, achieved with some brilliance despite Prohibition. The unlit halls and stairways in Cushing Hall made it difficult for them to navigate to their rooms. In return for Fran's coming to their assistance at the yell of "Philly," they agreed to be roused and taken to church on Sunday mornings. Assistance included undressing them, pushing them under a cold shower, and steering them to their beds. Fran would use the quiet Saturday evenings to study, determined to keep at it until the last of the lads was back. His motivation back then, as it was later in life, was an anguished sense of the lostness of people without God, coupled with meeting them in their particular need. Describing his application to his studies, Edith Schaeffer commented nearly fifty years later, "All through life Fran's best quality has also been his worst feature: such severe concentration on what he is doing, come wind or come weather, that nothing stops him."[22]

A few months after starting at Hampden-Sydney Fran became aware of the existence of a Sunday school for black children in a plain and cramped wooden building. The church was called Mercy Seat. It was deep in the countryside surrounding the college, and Fran began making his way through fields of corn and woods to help out. Through the remainder of his four years at Hampden-Sydney he barely missed a Sunday. He befriended an elderly black man named Johnny Morton who cleaned the college rooms, went to his shack to see him when he was ill, and visited his grave when he died. There were normally between eight to twelve in the Sunday school classes that he taught, their ages ranging from eight to thirteen. One of the girls corresponded with him for years as she grew up and became a nurse.

Fran was a straight-A student who eventually achieved a BA. As well as active involvement in the Ministerial Association, the League of Evangelical Students, and the Literary Society, Fran continued to jot

---

[22]Edith Schaeffer, *The Tapestry*, 127.

down poems in his notebooks, struggling with his spelling. His basic outlook in theology was developed in those college years, before he went to seminary.[23] At that time there was no chapter of Phi Beta Kappa. Had there been, his college acknowledged late in Francis Schaeffer's life, he would have become a member on the basis of his academic record. As it was he was made an honorary member in 1980 for his contributions to human knowledge. Fran deeply appreciated his teachers, including David Wilson (Greek), J. B. Massey (Bible), and Dennison Maurice Allen (Philosophy).

The philosophy professor made a particular and lifelong impact on the young Schaeffer. Fran recalled in an interview toward the end of his life, "I had a philosophy professor in college, Dr. Allen, who was brilliant. I was his favorite student, because I think I was the only student in the class who understood him and stimulated him. He used to invite me down at night to sit around his potbellied stove and discuss. He and I ended up in two very different camps: he became committed to neo-orthodox thinking, but he was very important in stimulating my intellectual processes."[24]

A year after starting at Hampden-Sydney, Francis Schaeffer met Edith Seville, while he was home on summer vacation. Edith was one of three daughters of missionaries who had spent many years in China. Her mother had lived through and narrowly escaped death in the bloody Boxer Rebellion, in which many missionaries and their children were massacred. They had served with the China Inland Mission (now known as the Overseas Missionary Fellowship), founded by Hudson Taylor. Its ethos included "living by faith" without advertising for funds and attempting to adapt to Chinese culture not only by learning the language but by adopting Chinese dress. Some of this ethos, via Edith, would carry over into the work of L'Abri many years later and into Francis Schaeffer's emphasis upon listening to and "speaking" the culture of modern people in the twentieth century.

The missionary family had recently located to Germantown, where George Seville, Edith's father, worked at the CIM headquarters. His

---

[23]Yancey, *Open Windows*, 116.
[24]Ibid.

job was editing *China's Millions*, the mission's magazine. Edith began attending Germantown High School in her senior year, from which Fran had graduated. Her mother's first marriage had been to Walter Greene, and they had planned to go to China together. At his untimely death and that of their baby son one year into the marriage, she had vowed never to remarry but rather to devote herself single-mindedly to mission work with the China Inland Mission. Four years later, after training in Toronto, she had sailed for Shanghai. George, however, won her heart after several years in China. Edith Rachel Merritt Seville was born on November 3, 1914 in Wenchow, joining a family of two older sisters and learning Chinese as an infant. As a child she had resolved, "I may be a missionary when I grow up, but I'm not going to look like one."[25] She grew to love beauty in all forms, whether in textiles and clothes, the creation of a home, or movement and dance.

Edith graduated from high school in June 1932, and on Sunday, the 26th of the month, untypically she attended the Young People's meeting at the liberal First Presbyterian Church in Germantown. Francis had just returned from his first year at Hampden-Sydney College and headed for the same meeting, prepared for a fight. The speaker was Ed Bloom, a former member who had joined the Unitarian Church. His chosen title was, "How I know that Jesus is not the Son of God, and how I know that the Bible is *not* the Word of God." As Edith listened, she recalled:

> . . . my reaction was to jot down things in my head to use in a rebuttal—things I had gathered from lectures about the original manuscripts that I felt might help people who were listening, even if they did nothing to convince Ed Bloom. As soon as he had finished I jumped up to my feet and started to open my mouth . . . when I heard another voice, a boy's voice, quietly begin to talk. I slid back into my seat and listened, startled.[26]

She heard him say that although those there might think his belief that the Bible is the Word of God was influenced by a Bible teacher at college whom they would term "old-fashioned," he himself knew Jesus is the Son of God and his Savior who had changed his life. Although he

---

[25]Edith Schaeffer, *The Tapestry*, 130–131.
[26]Ibid., 131.

could not answer all the things Ed Bloom had said, he wanted them to know where he stood.

Edith hastily asked her friend beside her, "Who's that boy?" and Ellie Fell replied by briefly telling her of Fran's parents' resistance to his becoming a pastor. After mentally resolving to comfort the poor boy somehow, Edith then rose to make her points. She did this by quoting from Dr. Gresham Machen and Dr. Robert D. Wilson, both on the faculty of Westminster Seminary nearby, known to Edith through her father. The quotes encapsulated, in Edith's words, "that type of apologetic for the truth of the Bible which I had heard in lectures and read."[27] Fran was astonished to hear her speech and asked the lad sitting next to him, "Dick, who is that girl?" He had not known anyone in that church was familiar with Old Princeton apologetics. Dick knew Edith and briefly filled him in.

As was the custom, the young people went to someone's home after the meeting, which they considered the real event. As they prepared to go, Fran and his friend pushed their way through the chattering group to Edith, where Dick introduced the two. Fran did not waste the opportunity and immediately asked Edith if he could walk her home. She said she already had a date (meaning she had promised to go to Ellie's house afterward). Fran said, "Break it." Edith's curiosity had been so aroused by this boy who had the courage to declare his belief that she uncharacteristically agreed. They both saw it later as meeting "on the battlefield."[28] Typically, Edith encouraged Fran to read J. Gresham Machen's *Christianity and Liberalism*. In her Fran had discovered an essential ally against liberal attacks upon the integrity of Scripture. Throughout the summer vacation Fran worked selling silk hosiery door-to-door and seeing much of Edith. Their shared activities included visiting the Philadelphia Museum of Art.

During his remaining three years at Hampden-Sydney Fran and Edith were soon writing to each other almost daily, their newfound love deepening into plans for marriage. In the letters it is clear that each had met an intellectual equal, someone with whom each could share

---

[27]Ibid., 132.
[28]Ibid.

deepest aspirations and who would give encouragement in the Christian life. In the fall of 1932 Edith entered nearby Beaver College, enrolling for a degree in home economics, which was cross-disciplinary and stimulating. It was a science degree as it included chemistry, microbiology, psychology, and philosophy of education. It also involved English, philosophy, and ethics. Unlike arts degrees of sixteen hours per week, the course required thirty-two hours. Those hours were crammed not only with the basic scientific elements but classes on foods, dietetics, dressmaking, interior decorating, art appreciation, and other subjects. Edith was in heaven. She was not discouraged by the fact that her family could only afford for her to be a day student, which meant commuting to college by bus and train.

Fran graduated in June 1935, BA *magna cum laude*, a fact that pleased his father when Edith explained its significance—for him it meant that his son had worked harder than most of the other students. Edith had decided to forgo her fourth year of studies at Beaver College so she could fully give her support to Fran, who was poised to enter Westminster Theological Seminary in Philadelphia to complete his ministerial training.

CHAPTER TWO

PASTOR AND
DENOMINATIONALIST

(1935–1945)

ᘒᘒᘒᘒᘒ

Theological turmoil mingled with anticipation in the months leading up to the marriage of Edith Seville and Francis Schaeffer. Its heart was a "fundamentalist-modernist" controversy that six years earlier, in 1929, had already led to the foundation of Westminster, the seminary in Philadelphia at which Fran had decided to enroll.

Fundamentalism then was very different from the fundamentalisms of the early twenty-first century, and so was theological modernism. The fundamentals of Christian faith—including the supernaturalism of the virgin birth and resurrection of Jesus—were under attack from increasingly influential biblical scholars who sought a natural, human origin for the scriptural texts. An outstanding evangelical scholar, John Gresham Machen, argued in his *Christianity and Liberalism* (1923), a book that Edith introduced to Fran early in their friendship, that historic Christianity and theological liberalism were in fact separate religions, inevitably resulting in conflict, not inclusion.

> In the sphere of religion . . . the present time is a time of conflict; the great redemptive religion which has always been known as Christianity is battling against a totally diverse type of religious belief, which is only the more destructive of the Christian faith because it makes use of traditional Christian terminology. . . . [T]he many varieties of modern liberal religion are rooted in naturalism—that is, in the denial of any entrance of the creative power of God (as distinguished from the ordinary course of nature) in connection with the origin of Christianity.[1]

---

[1] J. Gresham Machen, *Christianity and Liberalism* (Grand Rapids, MI: Eerdmans, 1923), 2.

The consensus of "new" scholarship was so strong at the Presbyterian-based Princeton Seminary, which had been an evangelical bastion, that in 1929 it was reorganized to be more inclusive. Leading faculty members there, including Machen, left and set up Westminster. The faculty at the new institution soon included Machen, Cornelius Van Til for apologetics, R. B. Kuiper for systematic theology, Paul Woolley for church history, Ned B. Stonehouse for New Testament (with Machen), and a frail Robert Dick Wilson, assisted by Allan A. MacRae, and Oswald T. Allis, for Old Testament.[2] The institution saw itself keeping the flame burning that had previously shone for so long at Princeton. Machen put it dramatically in his address upon the opening of the seminary in 1929: "My friends, though Princeton Seminary is dead, the noble tradition of Princeton Seminary is alive."[3] Unlike Princeton, however, Westminster chose to be free of church control, seeking to be controlled primarily by the tradition of historic Christianity, as focused by Reformed faith. This meant that faculty could be drawn from other denominations. It also meant that the seminary was founded on a wider basis than the recent modernist controversy and separatism—a broad foundation that would soon lead to division among both staff and students.

Machen and other leading evangelicals, having established an advanced teaching institution with the highest standards, were now anxious about wider mission. Machen saw that the Independent Board for Presbyterian Foreign Missions was in contravention of the church's constitution in not upholding the necessity of historic Christian faith. A new Independent Board of Foreign Missions was established in 1933, with Machen being elected president, a move that would soon result in his defrocking. It is this Board for whom Francis Schaeffer would undertake a survey of Western Europe in 1947.

The existence of the Independent Board created a storm of controversy within the Presbyterian Church in the USA. The following year the general assembly proscribed it. Machen refused to abandon it, and throughout February and March 1935 he was tried and then suspended from ministry. His appeal the following year was unsuccessful, and, now

---

[2]Ned B. Stonehouse, *J. Gresham Machen: A Biographical Memoir* (Edinburgh: The Banner of Truth Trust, 1987), 446ff.
[3]Ibid., 458.

defrocked, he turned his energies to founding a new denomination that very year, initially called by the bold title of the Presbyterian Church of America, before being forced to change its name to the more subdued Orthodox Presbyterian Church.

These extraordinary and momentous events marked a decisive response by many evangelicals to theological modernism and provided the context for the young Francis Schaeffer's increasing separatism. Bryan A. Follis notes that "the historical backdrop against which Francis Schaeffer lived and worked [was] the retreat of evangelicalism from its position in mainstream society to being a fringe separatist movement."[4] The treatment of Machen and fellow dissidents by his church was very much in Fran's mind as he and Edith prepared for marriage in 1935. In a letter dated April 26, from Hampden-Sydney College, to Edith, his "dearest Sweets," he says, "Thanks for the clipping. . . . Let's put these men on our prayer list as they come to trial—Machen and [Carl] McIntire. The latter one especially as he is so young, and in such a position he should have our prayer help."[5]

Both Edith and Fran saw their relationship in the context of Christian ministry. Their activist approach—being close to Fran was like being on what he sometimes called an "escalator," Edith later reminisced[6]— would be tempered "into a much more mature understanding. We didn't know much about the deep afflictions of life by experience then, nor how short *time* is."[7] Inevitably they would discover the flaws in each other, living with which would become a daily reality, as in any marriage. Fran's characteristic mix of idealism and quest for realism is captured in the letter just quoted, even though idealism predominates:

> No one else can fulfil any side of mine, or even be totally sympathetic to any side, and here you are who can completely fulfil all parts of me, and you soon will be my wife. Think, dear, actually my wife! You are what I could sit down and coldly figure out that I wanted in a woman. But, how in the world, you so gloriously perfect for a Christian's wife have come to me I do not understand. But you have, and I give thanks

[4]Bryan A. Follis, *Truth with Love: The Apologetics of Francis Schaeffer* (Wheaton, IL: Crossway Books, 2006), 11.
[5]Edith Schaeffer, *The Tapestry* (Nashville: Word, 1981), 167–168.
[6]Ibid., 172.
[7]Ibid., 173.

for you. I do not understand why you have come to me any more than I
do not understand why *I* was called into the ministry, but I know both
are true, and I am glad for both—great are the mysteries—but how
much better we are cared for, than we could care for ourselves. How
fine it will be to know that we will be responsible to each other and
for each other and that everyone will expect us to put each other first.
How I hope we may have many many years of service together, and
finally entrance together into eternity. Perhaps Christ will return in our
lifetime, and then it will be for sure together—I hope He does![8]

The waiting was eventually over. On July 26, 1935, soon after
Fran graduated from Hampden-Sydney, the two cast their fortunes
together in marriage. Fran was twenty-three and Edith twenty years
old. The wedding took place at the Wayne Avenue United Presbyterian
Church, Philadelphia, Edith's father George Seville marrying them.
To simplify arrangements, Dr. Seville got a Westminster friend, Paul
Woolley, professor of church history, to give the bride away. Edith and
Fran were very different people, accounting for the real strengths and
weaknesses, tensions and mutual encouragements in their relationship.
Fran's proneness to anger and depression, for instance, did not sit easily
with Edith's tendency to cling to flighty ideas of what her "imagination had pictured as ideal."[9] Edith's culture and refinement, however,
complemented Fran's concern with personal relationships, which was
forged by his working-class background but was also a unique part of
his makeup. They, with their own individual emphases, stood together
as intellectual equals trying to interpret and respond to the contemporary world. The two together shaped the ten years they were to have in
pastorates and the later work of L'Abri. Edith's own books would add
dimension to Francis Schaeffer's writings in middle life, just as her "hidden art" would add to their home life from the onset. They set off for
what they hoped would be a zero-cost honeymoon in Fran's Model A
Ford, gripped by a romantic notion of overnight cabins along the roads,
into which they would bring their own cooking equipment and food.
Their destination was three hundred and fifty miles away—a camp on
the shores of Lake Michigan where they would work for that summer—

[8]Ibid., 172.
[9]Ibid., 231.

and they allowed themselves two weeks to get there. At the camp Edith made a nail-keg stool that would become familiar in later years to many visitors to L'Abri in Switzerland.

Their first home was a third-floor rear apartment in what was then basically a slum area on Greene Street, north of the Philadelphia Art Museum that Fran knew so well and regarded as rather "staid."[10] The museum would later house the best collection of work by Marcel Duchamp, a radical modern artist whom Schaeffer came to see as being particularly significant for understanding the intellectual and cultural climate of our times.[11] The apartment was also a vigorous walk away from Westminster Theological Seminary, which was at that time located in an unremarkable building at 1528 Pine Street in the center of the city. The young couple settled in happily, employing their skills in making their own furniture and accessories. Space was so scarce that the card table Fran employed for his nightly seminary work rested on the bed, with just two legs on the floor.

With marriage, as she had predetermined, Edith abandoned her studies at Beaver College (she had completed three of the four years) to devote herself to serving her new husband, making possible his preparation for ministry. Fran received a small grant from Westminster, which Edith supplemented by long hours of toil as a work-at-home seamstress, working with leather and linens, making dresses, and designing, manufacturing, and selling leather buttons and belts. She did this with a sewing machine and two leather punches. Fran studied late into the night, and she accompanied him as she sewed, sharing his discoveries in theology, philosophy, or the meanings of Greek or Hebrew words in the biblical text. As her fingers worked dexterously on leather and cloth, she benefited via Fran from what was virtually a seminary education, her mind quick and sharp. She became familiar with the names of the faculty, that of Cornelius Van Til standing out as another who "opened doors" for Fran, this time opening up wide vistas of thought. Another name that stood out was that of Allan MacRae, who particularly stirred his intellectual thought.[12] An element of Fran's study that was not pos-

---

[10]*The God Who Is There*, in *The Francis Schaeffer Trilogy* (Wheaton, IL: Crossway Books, 1990), 33.
[11]Ibid.
[12]Philip Yancey, *Open Windows* (Wheaton, IL: Crossway Books, 1982), 116.

sible to share was learning Hebrew. Battling with his dyslexia he used card after card of Hebrew vocabulary, inscribed in his small, clear handwriting, which he doggedly memorized, shutting out Edith and all else. Both gained the habit of working long hours and talking all things over, which made possible the future work of L'Abri, as well as the writing, lecturing, and film-making, a ministry by nature highly demanding and costly in human terms—and in addition bringing up a family. Though Fran often expressed behavior that we today would regard as rather chauvinistic,[13] reflecting assumptions of the time held by both men and women, it is fascinating that he participated fully in what Edith called "a weekly thorough housecleaning in which we polished everything, washed windows, shook out our little rag rugs, washed and waxed floors."[14]

The first year of studies at Westminster flew by, and as summer 1936 approached, employment during the vacation became a pressing issue. Fran and Edith were delighted to be offered charge of Camp Richard Webber, in the White Mountain area of New Hampshire. This is where their love affair with mountains and mountain climbing began. Their task was to care for a variety of small boys, teaching them, reading stories to them at night, hiking with them, as Fran had done with the Boy Scouts in Germantown, and generally being father and mother to them. The camp was part of an evangelical group whose mission was to reopen churches that had closed down. The camp site had a conference center, and here Fran made the acquaintance of Harold John Ockenga (1905–1985), who had been invited to speak. It may have been Ockenga who brought the shocking and sobering news that J. Gresham Machen's appeal had failed and that he had been defrocked. Machen had subsequently helped found the Presbyterian Church of America (later renamed the Orthodox Presbyterian Church.) Fran told Edith that he felt he must immediately resign from the main Presbyterian Church and place himself under the care of the new presbytery. Some years later he was still bitter at Ockenga's very different, more cautious reaction, failing to understand how some could take a principled stand without

[13]Interviews with Susan Macaulay, 2007 and Dick and Mardi Keyes, 1998.
[14]Edith Schaeffer, *The Tapestry*, 185.

embracing ecclesiastical separatism. Fourteen years later he wrote in *The Christian Beacon*, a separatist periodical founded by McIntire:

> The night that I heard of Dr. J. Gresham Machen's being put out of the Presbyterian Church, U. S. A., in the summer of 1936, I was at Dr. J. Elwin Wright's conference at Rumney, New Hampshire, directing the boys' camp there. Dr. Ockenga was one of the speakers that week and I talked to him soon after I heard about the outcome of Dr. Machen's trial in the Presbyterian Church. I told him that I was going to write to have my name erased from being under care of Presbytery right away. He said he was not going to do anything, but was going to wait for ten years and then by that time there would be a big movement that would either be successful in cleaning up the church or would resign in a body.[15]

Reflecting on this period of theological and ecclesiastical turmoil, the Schaeffers in later life were not happy with some of the decisions they made in their early career, particularly regarding the issue of separation.[16] They came to see that truth (both in theory and in relationships with fellow Christians) is more foundational than maintaining ecclesiastical separation, even though they continued to hold the view that they could not be part of a church that institutionally denied the unique beliefs of historic Christianity.[17] No doubt his comments about Harold Ockenga were some of the words Francis Schaeffer later regretted.[18] They became glad that they in later years did not put all their time and energy struggling against "liberalism" in their own denomination but concentrated on "a positive work."[19] As an attempt at healing wounds, they made a point of apologizing to people who had been hurt by an abrasive and unloving separatist stance.[20]

In his second year at Westminster, Fran threw himself into his studies again. On Tuesday mornings, for instance, he would join about twenty

---

[15]From "A Look to the Future," *The Christian Beacon*, written at the end of 1950 or early 1951, attacking latitudinous attitudes in church government. See Edith Schaeffer, *The Tapestry*, 188ff.
[16]See Edith Schaeffer, *The Tapestry*, 192–193.
[17]Late in his life Schaeffer was still exercised about latitudinarianism, as he was to call an attitude of compromise over essential doctrines such as the reliability of Scripture.
[18]In 1942 Ockenga went on to found the National Evangelical Association (NEA), a *bête noire* to separatists.
[19]Edith Schaeffer, *The Tapestry*, 192.
[20]See ibid.

other students at 8:40 A.M. for the Apologetics class with Van Til, a session Fran found particularly stimulating. We have a good idea of the content of the course in 1936, thanks to the Westminster archive.[21] Van Til had a habit of binding notes together. Class syllabi he prepared at the time were for classes on apologetics, systematic theology, and Christian theistic evidences. From his study of these early course notes, David R. Leigh believes that Schaeffer's analysis of St. Thomas Aquinas, central to his later historical analysis of the rise of modern thought, echoes Van Til's teaching from this period.[22]

It is likely that Van Til's teaching and writing (even though much of it was the unpublished class syllabi—albeit, widely distributed) was a significant influence in the distrust that evangelicals increasingly felt toward the great theologian Karl Barth, based particularly on his early commentary on Romans (1919, but not available in translation until 1935) and *The Word of God and the Word of Man* (translated 1928). In his years as a village pastor early in the century Barth had rejected theological liberalism, but his detractors felt that he had created a neo-orthodoxy that retained liberal views of Scripture. David R. Leigh argues, "Van Til's writings are one reason Fundamentalists (including Schaeffer) in the 1950s and 1960s were so agitated against Barth."[23]

However good his intentions and insightful his theology, Barth gradually was seen by many evangelicals opposing modernism as creating in effect a Gnostic-like dualism between the believer's faith in Christ and the fallen human person's existence in and knowledge of the world made by God. This was interpreted as a divorce between religious truth and evidential (and normal rational) truth, which bolstered neo-orthodoxy—an attempt to counter theological liberalism by accepting some of its criticism of the reliability of biblical texts while retaining their status as the authoritative Word of God. Barth's emerging theology was criticized by Dooyeweerd in his 1935 *De Wijsbegeerte der Wetsidee* (translated as *A New Critique of Theoretical Thought*) and by Oliver

---

[21]David R. Leigh, *Two Apologists: Cornelius Van Til and Francis Schaeffer* (M.A. thesis, Wheaton College Graduate School, 1990), 7.

[22]Ibid., 32.

[23]Ibid., 15. As well as his syllabus references to Barth, in 1948 Van Til critiqued Barth in *The New Modernism* and in 1962 in *Christianity and Barthianism*. Barth read both books and typically felt that Van Til had not understood a word of what he had written (in a letter to E. R. Geehan, quoted by Leigh, 15–16).

Buswell, one-time president of Wheaton College in a long article, "Karl Barth's Theology."[24] Dooyeweerd argued that faith has a central and integrating function in human life, whether a person is a Christian or not, and faith specifically in Christ operates within the same principles as a non-Christian faith, not outside of it. If this was not true, he reasoned, "unbelief or apostate faith could not be the opposite to Christian faith. It would belong to an entirely different order and could have no point of comparison with the belief in Jesus Christ."[25]

Coming to terms with Barth and the "new modernism" was part of the currency of discussion and teaching at Westminster and later Faith Seminary, despite the painful havoc wreaked by the old modernism that had forced them into being. The young Schaeffer was already convinced that there was a real point of contact between the believer and unbeliever, on the basis of truth and shared reality, a view that led to disquiet and protest on the part of Van Til even into his retirement years (though, significantly, he tended to avoid publicly criticizing his former student).[26] The Christian claims, Schaeffer articulated, were true in the world of history and science or they were wrong. These ideas slowly crystallized, culminating in a rather unsatisfactory meeting between Schaeffer along with others of his separatist group and Karl Barth in 1950 (see Chapter 4 of this book).

Many of the ideas familiar to readers of Schaeffer's books, written in his later fifties and beyond, were in seed during Fran's seminary years. Though he was exposed then to discussions and opinions on Aquinas and Barth,[27] both of whom are significant protagonists in his portrayal of the decline of the West, there seems to be little hint of the origins of

---

[24]J. Oliver Buswell, "Karl Barth's Theology: A Book Review," in *The Bible Today*, 1950, 261–271. The book reviewed was Barth's *Dogmatics in Outline*, Philosophical Library, 1950.

[25]Herman Dooyeweerd, *A New Critique of Theoretical Thought* (Philadelphia: P&R, 1953–1958), Part IV, 301.

[26]In an interview given late in life, Van Til does make rather a baffling criticism, given Fran's central concern for those lost without Christ and awareness of the effect of sin and the fall upon human beings: "I have not read Francis Schaeffer as warning his fellow evangelical pastors—as he quotes Ezekiel doing—to declare the wrath to come for those who reject God. And, again, with the best of will I cannot find in Schaeffer's writings what Paul says is the heart of his preaching: Christ and him crucified, and Christ and the resurrection. When I read Matthew 25:46 I shudder at what Jesus says. I know Francis believes that as well as I do. Should he not express himself on these his own convictions?" (David E. Kucharsky, "In the Beginning, God: An Interview with Cornelius Van Til," *Christianity Today* (December 30, 1977), 22.

[27]His knowledge of Kierkegaard may have come later, from his exposure to Europe in 1947 and following years.

his distinctive views on Hegel, which for him mark the most important historical turning point. Though he would have read Hegel, or about him, in his student years, we do not know the source for the connection between Hegel's view of history—with natural and human development as a process and evolutionary progress—and what Schaeffer called a decisive break with the logic of antithesis—a break that, in his view, led to modern relativism.[28] This is a brilliant connection, however one judges the full nature of the catastrophic break between the Old and Post-Christian West.[29]

The days and months of Fran's second year at Westminster passed quickly. That autumn of 1936 Edith had become pregnant, and soon afterward Fran had to have an emergency operation to remove his appendix, requiring two weeks' recovery in the hospital. The excitement of anticipation of their first child was further overshadowed. More denominational controversy forced big decisions upon Fran and Edith. They had been unhappy about a mismatch between declarations of holiness and "harsh and ugly" relations in the seminary. They also were troubled by a determinism that was present, they felt, at that time in the Reformed thinking at Westminster. This could be so extreme that it was considered worthless to ask the Sovereign Lord for anything specific and material. Fran and Edith at that time also had strong views on total abstinence, other don'ts, and premillennialist theology, seeing them as a requirement for holiness and sound doctrine. For many years his heavily annotated reading Bible was a Scofield Reference Bible, dominated by a popular dispensationalism originating in the nineteenth century. Fran, Edith, and a number of their colleagues began to overemphasize

---

[28]Robert D. Knudsen links Schaeffer's stress on non-contradiction with the influential apologists Gordon H. Clark and Edward John Carnell. He sees Schaeffer as a "presuppositionist" apologist and suggests that it is common for presuppositionalists to defend the law of contradiction. Knudsen, "Tendencies in Christian Apologetics," in E. R. Geehan, ed., *Jerusalem and Athens: Critical Discussions on the Philosophy and Apologetics of Cornelius Van Til* (Phillipsburg, NJ: Presbyterian and Reformed, 1980), 289–290. Schaeffer, however, gradually distanced himself from the label and saw non-contradiction as a principle of reality, not just of logic (rather as Hegel saw synthesis as a principle of the real universe). He did not view truth only as analytical—for him Christianity is "true truth"; the only reason for believing is that its claims are true to what is "there."

[29]C. S. Lewis, in his inaugural lecture upon taking up the Chair of Renaissance and Medieval Literature at Cambridge in 1954, *De Descriptione Temporum*, locates the break between the Old and New West more generally than Schaeffer and more sociologically, in the early nineteenth century. For an extended comparison of Lewis and Schaeffer, see Scott R. Burson and Jerry L. Walls, *C. S. Lewis and Francis Schaeffer: Lessons for a New Century from the Most Influential Apologists of Our Time* (Downers Grove, IL: InterVarsity Press, 1998).

secondary points of doctrine and Christian behavior. On January 1, 1937 the center of stability at Westminster was removed by the sudden, unexpected death of J. Gresham Machen. He was only fifty-five. In the previous days, months, and years he had pushed himself unmercifully, throughout conflict with the main Presbyterian Church, his defrocking, and founding a new church, all the time fulfilling his responsibilities at Westminster Seminary. On a trip to Baltimore to encourage support for the new denomination he succumbed to pneumonia.

Matters came to a head in May 1937 at a Synod meeting when tempers flared and accusations were hurled. A majority at Westminster emphasized "Christian liberty," while Fran's faction emphasized a list of behaviors unsuitable for the "separated Christian," such as drinking alcohol, smoking, theater attendance, and dancing. (Interestingly, Edith was a covert rebel when it came to dance—as an older teenager she had danced at high school events and other occasions without her strict parents' knowledge.) Tied to this was an insistence on the superiority of a premillennialist view of biblical prophecy. The result was another new denomination and a new seminary for the disaffected minority, led by Oliver Buswell and the youthful and driven Carl McIntire. The new denomination was called the Bible Presbyterian Church and the seminary, Faith Theological Seminary, to be located in Wilmington, a little over thirty miles down the Delaware River. Allan MacRae was to be president, and a number of faculty and students transferred from Westminster to Faith for the next academic year.[30] For classes the new seminary had been given the use of the Sunday school rooms of a church opposite the Baltimore and Ohio Railroad Station in Wilmington. The need remained, however, for accommodation for faculty and students, with very little time to find it. The search was complicated by the fact that a large company, DuPont, was also seeking accommodation for its workers at that time.

R. Laird Harris was one of those who migrated to Faith Seminary, joining the new faculty. His two graduate years at Westminster had

---

[30]According to R. Laird Harris (interview, 1998), a little-known factor in the divorce from Westminster was Allan MacRae's dissatisfaction with Van Til's Presuppositional Apologetics. MacRae respected the Princetonian Evidential Apologetics of Machen and that tradition. Harris said, "He felt it [Westminster Presuppositionalism] undercut a great deal of his Old Testament evidences for the truth of Christianity."

coincided with Francis Schaeffer's first and second years, where he got to know him. Harris recalled Fran being "very energetic, as he always was, very personable and a fine fellow, and he had ideas." He takes up the story:

> I remember that we were told that it would be very difficult to find housing for students [in Wilmington] because DuPont was bringing in a bunch of people. But the apartments the DuPont people were looking for were above the apartments we were looking for, [which were] for students. So we did find apartments for students, and Francis Schaeffer was active in that, he and a man named John Krause. . . . He and John Krause looked around and found several houses just a block away from the independent church where we were holding classes for the first few years.[31]

Schaeffer and Krause found four houses in all, each with three stories.

As well as searching out accommodations, Fran suggested his father-in-law, George Seville, as a faculty member, to teach beginning Greek and missions. He was semi-retired but had great vitality. (In fact, he lived to be over one hundred and would teach at Faith for seventeen years, before taking on the task of home secretary for the newly formed L'Abri Fellowship at eighty.) Seville remained close to the unfolding concerns and ministry of his daughter and son-in-law for the rest of his life.[32] Edith was glad to have her mother and father living across the street from them, providing support in early motherhood.

Fran had energetically helped in this practical way in the foundation of the seminary on top of his new responsibilities as a father, his engagement in the all-consuming task putting pressure on the family. Janet Priscilla Schaeffer had been born on June 18, 1937. Fran rushed Edith to the hospital a week before, police providing an escort after first stopping him for speeding. He was decidedly annoyed with Edith upon discovering that it was false labor—he had a lot to learn, and his attitude was not easy for Edith to absorb. A new crisis brought reality. At birth the new baby did not breathe for half an hour. Giving oxygen failed to help,

---

[31]Interview with R. Laird and Ann Harris, 1998.
[32]Edith in fact began writing her "Family Letters" for her parents' benefit in 1948.

but a doctor's mouth-to-mouth resuscitation finally worked. Against expectation baby Priscilla did not suffer brain damage.[33] Fathers in those days were allowed little visiting time, and even that was eroded by Fran's practical involvement in setting up the seminary. Though this was a struggle for Edith, she gamely supported him. Soon she would be leaving the baby with her mother while she and Fran traveled to Wilmington to find plumbers and electricians and to search for furniture and accessories, so accommodations could be ready for the start of the semester, all on a tiny budget provided by the seminary administrators.

The following year Fran graduated, among Faith's first graduates, and was the first to be ordained in the new Bible Presbyterian Church. So it was that nine months after going to Wilmington, the family was on the move again. Their destination was about three hundred and fifty miles away, in Grove City, Pennsylvania. Grove City was, and still is, a small town, its population then about six thousand, surrounded by rural landscape and farms. It is located about fifty miles north of Pittsburgh, with Lake Erie less than eighty miles to its north. In the late thirties Grove City prided itself on being a "dry town," which suited the conservative Schaeffers.

Francis Schaeffer was to be a pastor for over ten years, three of them in Grove City, and his small-town followed by larger-town experience deepened his theological knowledge. At first, for instance, his belief in human responsibility was overly simplistic. His closest friend in later years, Hans Rookmaaker, remembered:

> That God is at work in people has implications for the evangelist as well. Schaeffer once told me that when he had just become a pastor, he worked very, very hard. He was always completely exhausted. Why? Because when he was talking to somebody, he felt he had to convince that person. If he was not able to do that, he felt it was his fault that the other person did not accept Christ. But then one day he found out he had been wrong. That is not the way to do it. After all, nobody can make anyone else a Christian; that is beyond us. So what do we do? Well, if God calls us to speak to somebody we try to give the best possible answers, but at the same time we pray that God will work in that

---

[33]Edith Schaeffer, *The Tapestry*, 194–195.

person's heart so that whatever we say right will make itself felt and continue to work, and whatever we say wrong will have no impact. We acknowledge that it is first of all God's work rather than our work. Then the pressure is gone and because of that it is not so exhausting.[34]

This was an issue, however, with which Fran agonized until his dying day.

Grove City's busy industry belied the town's small size—including the manufacture of locomotive engines, carriages, and other engines as well as trucks. It also was home to a liberal arts college. The first challenge awaiting the new minister and his wife was a tiny congregation at the Covenant Presbyterian Church (then called the Westminster Presbyterian Church), which had separated the year before from the "big liberal Presbyterian Church." The congregation at that time met in the American Legion hall and did not bring their children, who remained in the larger Sunday school of their old church with their friends. In contrast to their hopes while Fran studied first at Westminster and then at Faith, Grove City was a shock. Late in life Edith remembered it not being "an idyllic time" and as seeming "unromantic."[35]

Today the church is thriving and tells on its modern web site what transpired some time after the arrival of the new pastor.

During his three years in Grove City, the new church began to thrive. The town of Nebraska, PA, was about to be flooded to create the Tionesta Dam, and in the middle of the doomed site stood a charming little white frame church. The session bought the building and dismantled it, piece by piece, for transportation to Grove City.

Schaeffer and the session helped to rebuild the church—until time came for the steeple-raising, when most of the crew suddenly scuttled away. One elder and Schaeffer were the only two with "heads that would take heights," Mrs. Schaeffer notes, so minister and elder painted their new steeple a gleaming white.

While Schaeffer was painting outdoors, his wife was also trying her hand at painting. The building committee had wanted to create a

---

[34]Hans Rookmaaker, "Predestination," in Marleen Hengelaar-Rookmaaker, editor, *Our Calling and God's Hand in History: The Complete Works of Hans Rookmaaker*, Vol. 6 (Carlisle: Piquant, 2003), 292.
[35]Interview with Edith Schaeffer in *Hearts on Fire: The Story of Francis and Edith Schaeffer*, a video production by RBL Ministries for Day of Discovery, USA, 2003.

ceiling piece to match the building's four stained glass windows. The colorful design, with narrow black outlines, creates a stained glass effect and did indeed match the windows. . . .[36]

When the new church was dedicated, every seat was full, and membership was 110. There were many children to be seen. They had not started to come to church, however, by accident.

Fran had been concerned about the lack of children from the beginning. He had found a secluded section in the town park that had once been a strip mine, and he came up with the idea of trying hot dog roasts. The church provided a small budget for food, and he went scouting for boys, calling out, "Hey, there—how would you like to come to a hot dog roast?" Boys, who soon nicknamed him "Rev.," would pile into his Model A Ford and be taken to the park. On one memorable occasion twenty-one boys squeezed into the car. After several weeks of the roasts Fran and Edith asked for volunteers from the church to help with a Summer Bible School. As there were no children in the Sunday school, there was some skepticism. The hot dog roast boys, however, proved to be the key to the success of the Summer Bible School, which ran mornings for two weeks. Fran took boys as part of his "visiting team" and would drive up and down streets, stopping wherever the boys knew a child, and knock on the door to offer an invitation. Edith supplemented his efforts by painting a big poster. The school was held in an adapted Legion Hall, and seventy-nine attended the first morning, swelling to a high of more than one hundred.[37]

Both Fran and Edith were never short on invention, and the school was packed with songs, vividly retold Bible stories, memorization of Bible verses, and catechism. The event was solid with content but obviously enjoyable to the children, who needed little encouragement to respond enthusiastically.

Fran spent much of his time on pastoral visits, not only to church members, but to parents of the children with whom they were working, and also people with an obvious need. It was clear to Edith early on that he had a talent for pastoral calling.

---

[36]See http://www.covenantopcgrovecity.org/history.html.
[37]The story of these events is recounted by several who were children at the time in the Day of Discovery documentary on Francis and Edith Schaeffer.

Attempts to make contact with students at the town's college was a failure, but more successful was a Miracle Book Club in their home. This came out of meeting Evelyn M. McClusky,[38] the originator of the national club by this name, which had been started to provide home Bible studies for high-school young people. Looking back over forty years later, Edith Schaeffer observed:

> This was the beginning of our work with young people that later grew into L'Abri, even as the Bible School was our beginning work with children that was going to include our "Children for Christ" work later. Many seeds were planted in Grove City.[39]

Edith was pregnant again, expecting their second daughter, Susan, who was born on May 28, 1941. Fran was not only fully involved with his local congregation and his young family but with the fledgling denomination. He had become moderator of the Great Lakes Presbytery of the Bible Presbyterian Church and a member of the Home Mission Committee of that denomination and served on the Board of Directors of the Summer Bible School Association. It was through the Association that he got to know Dr. A. L. Lathem, its elderly founder.

Abraham L. Lathem was Senior Pastor of the Bible Presbyterian Church in Chester, on the Delaware River, a mere fifteen miles downriver and southwest of Philadelphia. Wilmington, with its happy memories of Faith Seminary, lay a further fifteen miles or so downriver. Francis Schaeffer was invited to Chester, the oldest city in Pennsylvania, not long after Susan's birth to preach as a prospective move. He then received a formal invitation to be assistant pastor to Lathem. He and Edith by now had been three years at Grove City, had seen the church established on a healthy foundation, and felt that it was time to move on. They spent the summer of 1941 based in nearby Wilmington while they house-hunted, eventually taking out a mortgage on a newly built house in a suburb.

In contrast to Grove City, Chester was large, around sixty-five thousand at that time (it has since sharply declined), and the church had a membership of more than five hundred. The new minister quickly iden-

---

[38]Evelyn M. McClusky (1889–1994), author of many books, founded the movement in 1933, which rapidly spread around the world. She became a lifelong friend of the Schaeffers.
[39]Edith Schaeffer, *The Tapestry*, 207.

tified with the many working-class members of his congregation, both city and country folk. His building skills were soon utilized in helping complete necessary building work on the church. He happily climbed scaffolding to join members of the church who were giving their time to do the construction. Fran was not so happy, however, about further ambitious building plans that he felt were unnecessary.

They were settling in to the new situation when the American Council of Christian Churches was founded on September 17 in New York City, during a meeting between the Bible Protestant Church and Schaeffer's denomination, the Bible Presbyterian Church. It was set up as an agency to represent separated fundamentalists. In the years that followed, other denominations joined the ACCC. The agency was set up as an alternative to the Federal Council of Churches (now known as the National Council of Churches), which had strong affinities with the World Council of Churches, the formation of which had been delayed by the onset of war in Europe. The first elected president of the ACCC was the increasingly militant Carl McIntire.[40] Schaeffer would develop close ties with the ACCC while gradually disassociating himself from McIntire, who eventually called him a Communist![41]

Not long after their arrival the hideous war that had devastated much of the world since 1939 awoke American consciousness with the surprise attack on Pearl Harbor on Sunday, December 7, 1941 by Japanese bombers. The shock would be paralleled by the 9/11 attack on New York in 2001 by an Islamic terror cult. By autumn 1942 blackouts were imposed, and air raid drills in Chester became commonplace. As a minister Fran was allowed to use very limited lights on his car for pastoral visits. In the enforced darkness the last scenes of Fran's father's life played out. Much to the joy of Fran and Edith, "Pop" not long earlier had put his faith in Christ after the first of a series of strokes. Susan, who was a precocious infant at the time, takes up the story:

> It was in the Second World War, when there were blackouts, and the hospital didn't have blackouts, so they couldn't turn on the lights, and

---

[40]After many clashes within the organization as a result of his strong and abrasive views, McIntire's leadership was rejected by the ACCC in 1968.
[41]Interview with Susan Macaulay, 2007.

he was dying, and my father said to me—I came into the room and
he'd been praying for his dad—[that] suddenly his voice came out of
the blackness, "Boy, tell me about your Jesus." . . . With that sort of
thing, my father was a very emotional man, very strongly. So he would
never tell the story without it touching his own emotion. These stories
went very deep for us because they became almost as if they were our
own experiences.[42]

"Pop" Schaeffer died in the darkness of a blackout early one morning in June 1943.

Two incidents from their period in Chester illustrate the complexity
and unpredictability of Francis Schaeffer the man, belying the simple
theory that there were two or even three Schaeffers over the course of
his life, early and later, perhaps with an intermediate stage—a golden
age of L'Abri.

One concerned a small girl in the congregation. Fran rushed into his
house one day while he was making pastoral calls. "Edith," he asked,
"fix me a little bottle of sweet oil, will you?" He quickly explained,
"There is a little girl who has an incurable tongue disease. They say the
doctor doesn't give any hope for her life, and the mother has asked if I
would come and pray with her and anoint her with oil. I've called some
of the elders, so several of them are going to come with me now."[43] Later
he reported to Edith that he read the passage about anointing with oil
from James 5:13–18 at the girl's bedside, poured oil on her head, and
prayed simply that the Lord would give the little girl back to her parents.
Then he and the elders placed their hands on her. Each day after the
anointing the girl got a little better until she was completely well. The
doctors had no medical explanation for the change.

Another incident involved a Down's syndrome child named Ralphie.
His parents had no means to pay for special education. Fran spent time
with him twice weekly, taking along a variety of blocks in different
colors. He would patiently teach him. Soon a girl with similar learning
difficulties joined Ralphie for the lessons. Edith remembers that Fran got
as excited about any progress as if they had been PhD students work-

---

[42]Ibid.
[43]Edith Schaeffer, *The Tapestry*, 222.

ing on a thesis. "To Fran," she observed, "this was as important a part of his work as talking to any university student about his intellectual problems."[44]

Through the period at Chester, Fran continued to have a shaping role in the fledgling separatist denomination, in 1942 giving a paper on "Our System of Doctrine" to the General Synod of the Bible Presbyterian Church, meeting in St. Louis, which spelled out theologically the basis of separation and purity in the church. This he later adapted into a booklet published by the denomination.[45] He argued that they were a doctrinal church, "the value of a clear, strong, vibrant doctrinal position" being demonstrated by their break from the Presbyterian Church in the USA. "Other denominations which were weaker in doctrinal emphasis," he dramatically claimed, "fell into the hands of Modernism with barely a ripple of opposition." He defined their doctrinal position as Protestant, supernaturalist, evangelical, particularist (as opposed to universalist), and premillennialist (even though premillennialist statements were not formally part of their System of Doctrine). Their formal doctrinal position, he pointed out, is that which is commonly named "Reformed." Each element of formal doctrine inevitably brings separation; that they were supernaturalists, for instance, necessarily separated them from naturalists. Some elements involved a less emphatic separation than others; they could as evangelicals have a wider fellowship with certain sacerdotalists. He concluded with characteristic realism, "It must be doctrine, not merely on a sheet of paper, but *doctrine in action*" (his emphasis). It is clear from his words that even then his notion of separation was not totally exclusive and was not shaped only in the context of the recent crisis created by theological liberalism but was rather founded on historic Christian faith, epitomized for him in the Westminster Confession of 1646.

In all he and Edith served in Chester for less than two years before moving on to work in St. Louis. Edith remembered, "We loved the people in Chester and felt their sorrows as well as joys, longing in many

---

[44]Ibid., 223. Interestingly, at roughly the same period, C. S. Lewis, in his Oxford home, was giving lessons to an evacuee with severe learning difficulties, a lad with a mental age of about eight. Lewis made drawings and letter cards as he gave him lessons in reading. See Colin Duriez, *Tolkien and C. S. Lewis: The Gift of Friendship* (Mahwah, NJ: Paulist Press, 2003), 114.

[45]F. A. Schaeffer, *Our System of Doctrine* (Philadelphia: Bible Presbyterian Church, 1942).

ways to keep on being a part of their lives."[46] They took over the First
Bible Presbyterian Church from John W. Sanderson Jr., who had gradu-
ated from Faith Seminary in 1940 and who later went on to teach at
Covenant Seminary.

Edith's excitement in moving to St. Louis, deep in the Midwest, is
captured in a thumbnail sketch of the city that she wrote nearly forty
years later.

> St. Louis—with its Forest Park—a wonderful park with rolling ground,
> trees, a lake, an art museum on top of a hill, a complete zoo, and a
> marvelous and constantly changing greenhouse where large trees and
> basic plants remained, but where flower displays were a kind of suc-
> cession of "shows" fitting the season—was to be our home city. St.
> Louis—with its Kiel Auditorium and emphasis on symphony concerts,
> with its lovely big downtown stores (before shopping malls began),
> when errands could be done so efficiently and one could have special
> luncheons or a refreshing "bite" (a salad and an iced coffee) when
> meeting someone for conversation—was to open new doors for us.
> St. Louis—where "city homes" were solid red brick or stone, on tree-
> lined streets, some of the more affluent "private streets" with their
> magnificent old wrought-iron gates taking one back to another period
> of history. . . . . St. Louis—a city with two universities, medical colleges,
> and especially good private schools, enormous hospital complexes,
> some very successful businesses, as well as Roman Catholic seminaries,
> and the Lutheran Concordia Seminary; a city with a wide cross-section
> of people from the country-club set to the underprivileged—was to
> be an education for us, in some new ways, as well as a challenge!
> St. Louis—called in travel guides "Gateway to the West" as it stands
> on the Mississippi River, which connects a fantastic range of places
> from Minneapolis to New Orleans—was to be our home city, and, as
> far as we knew, it was to be for a lifetime.[47]

Their ministry in St. Louis was to be their longest stint in any one
place as an ordinary pastor and his wife. Fran was now thirty-one and
Edith twenty-eight years of age. He wasn't so easily mistaken now for
one of the young people in the church because of youthful looks. Edith
looked even more beautiful now that she was older. People were drawn

---

[46]Edith Schaeffer, *The Tapestry*, 222.
[47]Ibid., 230–231.

to the lively couple with their six-year-old daughter and her two-year-old sister. They found a three-story house with thirteen rooms and a large basement, near enough to the park with its zoo to hear lions roaring during the quiet of night. Edith fell in love with the red-bricked church on the corner of Union and Enright, with its lofty ceiling arches, tapering stained-glass windows, large beams, paneled walls, pews of dark wood, and a pipe organ. Its congregation was large, too, which meant that Fran was thrown into a schedule that teemed with meetings, both services and administrative, preaching twice on Sundays, and presenting a Bible study on Wednesday evenings at the prayer meetings. The children, Priscilla the elder and Susan the younger, remember Sunday afternoons at that time fondly.

Though her memories are not as clear as her elder sister's, Susan recalled:

> He'd take us to the zoo again and again and again, a wonderful zoo. And he'd also take us into St. Louis, one of our favorite things, because we'd be at church in the morning. My mother would cook a wonderful Sunday lunch, laid out the way she says in her books, with flowers and everything. I remember one thing that left a huge impression on me. . . . He took us to a room [in the art museum] where the Spanish monastery garden was all set up, brick by brick, with the fountain in the middle, and there were cloisters, and I remember loving it. He wouldn't rush us out—he gave us sketch pads.

For Priscilla, who had many vivid memories of the family outings, the art museum was particularly important. Her father was sharing something that had become a necessary part of his life, giving him nourishment and a unique window into the cultures of the past. He was to write as early as 1951, "Modern Art fits into the general tone of thought of our day, just as the earlier art forms fitted into the thinking of the day. *There is no better way to understand the basic world view of a period of history than studying its art forms.*"[48] Her father's deep interest in art existed while he was deeply part of a separatist denomination with strong views on all kinds of abstinence from the world. For her, looking back over sixty

---

[48]Francis A. Schaeffer, "The Christian and Modern Art," *The Bible Today*, March 1951. Emphasis Schaeffer's.

years, this revealed a characteristic quality of the unexpected. Priscilla's comment is very significant.[49] This quality may be why he constantly slips through the nets of those who are his detractors.

Priscilla looked back on the St. Louis days so clearly that she could still picture the rooms in the art museum there. This is because she and Susan, and later Debby, went so often with their father. It was not simply for a walk-through. He would get them to sit there and play different games together relating to the exhibits. They were asked to decide in a particular gallery which paintings they liked, which was not a simple question because he genuinely wanted to involve them.

> There we were in St. Louis, and on his day off he'd take us children, we three girls, Franky wasn't born yet, paraded through the St. Louis Art Museum. I know it by heart even today after all these years, and he'd really get us involved. He had great respect, admiration, and insight, so he'd tell us about the history of the paintings, but then he'd also say, "Now, sit in this room. Look, which painting do you really like?" But then a different question, "Which painting would you really like hanging in your bedroom?" because that might be two different paintings. So we had this kind of attitude toward the arts, and Franky had the same thing when he came to Europe, because Daddy was parading us around the European art museums. It was this great interest in art that differentiated him from the run-of-the-mill pastors and the church government—all these things he was entangled in, with church separation and McIntire and all that—this love for the arts.[50]

Deborah Ann was born on May 3, 1945, nearly two years after the Schaeffers moved to St. Louis. Though she therefore has fewer memories of this period than her older sisters, she recalled two things that demonstrated the same kind of unexpectedness in her father as his passionate love for the arts.

The first was his attitude toward the church in the city, with its growing ethnic mix:

> One of the things that I always found so striking and un-understandable . . . was the fact that in St. Louis, in the forties, he had told his

[49]Interview with Priscilla and John Sandri, 2007.
[50]Ibid.

elders that he would resign if they moved the church out to the suburbs. When you read a history of America you see that was a defining event in American history—moving away from the city and out to the suburbs changed the culture and society completely. For some reason, I don't know why, my father felt very strongly about that. He felt that the church must stay where it was and serve the people there and not move out to where people now wanted to have a more comfortable suburban existence. Connected with that, I know at the same time he told his session that if any black person came to the church and was not only rejected but [even] made to feel unwelcome, he would also resign. Again in the forties in St. Louis, Missouri, this was not a common issue that was being discussed. It wasn't an issue that certainly Christians were talking about, it wasn't an issue that was central in American life, and yet he felt very strongly about it. Those were certainly two political issues, if you want to use that term, and those were when he was a very young man, and not surrounded by other people who had that view.[51]

The second memory that revealed her father's unexpected qualities was his attitude to the far-off world war.

I'd always heard this interesting thing from him that he used to say to the young soldiers going off from his church that he thought it was a really right thing for them to go and fight in the Second World War, but that it could be murder if they, in their heart, as it were, were revengeful; hated these people personally [to] hurt them. I deduce that is a very unusual point of view, a very unusual thing for him to be talking about, rather than just praying with the soldiers that "the church will pray for you—go with our blessings." . . . I mean that was already a very unusual thing, especially at the time of the Second World War, with the patriotism and so forth. So I deduce . . . that he must have been very concerned with what was going on in Europe; he must have been very aware. He must have been following it very closely, because otherwise he wouldn't have that kind of concern. And knowing him in later life . . . he was tremendously burdened—I think that's the correct word—with what went on in human history.[52]

Fran's concern for the war, clearly tied up with an awareness of Europe, may have partly come from his German ancestry (emphasized

---

[51]Interview with Debby and Udo Middelmann, 2007.
[52]Ibid.

by his family name). It might also have been strengthened in his consciousness by his long-standing concern about higher criticism of the
Bible in modernism, which had originated in Germany long before the
threat of Hitler or even World War I[53] and which, in his view, had contributed to the use of anti-human values.

Related to the Second World War, there is a further indicator of
the unexpectedness, compassion, and great depths of Fran's developing
character. This is demonstrated in his attitude toward Jewish people,
which resulted in a pamphlet published by his church in St. Louis in
1943, probably based on a sermon given there. It was entitled "The
Bible-believing Christian and the Jew," and it directly addressed the
issue of anti-Semitism. It was widely distributed. In the pamphlet he
quotes a Jewish journalist on one of the New York newspapers whom
he had met a few years previously. (The occasion in fact was a brief
vacation Fran and Edith had taken in the Bear Mountain Inn on the
Hudson River in the autumn of 1937.[54]) They had discussed Jewish and
Christian faith, and then the journalist had recited a verse that, he said,
was widely repeated among the Jewish community in New York:

> *How odd of God*
> *To choose the Jew,*
> *But not so odd*
> *As those who choose*
> *The Jewish God*
> *And hate the Jew.*[55]

The year before Fran preached that sermon on anti-Semitism,
a young Jewish woman died in Auschwitz in southern Poland on
September 30, 1942, soon after her arrival from Holland. She was
twenty-three and unstereotypically blonde. Her name was Hendrika
Beatrix Spetter, nicknamed Riki. She could have been a statistic, just
one of the fifty-five million casualties of World War II, the most sav-

---

[53]An observation made by Udo Middelmann, in ibid.
[54]The incident is recounted in Edith Schaeffer, *Christianity Is Jewish* (London and Eastbourne, UK: Coverdale House, 1975), 5–6.
[55]The text of the booklet was published as "The Fundamentalist Christian and Anti-Semitism," Francis A. Schaeffer, *The Independent Board Bulletin*, October 1943, 16–19. Available online at PCA Archives, www.pcahistory.org/documents/anti-Semitism.html.

age conflict in human history. But almost certainly she would become known indirectly to Fran via her fiancé, a young Dutchman incarcerated in an Officers' Prison Camp in southwestern Ukraine at that same time, and soon to come to Christian faith there rather as Fran did, by reading the Bible through and reading philosophy at the same time. That Dutchman, Hans Rookmaaker, was to become Fran's closest friend apart from Edith. Around the time of Fran's sermon in far-off St. Louis, Rookmaaker, now a Christian, prepared a study of God's working through the Jewish prophets of the Bible, subtitled, "God's way with Israel," which he dedicated to Riki Spetter on September 19, 1943, giving his location as Stanislau. He was unaware that she was dead.[56]

From the very beginning of their pastorate in St. Louis, Fran and Edith continued to have a concern for children. Throughout North America, Britain, and elsewhere missions to children was becoming more organized, with various parachurch organizations emerging or consolidating, such as Scripture Union in Britain and Child Evangelism Fellowship in North America. Sunday schools had long been established. Throughout their years in St. Louis the Schaeffers gradually developed a wide strategy for missions to children, which was to open up on a scale they little imagined. Just one aspect of it was their enthusiastic rallies and Summer Bible Schools, which were vividly remembered many decades later by those who participated as young children, a number of whom became Christian leaders. One person with such memories is Hurvey Woodson, who was to join the work of L'Abri in its early years in the next decade. He was particularly struck by the enthusiasm Schaeffer displayed in his work with children and young adults.

> Mr. and Mrs. Schaeffer were quite young at that time. He had an outstanding Summer Bible School here at St. Louis; [it] was four weeks long. At a certain point, we had three or four hundred kids going. We enjoyed it so much that we started going to Young People's and going to their church. They were always dynamic, high-energy, and we had just a lot of fun. You got all these awards, your red ribbon and your blue ribbon, and all these sort of things. We learned reams of material. In those days, a Summer Bible School went right on through high

---

[56]Despite searching and waiting for her several years after his return to the Netherlands, Rookmaaker did not discover the facts about Riki's death during his lifetime.

school [ages, taking in children and young adults]. We took geography
of Palestine, all sorts of subjects. It was not a large church, but we had
a huge summer Bible school. Kids would come from all over St. Louis.
As a matter of fact, there was a large picture of all the Summer Bible
School in the *St. Louis Post Dispatch*. It was really pretty phenomenal.
The young people liked him a lot.[57]

The younger children also enjoyed it. The Schaeffers' second child,
Susan, was totally caught up in the Summer School. She remembered:

> Every morning they sent school buses all over the city of St. Louis and
> would bring in [children]. In the forties there wasn't any amusement,
> and we'd go. They made them so we really enjoyed it. We'd sing,
> we'd all belt it out like some kind of Spring Harvest [meeting], "[And
> when the] saints come marching in," and she'd [Mother] do great
> big pictures and be up on the platform, all very charismatic, and my
> father planned Bible teaching, so that we were really learning from the
> Psalms, memorizing and getting a star. . . . [58]

The horizons of Fran and Edith's future work began to open up
with the response from children to the Summer Bible Schools and rallies. They also developed an explicitly Christian version of Boy Scouts
and Girl Scouts, resulting in the first publications Schaeffer later listed:
Empire Builder for Boys and *Empire Builder for Girls*, 1946.[59] They
were adapted from Robert Baden Powell's famous book, *Scouting for
Boys*. As part of a careful strategy for outreach to children and young
adults, they also began an organization called Children for Christ. This
at first small evangelistic mission to children was the stimulus that
would lead Francis and Edith to Europe in the crucial years following
the Second World War.

---

[57]Interview with Hurvey and Dorothy Woodson, 1998.
[58]Interview with Susan Macaulay, 2007.
[59]Listed about 1968 by Schaeffer in a form filled out for IVP UK (IVF Publications: Index of Authors).

CHAPTER THREE

NEW VISTAS

(1945–1948)

രരരരര

During the five years in St. Louis Francis Schaeffer continued to
be involved heavily in the shaping and administration of the
new denomination, the Bible Presbyterian Church. He served
as moderator of its Midwest Presbytery. He also developed close connections with the separatist American Council of Christian Churches,
serving on a national level but also setting up a local council for the
St. Louis area. With his constant burden over what was transpiring in
the World War, he took a great interest in the Independent Board for
Presbyterian Foreign Missions, which J. Gresham Machen had helped
found in 1933 and which was now closely connected to the Bible
Presbyterian Church and other separated denominations. Eventually he
became a member of its board.

In the development and future ministries of Francis and Edith
Schaeffer what is most significant in this era is not Fran's denomina-
tionalism (even though its separatism was very important to them) or
the pastoring of their St. Louis church but their work with children,
leading to the creation of Children for Christ, which existed formally
from 1945.

Children for Christ was a more thought-out and long-term mission
than their highly successful Summer Bible Schools that had started in
Grove City. It would soon take on an international dimension, beyond
their initial expectations.

Edith remembered the simple beginnings of Children for Christ
soon after the family moved into their new home at 5248 Waterman
Boulevard on Christmas Eve, 1943, some months after arriving from
Chester, Pennsylvania.

With Priscilla and Susan's small friends, we soon started a children's class in our basement, with children from a diversity of backgrounds coming—Jewish, Roman Catholic, Lutheran, Episcopalian, and those who had never been in any religious group. Simultaneously with my starting this class, Fran invited women of our church to come once a week to prepare to teach children's Bible classes in their own homes. Soon twenty such classes were started. We gave a weekly lesson as if to children, and the ladies took notes. Using the Ping-Pong table in the basement for a working surface, they cut out pictures for lesson illustrations and pasted flannel on the backs, so that the individual classes were prepared for, together. We then prayed for the children of our various neighborhoods, compared notes, exchanged ideas, and drank hot chocolate or tea. These very practical evenings were really the beginning of the work we were soon to call "Children for Christ."[1]

The classes were a straightforward and practical response to the question of how their church could reach out to the children of the city. They became the prime element in a seven-point strategy under the label of Children for Christ. The strategy lent itself to easy modification for particular circumstances, which, unanticipated by the Schaeffers, would turn out to include use in other countries.

1. The home Bible classes.
2. "Released Time Classes"—utilizing the one hour a week for which Missouri (and some other states) allowed children to be released from school for voluntary religious teaching at that time.
3. A program for informal gatherings of children on beaches and in parks (as allowed by some states)—these could include hymn-singing and retelling Bible stories.
4. Empire Builder Clubs, similar to Boy and Girl Scouts, but with added Christian teaching.
5. An annual Summer Bible School.
6. A camping program to follow the Summer Bible School.
7. A large annual children's rally, the purpose of which was so children could see that a large number of other children shared their Christian faith.

As the months and years passed in St. Louis, all seven points

[1]Edith Schaeffer, *The Tapestry* (Nashville: Word, 1981), 233–234.

became realities. The first rally alone was so successful that over seven hundred children attended—it was this event that was captured in the pages of the *St. Louis Post Dispatch*, as remembered by Hurvey Woodson.[2]

Word about Children for Christ got around, and its work spread to other churches, and even to other denominations. At this time, however, the movement was still strongly separatist. It was only through Fran's and then Edith's exposure to Europe that Children for Christ became more widely taken up. Edith admitted, "I must say very frankly that at that time Fran was in the American Council for Christian Churches, and our Children for Christ was made available only to churches in this 'separatist circle.'"[3] She recalled that in those St. Louis days they were unable to achieve a balance between dealing with "false teaching" and not negatively attacking people. They were aware, however, of a "vague uneasiness"[4] about the limited access they allowed other churches to participate in Children for Christ.

The organization was not set up formally until 1945, and this was in reaction to developments in the Child Evangelism Fellowship, according to an explanatory sketch in the PCA archives:

> During the meetings of the American Council of Christian Churches in St. Louis, Missouri, in 1945, a movement for child evangelism was launched on a national basis. Children for Christ, Incorporated, was a local organization in St. Louis which had its beginnings because of the reorganization of the Child Evangelism Fellowship program in that city earlier in 1945. On October 20th, in a meeting at the First Bible Presbyterian Church of St. Louis, a national board of trustees was formed, with the Rev. Francis A. Schaeffer appointed as director. Such men as the Rev. Carl McIntire, the Rev. R.T. Ketchum, and the Rev. E. G. Zorn were included as members of the national board.
>
> With the enlargement of the work to a national scale, an aggressive program began to be put in place. Already the program was ministering to thousands of children in the St. Louis area through child evangelism classes in the neighborhoods and through released time classes in the public school system. A work in Columbus, Ohio soon reported

---

[2]See note 57, Chapter 2.
[3]Edith Schaeffer, *The Tapestry*, 235.
[4]Ibid.

the organization of a work along similar lines, and other similar works were quickly replicated across the country.[5]

Fran, according to historian Forrest Baird, had been a prime mover in the local Child Evangelism Fellowship branch until the national CEF Board ordered him to stop running it as a separatist organization. They wanted evangelical pastors and churches outside of the American Council of Christian Churches to be involved. He had refused and resigned, formally instigating Children for Christ on separatist lines.[6]

Looking back to that time, Edith acknowledged that the formation of Children for Christ was a factor in their eventual move to Europe in 1948. It was certainly an important part of their work together in St. Louis and easily could have developed into a full-time occupation for them both.[7] This evangelistic outreach to children, in fact, was one of two important stimuli that eventually led Francis and Edith to Europe in the crucial years following the Second World War. The other was Fran's deeply felt concern over the impact of theological liberalism in U.S. churches, which had come from Europe. He was also very concerned about the new face of such liberalism—neo-orthodoxy—which he regarded as nothing short of a wolf in sheep's clothing. Its use of ortho-dox terminology and emphasis on the Word of God gave it a fatal attrac-tion.[8] In the spring of 1947 the Independent Board for Presbyterian Foreign Missions discussed the situation in Europe following the recent war. Fran expressed interest in the state of children's and youth work and the danger of infiltration of theological liberalism in Europe. Edith reports him as saying to the Board, "It seems to me that we should find out just what the situation is in the churches. So many have been isolated in those countries during the war—isolated from the new sweep of dan-ger, theologically—and are sending their theological students to study in America without any knowledge of what is being taught. We also

---

[5]PCA Historical Center Collection; www.pcahistory.org/findingaids/childrenforchrist.html.
[6]Daymon A. Johnson, *Francis A. Schaeffer, An Analysis of His Religious, Social, and Political Influence on the New Christian Right, 1990*, MA dissertation in history, California State University, 1990, 30, citing Forrest Baird, "Schaeffer's Intellectual Roots," in Ronald Ruegsegger, *Reflections on Francis Schaeffer* (Grand Rapids, MI: Zondervan, 1986), 58.
[7]Edith Schaeffer, *The Tapestry*, 235.
[8]Schaeffer outlines the geographical spread of the new orthodoxy, with Karl Barth as its "door," in his *The God Who Is There* and *Escape from Reason*.

ought to find out how children can be given Bible teaching, apart from the churches—something like the Children for Christ work."[9] After a lengthy discussion the Board invited him to make a fact-finding tour later that year, that summer in fact, to last three months. They asked him to visit thirteen countries and to make a detailed report. Not only was he to represent the Board as a member, but he was to be the American Secretary, Foreign Relations Department, of the American Council of Christian Churches.[10] This tour would change his life—and eventually the lives of countless others throughout Europe and the world.

The summer was very close, and it was a daunting task to arrange such a complex itinerary, involving air, sea, and train travel—not to mention local buses, trams, and cog-and-rack railways in Switzerland. Planning and booking was made far more difficult, however, by the lingering impact of the war on Europe, with militarized zones and the Soviet Union poised to take over Czechoslovakia (now the Czech Republic and Slovakia). The bustle of preparation strengthened a feeling the Schaeffers had had for some time, that of being drawn toward wider vistas. As Edith remembered more than three decades later: "It is difficult to be completely certain as to the first 'stirrings' that lifted our eyes to the horizons. Our bedroom wallpaper was grey with pleasant patterned stripes of pale yellow and white. In the garage Fran had found a big mahogany frame (the mirror it contained was broken) and had polished it and backed it with cardboard covered with this wallpaper. In this frame we had placed black and white prints from the old *Asia* magazine—a fisherman casting his nets, tall dignified-looking women carrying loads on their heads, Asian beauty of fields and boats. I had printed with white tempera paint the words, 'Go ye into all the world.' It was a balanced poster on our bedroom wall. . . ." Fran, as part of this same stirring, had asked Edith on one occasion whether she would be willing to take on all the difficulties of going somewhere like Edinburgh in Scotland, if the Lord opened the way for him to study further.[11] As it happened, Fran's three months in Europe would lead to extensive mental and physical exhaustion. It also, however, in Edith's

---

[9]Edith Schaeffer, *The Tapestry*, 246.
[10]Ibid.
[11]Ibid., 245–246.

words, "opened his eyes to a brand new world of understanding as the walls of provinciality were pushed down in a variety of ways."[12]

The travel plans were eventually in place. In all Fran would visit countries in northern, central, and southern Europe, involving around two interviews a day for three months, July to September, mainly with key Christian leaders in the thirteen countries. He would sleep in fifty-three places in France, Switzerland, Norway, Denmark, Germany, Czechoslovakia, Austria, Italy, Greece, Holland, Belgium, England, and Scotland. But there were not only these plans for Fran. Another pastor was arranged for the summer to look after the St. Louis church in Fran's absence, Elmer Smick, with he and his wife Jane occupying the Schaeffers' house. (Elmer Smick would become a lifelong friend of Fran's.) Edith and the three girls found summer accommodations at Cape Cod, in an old schoolhouse in Brewster. The plan was to share it with her sister Janet Bragdon and her two boys, David and Jonathan. They would be joined for two weeks by her other sister, Elsa Van Buskirk, with her daughters, Lucinda and Lydia. The family get-together, in retrospect, turned out to be a very special vacation as the next year would find the Schaeffers beginning a nomadic life in what seemed far-off Europe.

After a flight to Paris that hauled its way via Gander in Newfoundland and Shannon in Ireland, Fran's first month was mainly taken up by engagements in France and Switzerland, much of his traveling in crowded trains. I have his schedule before me. Monday, July 7 to Friday the 11th was spent in Paris, the 12th in Bordeaux, the following two days further south in Nimes, and Tuesday, the 15th in Marseille. From there he visited the Reformed Seminary in Aix-en-Provence, an hour's train journey away. From Marseille he took a midnight train on Wednesday, July 16 to Switzerland (he could not get a sleeper, so he sat up all night), rushing around Geneva on the 17th, and attending a conference in the heart of the country, in Beatenberg near Interlaken, from Friday the 18th to Sunday the 20th. By the 21st he was in Basel, and from there the next day he took the sleeper train to Paris.

In frequent letters back to Edith he shared delighted discoveries, the

<hr />

[12]Ibid., 250.

frustrations of travel, and vignettes of meetings with Christian leaders. He described Geneva. After many hours sorting out travel documents, he wrote, "I put on old clothes and in the pouring rain went looking for the pastor whose address had been given me in France. The address was incomplete and I didn't find him. However, as I was up in the old city I saw the site where Calvin had died. I also saw the great cathedral, St. Peter's, the church where Knox had preached, old Calvin College, and the Reformation monument—I found it all so thrilling! We have a great heritage and I am glad for whatever part I have in carrying it on. Soaking wet I walked along the rushing blue river in the rain. . . ."[13] He was enraptured about the train journey between Lausanne and Berne, the most beautiful ride he had experienced, he said: "The towering mountains on the other side of the wide blue lake just do not seem possible, even when looking at them."[14] Later, on the last leg of his journey to the Bible school at Beatenberg, he described the vista from the cable car as they soared up the mountainside: "The lights of the villages were like a thousand stars."[15] His letters show that his meetings with people were as memorable. At the conference in Beatenberg, he wrote, "After lunch I talked with the director of Emmaus Bible Institute—Dr. de Benoit. He knew Karl Barth as a boy. He sees the need of separation clearly. . . ."[16]

During the last part of July Francis Schaeffer flew from Paris to Oslo for what turned out to be a pivotal experience of the danger of neo-orthodoxy—the new theological liberalism. It also confirmed for him the need for separatism in church life. The event that took him to Oslo was the Young People's Conference of the World Council of Churches. The day after his arrival he heard Dr. Visser 't Hooft speak. It soon became clear to him that the strategy was to encourage younger people to assume leadership in churches, driving out "the greyheads" who resisted the new World Council. His feelings of horror and disquiet contrasted sharply with the pleasure of Scandinavian food and climate, where the sun stayed high in the sky long after it would at home. He

---

[13]Ibid., 253.
[14]Ibid., 254.
[15]Ibid.
[16]Ibid.

wrote Edith, "There is little or no time when there is not light in the sky, and the sun sets and rises less than a quarter of the way around the horizon."[17]

On the following day he attended an early press conference, at which the theologian Reinhold Niebuhr spoke, whom Schaeffer realized was "the thinker for this group." Fran reported to Edith in his daily letter that Niebuhr's "interpretation of Barth provides the bridge for a socialistic conception of Christianity, but keeping some of the religious context. Fosdick is considered to belong to the Dark Ages."[18] Fran's reference to Harry Emerson Fosdick (1878–1969) goes to the quick of what he understood from Niebuhr. Fosdick was an old theological liberal, a modernist at the heart of recent conflict between liberals and fundamentalists. Something new was happening. Not only were the old guard of fundamentalists in the denominations to be superseded, but also the old-fashioned modernists. Henceforth Fran was determined to battle the real enemy, neo-orthodoxy, riddled with what he in later years was to call its "semantic mysticism," by which it retained the richly allusive "religious context" of the Word of God while accepting higher criticism of Scripture. The Bible was understood to be fallible, conditioned by the finitude of its human authors, inevitably making it historically and scientifically misleading or untrue. Neo-orthodoxy said "So what?" to the higher critical view of the factual unreliability of the Bible while affirming Scripture's "religious" truth. That afternoon Fran retired to his hotel "tired and lonely. The loneliness was more than personal. The whole Conference makes me desperately lonely for some Christian contact."[19]

After worshiping in a Baptist church the following day (Sunday), which encouraged him even though the service was in Norwegian, he attended a Greek Orthodox Communion in the Cathedral the next morning that had been laid on for the young people. Though dismayed to see hundreds of Protestant youth participating, he felt far worse with the realization that the service, with its incipient orthodoxy, was nearer to his heart than what was being given by Conference leaders like

[17]Letter to Edith Schaeffer, July 25, 1947, quoted in ibid., 257.
[18]Edith Schaeffer, *The Tapestry*, 257.
[19]Ibid., 258.

Niebuhr and Visser 't Hooft. He confessed in his letter that day to Edith: "At least the liturgy had Christian elements in it. I could have wept, and I guess I was weeping but it was out of the depth of soul for more power to speak with a tongue of gold and fire for the cause of Christ in this age. Never have I realized more that nothing is worth the lessening of that power. I prayed for the filling of the Holy Spirit as I have never prayed before."[20] This was a prayer that anticipated the crisis he would go through as his convictions started to be tested in earnest three years later.

A high point in his visit to Oslo was meeting Ole Hallesby, author of a famous book simply called *Prayer*. To meet him meant being driven seventy-five miles from Oslo over bumpy, potholed roads to his attractive, old farmhouse. A leading theologian, Hallesby had been staunch in his opposition to theological liberalism for decades. Fran was encouraged to discover that Hallesby shared his view of Karl Barth's importance in the rise of neo-orthodoxy. His conviction that evangelicals must separate themselves from liberalism and its embodiment in the spreading ecumenical movement intensified.

When Fran awoke the next morning in his hotel in Oslo, he felt weary. As the day went on he felt worse, his throat very sore. When his temperature was discovered to be 104 he was admitted to the hospital for several days of penicillin injections. This meant his planned visit to Sweden had to be canceled. By the week's end, however, he was able to fly to Copenhagen as scheduled for a Conference of Lutherans.

During the next two months Fran left Copenhagen for a brief stay in Paris, after which he visited Germany, Czechoslovakia, Austria, Italy, Greece, Holland, and Belgium, including a brief return to Switzerland, before finishing his journey in England and Scotland. Everywhere he went he made a point of visiting art galleries and searching out places of historical interest. His exploration of the art and culture of these old countries was not scheduled into his crowded itinerary. While busy getting papers to allow him to enter restricted parts of Germany he revisited "the Louvre in all his spare moments, as well as the Jeu de Paume,

---

[20]Ibid., 259.

standing long in front of his recently discovered favorite paintings."[21]
His daughter Deborah commented:

> He used all his spare time until late at night always walking around
> the cities looking at the buildings, looking at the architecture. He went
> to the art museums all over, which was not part of the trip schedule.
> I think he was on his own, because the pastors who were with him
> wouldn't have gone with him, I don't think. He came back with a
> great appreciation. It hadn't started there, because those memories
> of Priscilla, in the St. Louis art museum, were before that time. This
> was not a new thing. It's rather that suddenly here he was in Paris and
> London, and he wanted to enjoy all that.[22]

Priscilla Sandri, from her older memories of the period, considers
her father's exuberant exploration of old Europe the mark of a profound
change in him. "That's when he fell in love, absolutely in love with
Europe. [Art] was one of his burning loves of life, and suddenly he had
this whole European art, history, culture, [taking to it] just like a duck
to water."[23]

Besides Ole Hallesby in Norway, Fran met many other significant
Christian leaders and theologians, such as Gerrit Cornelis Berkouwer
in Holland, Frank Houghton and Martyn Lloyd-Jones in England, and
Francis Davidson in Scotland. Dr. Lloyd-Jones famously was to take a
separatist path in 1966, almost twenty years later, when, controversially,
he called upon fellow evangelicals in denominations affiliated with
the World Council of Churches to come out from among them. As in
the 1930s in the USA, many evangelicals took a principled decision to
remain. Lloyd-Jones, however, rejected a harshness of spirit in separating, a harshness of which Francis Schaeffer would repent, retaining
warm relations with many evangelical leaders who stayed in "mixed"
denominations, such as the Presbyterian and Anglican.

Great swaths of ruin in cities, bodies of people who had fallen from
greatly overcrowded trains, severe rationing, and other legacies of the
recent war deeply moved Francis Schaeffer as he traveled with difficulty

---

[21]Ibid., 263.
[22]Interview with Debby and Udo Middelmann.
[23]Interview with Priscilla and John Sandri.

around the continent. In Prague, Czechoslovakia, he felt physically sick at the realization that the Americans had held back so the Soviets could take over. The population largely was in dread expectation of their imminent arrival. A letter to Edith tells of a pastor in Prague taking Fran to see flowers placed in walls at various points throughout the city. Fran records him as explaining, "These are places where our people were killed as they tried to resist the German takeover, waiting for the Americans to come and free us."[24]

As so often happened in Francis Schaeffer's life, he saw the supernatural converge upon natural events. This happened dramatically on his flight back to the USA from Paris. The TWA aircraft, a DC-4, left France on the morning of Thursday, October 2, due to reach its final destination in New York more than twenty-four hours later. Fran was sitting near a woman with two children. He takes up the story after they had stopped at Shannon Airport, in Ireland:

> As we started across the ocean, the Northern Lights stretched like a great bow on our right. Halfway, almost to the minute, between Shannon and Gander, both motors on my side of the plane stopped at once. We fell about 3000 feet in a very few minutes. . . . [25]
>
> I had already flown a lot, and so I could feel the engines going wrong. I remember thinking, If I'm going to go down into the ocean, I'd better get my coat. When I did, I said to the hostess, "There's something wrong with the engines." She was a bit snappy and said, "You people always think there's something wrong with the engines." So I shrugged my shoulder, but I took my coat. I had no sooner sat down than the lights came on and a very agitated copilot came out. "We're in trouble," he said. "Hurry and put on your life jackets."[26]
>
> I fully expected to spend the night on the wing of the plane! My chief concern was my notebook, which had grown thick and heavy during the ninety days, and I was glad I had lost so much weight so that I could stuff it under my belt into my pants. I assured a woman with two children that I would take one of them.[27]
>
> So down we went, and we fell and fell, until in the middle of the night with no moon we could actually see the water breaking under us

---

[24]Edith Schaeffer, *The Tapestry*, 264.
[25]Ibid., 270.
[26]Francis Schaeffer, *Death in the City*, in *Complete Works*, Vol. 4, 290–291.
[27]Edith Schaeffer, *The Tapestry*, 270.

in the darkness. And as we were coming down, I prayed. Interestingly enough, a radio message had gone out, an SOS that was picked up and broadcast immediately all over the United States in a flash news announcement: "There is a plane falling in the middle of the Atlantic." My wife heard about this immediately, and she gathered our three little girls together and they knelt down and began to pray. They were praying in St. Louis, Missouri, and I was praying on the plane. And we were going down and down. . . . We could see the waves breaking beneath us and everybody was ready for the crash.[28]

As the aircraft sank, the silent motors began droning again, the propellers on Fran's side started spinning, and the plane steadied and climbed high into the sky. After the craft landed in Gander, the pilot, when asked by Fran, was at a loss to explain how the motors started up again. Schaeffer later recalled:

"Well," he said, "it's a strange thing, something we can't explain. Only rarely do two motors stop on one wing, but you can make a rule that when they do, they don't start again. We don't understand it." So I turned to him and I said, "I can explain it." He looked at me. "How?" And I said, "My Father in Heaven started it because I was praying." That man got the strangest look on his face and he turned away. I'm sure he was the man sitting in the materialist's chair.[29]

The unsettling event only underlined Fran's sense that his journey to Europe had been of deep significance. His final letter of the trip, written on the train from New York to St. Louis, concluded:

The trip is ended. This has been the great spiritual experience of my life, second only to my conversion. It has been wonderful to realize the unity of the church of Christ, and I have realized anew how right we have been in separating ourselves from the modern unbelief which is the new paganism. I have never felt more sure that our stand in the last twenty years has been the right one. Daily I have felt the Lord's hand upon my shoulder.[30]

---

[28]Francis Schaeffer, *Death in the City*, in *Complete Works*, Vol. 4, 290–291.
[29]Ibid.
[30]Ibid., 271. "The last twenty years" refers to the conflict with modernism spearheaded by Machen and others, with the iconic break from Princeton in 1929. He refers further to the personal impact of his trip in "The Needs of Europe," in *Here We Stand*, a booklet by Schaeffer (Philadelphia: International Board for Presbyterian Foreign Missions, 1948).

This high note was followed by a low one. When Fran arrived back in St. Louis, the weeks and months of constant traveling in difficult, post-war circumstances, the numerous meetings, the responsibility of evaluating and recording in his notebook, and poor diet and sleep caught up with him. He suffered physical collapse, mentally and bodily exhausted. He had desperately missed the support and physical closeness of Edith. At this time, as in later years, Fran almost desperately depended upon Edith. As Os Guinness commented about this unique and remarkable woman: "In many ways she was the secret of L'Abri."[31] Edith remembered that upon his return home, "He needed long hours of sleep, his favorite food, fireside times of talking and reading together, and privacy with me."[32] His body would always remember the shock and debilitation of his collapse, deepening the low periods of depression he suffered from time to time. Fran's tough, self-reliant, organized nature mixed uneasily with his sensitivity and with his realism about the malaise and vulnerability at the heart of modern life and culture. As Fran slowly recovered, Edith pondered the cost of the call to ministry to those in need. She wrote, "It is the *answer* to prayer [to be used by God] that brings exhaustion of a variety of kinds, and that brings a cost to be paid that almost smashes you, and me."[33]

Demands on Fran in his role as moderator of the Bible Presbyterian Church, pastor, and board member had to be resisted; the home had to be organized so that he had quiet for rest and the children's needs were not neglected. Finally the time came when he was able to accept a request to speak at a banquet in Philadelphia about his survey trip to Europe. The proviso was that Edith arranged everything, took care of the travel plans, and accompanied him. He was able to talk and illustrate his words with a slide show without breaking down.

Soon he was giving his illustrated talk widely. Opinions about the quality of the slides he had taken varied greatly. Fran himself thought that some were good enough to send to *National Geographic* magazine. His daughter Prisca was more realistic about them.

---

[31]Os Guinness, "Fathers and Sons," in *Books and Culture,* March/April 2008, Vol. 14, No. 2, 32.
[32]Edith Schaeffer, *The Tapestry*, 272.
[33]Ibid., 272.

He took over two thousand slides and showed them all to us. A lot of
them were interesting old buildings and history. He even tried to sell
some of them to *National Geographic*. They weren't that good![34]

For Ann Harris a slide show that Francis Schaeffer gave at Faith
Seminary in Wilmington was memorable, but not always for the right
reasons.

I remember the time he came back to the seminary when I was a
student. It was after his first trip to Europe, and he had taken lots
of pictures. He would show them. "Now this doesn't mean much to
you, but that is the collar of so-and-so whom I met in Sweden, and
oh, what a wonderful man he was." He kept talking, and he kept our
attention.[35]

Fran also kept the attention of both the Independent Board for
Presbyterian Foreign Missions and the American Council of Christian
Churches. He was pleased by their reception of his detailed report of
his three-month survey. He summed up his report in a booklet the following year: "To meet the basic need of Europe we need two things—
missions, and an international Council of Bible-believing Churches."[36]
It seemed to him, however, that this trip was a valuable anomaly, now
behind him. He had done the work of reporting, and so he returned
with his usual enthusiasm to his life before Europe—pastoring and his
denominational involvement, although he continued to give his special,
slide-illustrated talks about Europe. Soon, however, he and Edith faced
hard decisions. He was beginning to receive what became a stream
of mail from the countries he had visited, both from people he had
met and from those who had been unable to meet him. These letters
contained questions, a desire to meet in fellowship, and invitations to
speak. For Fran and Edith they had something of a Macedonian call
to them—"Come over and help us." The Independent Board was concerned about building upon what was tangibly there, as was evident in
Fran's report. They presented the young pastor with a challenge: "We

[34]Interview with Priscilla and John Sandri.
[35]Interview with R. Laird and Ann Harris, 1998.
[36]Francis Schaeffer, *Here We Stand*, 14.

find from what you have given us in your report that we feel strongly that we should send someone to Europe to help strengthen the things that remain, and the consensus is that the only ones we would send would be you and Edith."[37] Fran and Edith were being asked to be missionaries by the Board. As they thought about it, the poster Fran had made in their bedroom on Waterman Boulevard looked down on them, "Go ye into all the world . . ."

Before Christmas that year the request had been clarified by Fran's careful questions, and he and Edith agreed to go. Their mission would consist of two parts, one short- and one long-term. The long-term task was to represent the Independent Board in Europe wherever the Lord led them, described by the General Secretary of the Independent Board, J. Gordon Holdcroft, as a "broad commission."[38] The short-term task was to go initially to Amsterdam in the Netherlands to prepare meetings to form a new International Council of Christian Churches, meetings that would be held in August 1948. The intention was that this would extend the existing group of separated churches internationally. Moving abroad would be preceded by six months of traveling and speaking around the USA about the trip Fran had made to Europe and this new step. For those six months, from February to July 1948, Edith was to be Fran's secretary, which required that she learn shorthand and typing. Later Holdcroft summed up Fran's work over that period:

> Mr. Schaeffer, temporarily lent to The American Council of Christian Churches as American Secretary of that Council's Foreign Relations Department, has travelled all over the United States where his searching analysis of the movements which today are bidding for the support of Christian Churches of Europe and America, and in a very real sense of the world also, have startled and shocked, and also have convinced, thousands of American Christians that Christianity in Europe is fighting for its very life against many foes. Among these foes the most subtle is that form of unbelief which in present day Protestantism has come to be known as modernism. Mr. Schaeffer has shown that modernism is at heart nothing other than a cultured paganism as are [sic] also the system from which Protestantism separated long ago but with which

---

[37] Edith Schaeffer, *The Tapestry*, 275.
[38] Foreword to Francis Schaeffer, *Here We Stand*, 3.

modernism would now join hands in an "ecumenical movement" to embrace all Christians.[39]

Francis Schaeffer, according to this summary, was pointing out dangers from the Roman Catholic Church as much as from neo-orthodoxy. Fran had often preached against the errors of "Romanism" from his St. Louis pulpit, his distrust being deepened by his three months in Europe, even though he acknowledged sound credal elements in Orthodox and (presumably) Roman liturgy. In late 1950 he would visit Rome for the occasion of the proclamation of the Assumption of Mary.

Those six months were not easy, particularly for Edith. They stayed with Fran's mother in Germantown, paying her rent, so she could have time with her grandchildren before they went away. She was a difficult person, with exacting standards, and Fran was away much of the time. To cap it all, Priscilla became ill for months with a mysterious ailment. With no diagnosis she was about to be referred to a psychiatrist, the thought being that she was reacting to the prospects of going to Europe (even though she was delighted at the idea). A young pediatric surgeon at the Philadelphia Children's Hospital had a specialist's knowledge of mesenteric adenitis and happened to see Prisca waiting for a barium X-ray. He decided to check her right away and told Edith she had recognizable symptoms, arranging to remove the appendix the next day. The surgeon was C. Everett Koop, and that was the origin of his long friendship with the Schaeffers, which would in the 1970s result in his collaboration with Fran on the book and movie series, *Whatever Happened to the Human Race?* Priscilla, who was ten at the time, remembered, "Koop was my old doctor; he took my appendix out in Philadelphia, just before we went to Europe. Over my stomach he was talking to Mother. He said, 'I've just become a Christian.' They started talking, and that was the beginning of the friendship."[40] As Koop wheeled Priscilla's cart to the operating theater (an unusual act for a surgeon) he read aloud to her a telegram that had just arrived, from Fran, away on denominational business in

---

[39]Ibid.
[40]Interview with Priscilla and John Sandri.

Nashville, Tennessee: "Dear Priscilla, Remember underneath are the everlasting arms. Love, Daddy."[41]

Despite her affliction, leaving her thin and pale from months of nausea and stomach pains, Priscilla remembers vividly her feelings of excitement at the prospect of moving to Europe, unaware of consequences over which she later had no regrets, such as becoming a European: "I remember looking in an encyclopedia: pictures of Switzerland and what it was like. But I had no idea, now looking back as a seventy-year-old, [of] the two great things, personally, that my father gave to me: one, my love for art, and secondly, bringing me to Europe, because I'm not an American in any way, shape, or form." She added that, had the family not gone, "My life would have been so totally different—whereas Mother and Daddy weren't as European as [their] children, though that's natural."[42] Prisca was particularly interested in Switzerland because that is where they planned to have their base after the August conference in Amsterdam was over.

Within days of Priscilla's appendectomy the "nomadic life," as Edith called it, of the Schaeffer family began as they set sail for Europe. The *Nieu Amsterdam* brought them to Rotterdam, Holland, via Southampton. There were wide, flat spaces in the cityscape, a reminder that much restoration had to be done after the recent war, with its carpet bombings of strategic cities. The excited family lodged in a cheap boardinghouse on the coast nearby in Scheveningen and endured food rationing. Edith was amused to meet a Dominie—a Christian minister—who smoked black cigars as he chatted to Fran and her, yet had walked several miles from church to avoid using a tram on Sunday. He was one of many smoke-emitting Dutchmen who would attend the conference. Scheveningen was close enough to Amsterdam for Fran to commute via The Hague to work on the arrangements for the international conference. One of his responsibilities throughout the conference was to be recording secretary. The American Council of Christian Churches had issued "an invitation to the evangelical and reformed Churches of the world to meet in Amsterdam, Holland, August 12 to 19, 1948, there to

---

[41]Edith Schaeffer, *The Tapestry*, 282.
[42]Interview with Priscilla and John Sandri.

form, if it please God, an International Council of Christian Churches, for The Word of God and for the testimony of Jesus Christ."[43] The invitation was timely, in tune with the concerns of evangelicals everywhere in that post-war world. Delegates came from fifty-eight churches of various denominations, representing twenty-nine countries.[44]

Amsterdam had been chosen for its symbolism—the World Council of Churches was to be formally inaugurated there that year in its First Assembly, which ran just after Fran's conference, from August 22 to September 4, under the leadership of its General Secretary W. A. Visser 't Hooft. There, in fact, its initial doctrinal basis, both inclusive and minimalist, was ratified: "The World Council of Churches is a fellowship of churches which accept our Lord Jesus Christ as God and Saviour." The ICCC was intended to be both an "evangelical and reformed" alternative and a protest call.

The meeting place for the Amsterdam conference was even more heavy with symbolism. It was the *Kloosterkerk*, the church favored by the Puritan Pilgrim Fathers as a place of worship before they set off for the New World. As the conference opened, the delegates perched on the narrow pews, their faces uplifted to watch as the welcome speech was given by Arie Kok. He had been Dutch Chancellor to Peking at the time war engulfed China. The Ambassador compared the call of the conference with Gideon's stand against the host of Midian. The ancient building (it was built in 1400) was also the setting for one of the most remarkable encounters in Fran's life. Edith remembered the moment vividly.

> Leaning against this historic wall, a young art critic for two Dutch newspapers, who was still taking his studies for his doctorate, chewed on his pipe and thoughtfully began to talk to Fran about art. They talked about art and history, art and philosophy, art and art, and the time went by and the recording secretary was missing from his meeting . . . a small blaze had started as two minds set each other on fire! It was Hans Rookmaaker's and Francis Schaeffer's first conversation,

[43]J. Gordon Holdcroft, Foreword to Francis Schaeffer, *Here We Stand*, 3.
[44]Laurel Gasque, *Hans Rookmaaker: An Open Life*, in Marleen Hengelaar-Rookmaaker, editor, *Our Calling and God's Hand in History: The Complete Works of Hans Rookmaaker*, Vol. 6 (Carlisle: Piquant, 2003), 346.

and Hans in student brashness had remarked, "These people in here," pointing with his pipe, "don't understand anything. But you and I, we can talk and understand each other."[45]

Rookmaaker, ten years Fran's junior and still an undergraduate, was not an official delegate, though it is likely that later he attended some sessions. He had dropped in on his fiancée to escort her home, a young Dutch woman named Anky Huitker. She was one of several people who had been recruited to work temporarily for the international conference. The event was a turning point for her, too, as she also got to know and become friends with the Schaeffers. Looking back, near the end of her life, she remembered:

> I was helping in the office, and one night [Hans] came to the office to pick me up, and he saw there an American. Hans was very fond of negro music. So he said to me, "I go to that man"—that was Schaeffer—"and ask him about jazz music." Then they started to talk, and they left without me. They walked the whole time through Amsterdam, and they came home at 4 o'clock [A.M.], I think. They never talked about American jazz music, but they had all other kind of things to talk about, mostly about religion, and art, of course. I think it started the interest of Dr. Schaeffer in art. . . . Mrs. Schaeffer was there [at the conference] also, and she talked to me about the work with children, Children for Christ, and she got me enthusiastic for it, because I had for years a group of children coming to my house and hearing about the Bible.[46]

As Fran and Hans Rookmaaker paced the empty night streets, crossing the frequent canal bridges and eventually going to Hans's student lodging to continue their discussion, they found a meeting of minds, though much about them was different. The range and depths of Hans Rookmaaker's brilliance can only now be gauged, with the publication of the six extensive volumes of his *Complete Works*, ranging from art criticism and theory, to learned philosophical aesthetics, to

---

[45]Edith Schaeffer, *The Tapestry*, 285. Edith's memory is mistaken here—at this time Hans was an undergraduate at the University of Amsterdam and had not yet started reviewing for *Trouw*. He was much older than the normal undergraduate and mature even beyond his actual years, having passed through the fire and waters of wartime, imprisonment, and grievous personal loss of a loved one.
[46]Interview with Anky Rookmaaker.

Bible study, to popular music and jazz. A deep friendship was forged that, not surprisingly, began with a conversation, like so much in Francis Schaeffer's life. The two men were shaped and enriched by each other's ideas and biblical understanding. Both had been converted in isolation largely by reading through the Bible with philosophical questions in mind. Rookmaaker's questions had been sharpened by his agony over the fate of Jewish people, including his close friend. At the time of the meeting with Schaeffer, Hans and Anky did not know of Riki Spetter's fate. They waited years before getting engaged in the hope that she would return. Later he and his wife Anky were to become members of L'Abri Fellowship, leading its distinctive and influential work in the Netherlands.

L'Abri was not even a dream in 1948, but the spiritual unity between the two men was real, potent with the future. Many years later, in his inaugural lecture for the Chair of Art History at the Free University in Amsterdam in 1968, Rookmaaker paid public tribute to his friend:

> It seems to me a token, not only of our friendship but also of our spiritual unity, that you have come from Switzerland for this occasion. Since the first time we met, in 1948, we have had many long talks about faith, philosophy, reality, art, the modern world and their mutual relations. I owe very much to these discussions, which have helped to shape my thoughts on these subjects. I want to express my deep gratitude, and consider it a great honour and joy to be a member of L'Abri Fellowship.[47]

In a subsequent interview Rookmaaker told me of the tangible unity that bore so much fruit:

> It was in 1948 that I met Schaeffer. . . . I was a bit dissatisfied with Dutch Christianity, which I felt was in some cases below what it should be, particularly on the level of personal faith and way of walking with the Lord. On the other hand, I feel that Anglo-Saxon Christianity really lacks the intellectual insight we have developed in Holland. In a

---

[47]Hans R. Rookmaaker, *Art and the Public Today*, second edition (Huémoz-sur-Ollon, Switzerland: L'Abri Fellowship, 1969).

way, what Dr. Schaeffer and I have tried to do is to fuse the two things, to make them into something new.[48]

He revealed more about that first meeting in a lecture he gave many years later while doing one of his regular summer stints tutoring and lecturing at L'Abri in Switzerland:

> I came out of the prisoner-of-war camp as a Christian and with quite a bit of training in philosophy. After the war I started my studies in art history and began to wrestle with the problems of modern art which I traced back to the existentialist outlook on life that lies behind modern art. In 1948, as a young student, I happened to meet Dr Schaeffer. Humanly speaking we met by chance. At an international conference in Amsterdam I was looking for an American who could answer some of my questions about Negro spirituals, so I was looking for an intelligent-looking American, and I came across Dr Schaeffer and said, "May I speak to you?" He said, "Yes, I have half an hour before we start again at 7 p.m." So we went out of the building and he left my room the next morning at 4 a.m.! We just talked on and on. We discussed modern art and that brought us together.[49]

It was not as if either the older or the younger man dominated the conversation. Fran had already looked closely at art and paintings hanging in galleries in Philadelphia, St. Louis, and more recently all across Europe. He was already convinced that somehow understanding art was an important key to understanding a society. Hans, in his turn, had developed a philosophical understanding of biblical faith. Whereas Fran was steeped in Van Til, Hans was so knowledgeable of Groen Van Prinsterer, Abraham Kuyper, and Herman Dooyeweerd that he could discuss them with friends who were philosophers. Hans also at heart was a historian, who saw contemporary events as a direct consequence of the eighteenth-century Enlightenment.

Francis Schaeffer had spent three months traveling across Europe

---

[48]Colin Duriez, "Interview with H. R. Rookmaaker," *Crusade*, April 1972. A fuller version is published in "Interviews", in Hengelaar-Rookmaaker, editor, *Our Calling and God's Hand in History: The Complete Works of Hans Rookmaaker*, Vol. 6, 150–153.
[49]"A Dutch Christian's View of Philosophy," in Marleen Hengelaar-Rookmaaker, editor, *The Complete Works of Hans R. Rookmaaker*, Vol. 6 (Carlisle, UK: Piquant, 2003), 178.

the previous year, trying to assess the situation faced by its churches at a time of unparalleled change. Now he was back again and would soon make his base in Switzerland. He had learned a lot from his survey of Europe. He could give illustrated talks about it. Getting to know Hans Rookmaaker, however, introduced him to the soul of Europe.

CHAPTER FOUR

SWITZERLAND

(1948–1950)

ᔐᔐᔐᔐᔐ

The months living in Holland in 1948 deeply affected all members of the Schaeffer family. Susan, who was seven at the time, remembered vividly the little pension in which they lived, the scarcity of good food, the scars of war from heavy bombing. They were not able to change their sheets the whole time they were there, she recalled, because of shortages. Many of the children they saw had black teeth. She and her sisters must quickly have picked up some rudimentary Dutch as they were able to play with the local children. A mother and her children who lived in the same boardinghouse had been in a Japanese concentration camp in the east and were still recuperating from those years of captivity. They recounted some of their hideous experiences. One particularly pleasant memory Susan had, however, was of visiting the Rijksmuseum with her father. She was even then impressed with the fact that he "seemed to have an intuition of letting a person actually enjoy things, become involved, ask their own questions, think their thoughts, and work through their thoughts."[1]

It was soon time to make the journey to Switzerland and new ventures. They had already arranged accommodation in La Rosiaz, high above Lake Geneva to the west of Lausanne, which was to be their base and which in 1948 was still in the countryside. The family traveled by train through Belgium—stopping in Brussels for two days for a break—and into France, enjoying a holiday in Paris for eight days. Fran decided that they should go everywhere on foot, better to experience the city, their excursions centering on museums. They saw what they could of the

---

[1]Interview with Susan Macaulay, 2007.

vast Louvre, Debby, only three, joining in the experience by spotting the original paintings she had seen only on postcards. To their delight, Fran also took the three girls to sail miniature boats in the Tuileries Gardens. The family had a memorable vacation despite their tight budget.

A very early start allowed them to travel through France and into Switzerland to reach Lausanne in good time. There a taxi took them to La Rosiaz. They were all black with soot from the train journey when they arrived. Susan remembered

> getting out of the car: the smell of the Swiss air and sound of the cow-bells after Holland and France. The air was clean, a pure, good place, where in a way another whole real life started. We [the girls] only had this one little room, in a boarding, pension, guest-house place. Everybody else . . . was all old ladies. But the sunset! "Come, the sun's setting, come see the light, come see the mountains!"[2]

The days, then months quickly passed in their tiny accommodation—so cramped in fact that the rooms had to be rearranged for day or night. Fran's and Edith's room was both office and bedroom; the children's was a combined playroom and living area by day and bedroom for three at night. A touch of grace, however, was French doors in each room that led to a veranda just large enough for two people to stand to contemplate the sunset or the starry lights of Évian at night across the lake's expanse. In addition, they soon had use of a very small, viewless box room, which they dubbed "the little office." A complexity was that the boardinghouse residents included five elderly women, their landlady Madame Turrian and her husband, and a college student—meaning that the children constantly had to be quiet.

In one of her frequent letters home to her family Edith described the setting:

> The house is scrupulously clean. Madame Turrian is very kind and pleasant, and the view is a gift from the Lord! We are up in the highest part of Lausanne, just out of the town limits. The train line ends two houses away, so transportation is close. Yet we have country sounds and smells around us, the smell of hay and pine trees, and the constant

---

[2]Ibid.

sound of musical, tinkling cowbells. There is a farmer right behind
us, a small farm with a meadow and an orchard and about 20 cows
who wander about making music. . . . Priscilla and Susan and Debby
have very little indoor space, but Madame Turrian's front garden,
which goes downhill from house to wall, has a few pine trees with
lovely spots underneath them for pretend houses, etc. The back yard,
which goes straight up for about 30 ft., has a small vegetable garden
and a rabbit and chicken house. The children watch the rabbits and
chickens get fed each night, and Priscilla is allowed to gather 2 or 3
eggs which appear each day! This makes up a great deal for living in
one room.[3]

As they contemplated their restrictive living space, Fran recalled the
homemade poster that had hung in the bedroom in far-off St. Louis:
"Go ye into all the world . . ." That said nothing about living quarters
on such a venture.

Fran threw himself into his work each day as bedroom morphed
into office. He had numerous contacts from his visit to Europe the previous year to follow up. The Amsterdam Conference was still fresh in
his mind. As highly organized as ever, he networked efficiently, yet with
great warmth. This meant many letters to write, with Edith, transmuted
from wife to secretary, taking dictation and typing rapidly—she had
achieved a respectable speed as a result of her correspondence course
earlier that year, in the months before leaving America. As always,
Prisca, the eldest of the girls, was called upon to help. Edith notes in
her family letter for March 27, 1949 (when Prisca was almost twelve):
"Priscilla has been helping a lot with office work. Fran taught her how
to file. She has been spending some time each week filing all the carbons
and the incoming mail. She has also mailed all the letters on her way
to school, keeping a written record of the postage for each letter—and
settling accounts with her Daddy each night. This is good training for
her as well as a real help to the work."[4]

At weekends they had their Sunday school and church service in
their bedroom—it was not an office that day. Soon the tiny congrega-

---

[3]Edith Schaeffer, *With Love, Edith: The L'Abri Family Letters 1948–1960* (San Francisco: Harper &
Row, 1988), 36.
[4]Ibid., 69.

tion of three intent girls and their mother grew to include a diminutive Irish woman staying in their boardinghouse and an American with two children whom they had met on the street. Fran took as much trouble over his preparation as if he were preaching to four hundred souls.

The patterning of life continued with daily French lessons (except on Sunday) from 10 to 11 A.M. Following his earlier habits at college and seminary Fran carried meticulously inscribed cards, doing his vocabulary at every opportunity. German lessons followed, once the French ones were well established. (Switzerland is made up of four language zones; roughly, French in the east, German in the west, Italian at the southernmost tip, and the minority Romansch in the canton of Grisons [Graubünden] in the east.) Rather like C. S. Lewis, Fran tended to speak other languages without escaping his normal accent, instead of adapting to native intonation. The children, however, as might be expected, picked up French quickly and soon were relatively fluent. They had had to leap into deep water, having no choice but to enter their local school. Susan's early comment when she came home one day went into the family lore. She wailed, "I can't understand the children, I can't understand the teacher, and *now* I can't even understand myself."[5]

Gradually speaking engagements came, fulfilling the dual purpose of starting Children for Christ classes across Europe and preparing churches to stand up to the influence of neo-orthodoxy and ecumenism, particularly, in Fran's view, by becoming part of the International Council of Christian Churches. Fran and Edith were very much a husband and wife duo. At first they spoke in churches and evangelical institutions in some parts of Switzerland, which meant that the children easily could come along to sing, as part of initializing Children for Christ classes. A Scottish missionary admired by the Schaeffers, Hugh Alexander (1884–1957), invited them to Le Roc, his Bible school (L'Ecole Biblique de Geneva[6]), at Cologny above Geneva. Fran traveled alone to Holland in January 1949 for a meeting of the Dutch branch of the Executive Council of the International Council.

Later that year, in a cold, sometimes snowy April, Fran and Edith

---

[5]Edith Schaeffer, *The Tapestry* (Nashville: Word, 1981), 290.
[6]Part of *Action Biblique*, a Swiss evangelical mission; www.bible-ouverte.ch.

had three weeks of speaking engagements across Holland, taking the girls with them. To help their budget they arranged for their two main rooms in Lausanne to be rented out for the three weeks of the Easter vacation, which involved cramming all their belongings into the tiny box room, their "little office." Their journey to Amsterdam meant a four-hour wait in Basle, which the family spent visiting the zoo. Edith recollected how friendly the animals seemed as they greeted them in hope of being fed by the visitors: "To the sheer delight of us all, when we went to leave the cage of an owl, it said 'Whoooooo' in a deep bass voice. 'What did you say?' we all chimed forth, and the answer came right back, 'Whoooooo.' We had quite a conversation with this loquacious owl, though his answer was always the same."[7]

The weeks in Holland characterized Fran's work at that time. He gave talks on church history and the damage being caused to children by the influence of liberalism and neo-Barthianism on church teaching. The situation was so bad, he argued, that to have the Bible taught from the point of view of its full truth, children in fact needed to have it taught outside of churches. Edith supplied an answer as to how this might be done by demonstrating an actual Bible class, on the lines of Children for Christ. The Schaeffers spoke to individual dominies, or pastors, and to groups of them, getting a warm response. Among those they inspired to start children's classes in their homes were Hans and Anky Rookmaaker (they married two months later, on June 1). The Rookmaakers also began translating Children for Christ material into Dutch. To compensate the children for sitting long hours, uncomplaining, in cold churches, Fran and Edith fitted in some trips for them, such as to the tulip fields, which had appeared a little late that year due to the coldness of the weather.

Another trip for them was a special guided tour of the Rijksmuseum, conducted by Hans Rookmaaker, with help from Fran. Fran and Hans Rookmaaker, in fact, visited museums together throughout the three weeks, a mark of their deepening friendship. Rookmaaker wrote two years later about the involvement he and Anky had with children's Bible classes, in a strongly worded article in Dutch on "child evangelism,"

[7]Edith Schaeffer, *With Love, Edith*, 74.

reflecting their conversations and the teaching of Fran and Edith in those weeks. He asked about children who have not heard of God's saving love and went on to write of those who were misled even in their own churches.

> There are hosts of such children, in heathen countries, in Roman Catholic countries, yes, in our own neighbourhood. . . . We often talk about apostasy and write about the disobedience, about the unbelief of the liberals and the Barthians and about the heresies and errors of the day; but then do we ever think about all the children who with full trust listen to their teachers and leaders only to receive and believe a lie? We must be just as moved by compassion for children who are misled in this way as we are for those who are born into the darkest paganism.[8]

Such children, Rookmaaker continued, are victims of "erring spirits."

> If we can make our home a centre where the Way, the Truth and the Life is preached to the children from the immediate vicinity, from our own street, probably the little boys and girls who are friends of our own children, then we can also say that we have put the light on the candlestick, that we have not put the light we were given in grace under the bushel but have let it shine—then there is a possibility of saving children from the power of governments, from the powers and rulers of this darkness—for without God, that is what the world around us is. Perhaps the hearts of the parents can also be reached through these children.[9]

It is clear from Hans Rookmaaker's comments that in principle he was at one with Fran's concerns over liberalism and neo-orthodoxy and the modern "paganism" of Rome and that he clearly endorsed the strategy of children's neighborhood Bible classes, in the spirit of Children for Christ. This does not fit well with the theory that he helped to liberate Fran from his early separatism, preparing the ground for the

---

[8]In *Kerkbode van de Gereformeerde Kerken in de Provincie Noord-Holland* 7, 1 (1951), 1–2. This English translation is found in "Articles on Evangelism: Child Evangelism," in Marleen Hengelaar-Rookmaaker, editor, *The Complete Works of Hans R. Rookmaaker* (Carlisle: Piquant, 2003), 120–121.
[9]Ibid.

more enlightened work of the L'Abri era. The missing element, in fact, that would transform base metal to gold was love, love combined with a wild and reckless realism about the basis of Christianity. The crisis in Fran's life that was to supply this missing ingredient, however, was still a year or so away.

Though Fran's thinking had yet to go through the crucible, an article he wrote the previous year, probably just before leaving for Europe, remarkably carries the seeds of his mature thinking. "A Review of a Review" appeared in *The Bible Today*, a periodical linked to Fran's separatist denomination, published in October 1948. Edith Schaeffer, no doubt closely reflecting her husband's opinion on this important point, observed in *The Tapestry*: "This review, although short, amazingly enough was to give all the basic ideas which years ahead were to help him first in his own struggles concerning truth, and which, later still, were to be formed into an enlarged study to be called by some people 'Schaeffer's Apologetic.'"[10] Previous issues of *The Bible Today* had stimulated considerable interest by exploring the very different roles of presuppositions and Christian evidences in evangelism. The question of different roles alluded to unresolved tensions between the evidentialist approach of the Old Princeton School of Machen, Allan MacRae, and others and the presuppositionalism of Van Til in his apologetics syllabus at Westminster Seminary. Indeed this tension contributed to the founding of Faith Seminary as a breakaway from Westminster.

Schaeffer's starting point was a review of E. J. Carnell's *An Introduction to Christian Apologetics* by Oliver Buswell entitled "Presuppositionalism" in the May 1948 issue. Schaeffer's approach, as someone who admired both Van Til and the evidentialist approach, is irenic. He tries to demonstrate that a middle path can be taken between the two positions. In his words, "The problem is not insoluble."[11] For him the communication of the gospel should be the focus and priority, drawing upon whatever tools are appropriate in actual evangelism, whether one draws on the importance of presuppositions or upon evidences from history and archaeology or a combination. Schaeffer's

---

[10]Edith Schaeffer, *The Tapestry*, 314.
[11]Francis A. Schaeffer, "A Review of a Review," in *The Bible Today*, Vol. 42, No. 1, October 1948, 7.

position was relatively unchanged from his position in 1948 when he told me in an interview near the end of his life:

> I do believe [presuppositions] are crucial. . . . From my way of looking at them, presuppositions are not accepted by you unconsciously, as a prior condition to your first move of thought. For me, the proper way to get at it is that, if you are a thinking person, you decide what set of presuppositions are going to lead to the answers to the questions.[12]

For Fran, there is common ground between the Christian and the nonbeliever, allowing the use of intellectual argument and evidences. This is because, and only because, the non-Christian is inconsistent with his or her beliefs about reality. To say that there is common ground is not therefore to say that any part of the universe or human thought is neutral terrain, not requiring presuppositions that are Christ-centered in order to properly interpret it. As he put it in 1948:

> The average unsaved man has two parts to his world-view. (1) In as far as he is logical in his unbelief his "system" is hopeless and has no contact with the Christian system. This would include, if completely logical, a complete cynicism (or skepticism) to the natural world so that he could not be sure that the atoms which constitute the chair he sits on will not suddenly arrange themselves into a table, or even that the atoms may not disappear entirely. If logical he would have no contact with reality and I believe suicide would be the only logical answer. It would be completely "other" to the true world, which God has made. (2) Some men have come to the above state, but very few. The rest have much in their thinking which only logically belongs in the Christian system. There are all degrees of this intellectual "cheating." The modernistic Christian is the greatest cheater. The cynic, who is just short of suicide but continues to bring more life into this world by his, to him, a-moral actions when logically he should be erasing all life possible from this, again to him, hopeless world, cheats the least.[13]

Notice Schaeffer's unshakable realism. He is concerned with living authentically as the key to effective Christian apologetics, which meets

---

[12]Interview with Francis Schaeffer, September 30, 1980.
[13]Francis A. Schaeffer, "A Review of a Review," 8.

people both in their need and at the point of their inconsistency—whether this involves their large-scale "cheating," as he bluntly calls it, or being willing to be consistent enough to contemplate suicide as a consequence of their non-Christian worldview. Placing this authenticity at the center of apologetics soon led Schaeffer into his own crisis period, when he felt forced to lay his own faith on the table in a necessarily reckless realism. Unknown to him, he was halfway through his life—it seems now, as we look at the whole of his life, that this was a very appropriate moment for him to reflect upon it in this radical way. He was familiar with Plato's dictum, "Know thyself," and the opening of the Shorter Westminster Confession, "The chief end of man is to glorify God, and to enjoy him forever." He was following Calvin's footsteps in associating knowledge of oneself with knowing God.

The period of crisis was not short and simple, but its acute phase lasted through much of spring 1951. Though by then essentially resolved, the issues continued to trouble him until the point at which he decisively resigned as a missionary with the International Council of Christian Churches and founded L'Abri Fellowship in 1955 as a demonstration of what he had discovered in his struggles. In his preface to *True Spirituality*, completed many years later, he calls his difficulty at this period "the problem of reality."

> I faced a spiritual crisis in my own life.[14] I had become a Christian from agnosticism many years before. After that I had become a pastor for ten years in the United States, and then for several years my wife Edith and I had been working in Europe. During this time I felt a strong burden to stand for the historical Christian position, and for the purity of the visible church. Gradually, however, a problem came to me—the problem of reality. This had two parts: first, it seemed to me that among many of those who held the orthodox position, one saw little reality in the things that the Bible so clearly says should be the result of Christianity. Second, it gradually grew on me that my own reality was less than it had been in the early days after I had become a

---

[14]He begins the paragraph with "In 1951 and 1952." In *The Tapestry* Edith omits this when she quotes from the Preface and comments that "he is describing 1948, 1949, 1950." As she wrote *The Tapestry* with close reference to her husband, it seems that he agreed to the correction. Both sets of dates, the original and Edith's amendment, point to the period of crisis being extensive. It strongly seems that the onset of their exposure to life in Europe, leaving behind the "parochialism" (Edith's words) of their prior American experience, is a major context for the crisis.

Christian. I realized that in honesty I had to go back and rethink my whole position.[15]

Edith thinks that a significant article Fran composed at this time may have been written just before, or even marked the beginning of, his radical self-questioning. The quietly subversive article appeared in Carl McIntire's *The Christian Beacon* on February 2, 1950, just three months after the Schaeffers moved to the high village of Champéry from Lausanne. It simmered with passion and was entitled, "The Balance of the Simultaneous Exhibition of God's Holiness and Love." Fran isolated two dangers for the separatist movement, one from without and one from within. He briefly looked at the danger without—discouragement, resulting in compromise or retreat from the battle. Interestingly, he then focused at length on the danger within—"a will to win, rather than a will to be right." He explained that this "is the danger of losing the love God means us to have one for the other. Christ has commanded us to love one another. . . ." He quoted David Brainerd: "Oh that my soul might never offer any dead, cold service to my God!" Rather, Fran continued, "Soul-winning should mean self-denying and sacrificial work. The work of soul-building should mean the turning out of scholarly material and warm devotional material as well."[16]

The move from Lausanne had been precipitated by a wave of illness, ranging from flu to pneumonia, that swept through Madame Turrian's boardinghouse. It affected everyone, including all members of the Schaeffer family, with the exception of Fran, who splendidly played nurse to Edith and the girls. The grippe was part of an epidemic that had spread through Holland, France, and Switzerland. As a result their French teacher, Mme. Wildermuth, pointed out to Fran and Edith the importance of getting up to the mountains for the summer. It was necessary, she argued amid the coughs and sneezes, for the well-being of the children. Very practically, she offered to help in the quest for a chalet to rent. She knew a suitable location, Champéry, high up the west side of the Rhone, in a great bowl watched over by the giant peaks of the

---

[15]Francis Schaeffer, Preface to *True Spirituality* (Wheaton, IL: Tyndale House, 1972). Increasingly for Schaeffer, "the problem of reality" also included the fact that each person is confronted with the reality of his or her own humanity ("mannishness") and an external world with its definite nature.
[16]Edith Schaeffer quotes more fully from the article in *The Tapestry*, 315.

Dent du Midi. It was in a Roman Catholic canton (in Switzerland some administrative regions historically are Catholic, others Protestant), but the significance of this was not to become fully clear for some years. Quickly she selected some possible rentals, which Edith was soon able to examine, traipsing around the village in the crisp deep snow and biting air, choosing a chalet called Bon Accueil ("Warm Welcome"). Its landlady was Madam Marclay, who quickly became a family friend.

The family was entranced and delighted by their stay in the village during July and August. Fran had to be away some of the time, but he was enthusiastic when Edith realized (benefiting from Madam Marclay's advice) they could afford to rent a chalet here permanently at about the same cost as cramped accommodations in expensive Lausanne. From the garden they could look down the steep mountain slopes at the village houses dotted around, with the tip of the Temple Protestant directly below them—a church that was to play an important part in their lives for many years. When they returned to Champéry in November 1949, it was with their worldly belongings and to a different chalet that was to be home—Chalet des Frênes ("The Ash Trees"). It had been constructed twenty years before by a wealthy English woman for her comfortable use on winter vacations. Edith described it in a letter to her family, beginning with the grounds: "Enough place for a vegetable garden with plenty of space for the children to play—big trees, gravel path, a stone terrace where outdoor meals could be eaten, even a little summerhouse on the highest spot whose three sides and a bench would make a lovely playhouse for the children."[17] A new thought occurred to Edith and Fran as they looked over the chalet itself, a thought she shared with her supportive parents and family in that letter: "As we inspected the inside, finding central heat (furnace and radiators almost unheard of for a mountain chalet), finding ample space not only for our family and office needs but also for guests—we wondered if the Lord were not preparing to take us into a new stage of the work."[18] Unknown then to them both, it was the first glimmer of the idea of L'Abri, a shelter based on hospitality and love. Within two years they would move to another

---

[17]Edith Schaeffer, *With Love, Edith*, 101.
[18]Ibid.

chalet in Champéry, Bijou ("Jewel"), before being forced to leave the Roman Catholic canton in 1955 because of their missionary activities.

Having this much larger accommodation in Champéry allowed them at last to unpack their belongings, including furniture, which had been shipped from St. Louis the year before. Edith captured the excitement of this in her family letter at the time: "As all our trunks, boxes, etc., were dumped into the place, the halls became knee-deep with shredded paper. St. Louis barrels and boxes were sort of like a treasure hunt, for we had forgotten what we packed. The shrieks of delight at finding old book friends filled the house for a whole afternoon."[19] As their milk came crude from the local *laiterie*, they were glad to have their Sears and Roebuck's Home and Farm Pasteurizer.

Family life settled back into its routines, while all the time Fran visited churches and groups, or he and Edith went together to give their complementary presentations. They also assiduously worked on Children for Christ material based on the Gospel of Luke.[20] One extensive trip led them throughout Scandinavia. Their seven-week itinerary took them to Sweden, Norway, Finland, and Denmark. A Finnish newspaper photograph of the youthful couple shows Fran wearing a dark overcoat and a black beret at a rakish angle, with a Latin-looking Edith at his side in a dark suit, her long hair parted in the middle. The playful caption reads: "Rev. Francis Schaeffer is 100% Finnish. Mrs. Edith Schaeffer claims to be American, but we know that she's Italian."[21] In Champéry the younger girls attended a tiny local school, Home Eden, while Priscilla walked each day to *École Alpina* for high school, none of the children having any problem by now with speaking French. *École Alpina* was a boys' boarding school that Priscilla was allowed, by special dispensation, to attend as a day student. Home Eden doubled as a boardinghouse for children, so Fran and Edith could leave the girls there when making longer trips across Europe, such as the Scandinavian one, though at first little Debby was placed with the kindly Mme. Turrian in La Rosiaz.

Susan in particular found Home Eden a very odd education, though

---

[19]Ibid., 114.
[20]Much of this material was eventually incorporated into the Francis and Edith Schaeffer book, *Everybody Can Know* (Wheaton, IL: Tyndale House, 1975).
[21]Edith Schaeffer, *With Love, Edith*, 155.

it taught her French and mental arithmetic. Much of her education, in fact, came from their unusual family life and from her father, who took each of his children seriously as an individual human being who had not chosen to come into the world. One of Fran's sayings in the home was, "Never let school stand in the way of an education."[22] Susan, who later became an authority on the pioneering educationalist, felt she had had a Charlotte Mason type of education. Mason (1842–1923) is mentor for many in the homeschooling movement, as such the PNEU, Parents National Education Union, in Britain. She taught that "children are persons" in their own right and should be treated as individuals. From an early age they should experience a broad curriculum, not simply be taught the three Rs (reading, writing, and arithmetic). Their education should expose them to the best in art, literature, music, and science. Susan recalls an incident soon after they came to live in Champéry that illustrates her father's unusual attitude to children and education:

> Prisca and I were weeding. . . . It was our first year in Champéry and we were growing a vegetable garden [at Chalet des Frênes]; we needed to grow vegetables for financial reasons. We had a quarrel, just a normal, sisterly quarrel. I was nine and she would have been thirteen. I was really mad at her and I wanted to upset her. I wanted to have the last word. I stood up and I said, "Well, I'm not a Christian any more." "Oh, no," she had said to me, "don't behave like this; you'll be a bad witness to the villagers." She rushed into the house [with] "Susan's not a Christian." My mother cried. After I said it I thought, Why did I say I'm not a Christian?—because it had been very precious to me. I'd had a very alive experience from very young. There was something I think I really trusted and it was very real to me. [Yet] people [had] come [to our home] with loads of questions. Maybe these other ideas are better; maybe they're stronger. How do I know? I don't know. So then I strengthened in my thoughts about how much I didn't know. I was quite young.
>
> That night, I got ready for bed. Dad came in and he just sat down on the chair and said, "Now, Suz, what are you thinking?" Then, instead of saying to me, "Stop crying, you'll understand when you grow up," or something [similar], he started going through things, very like he did later on with anybody in Oxford or Cambridge, just taking [my

---

[22]Recalled by Debby, in interview with Debby and Udo Middelmann.

questioning] utterly seriously. He said [at one point], "That's a good question. I'm glad you've asked it. It's good to ask when you don't know; it's a good thing to think the questions through." He started talking to me about what he thought—why he thought it was true. I felt then that quality of respect, a respect for what I thought, taking it seriously and not being emotional about it. He may have, in other areas, been emotional. But, no, he actually liked it when somebody was asking questions.[23]

Much of 1950 in Champéry was dominated by preparations for a large summer congress in Geneva, to bring together churches and groups from throughout the world linked to the fledgling International Council of Christian Churches. As in the inaugural conference in Amsterdam in August 1948, Fran's responsibility was to organize it and also to be recording secretary. Delegates for the Second Plenary Congress would include friends and associates of Fran's from the Bible Presbyterian Church and Faith Seminary in the USA, as well as many with whom he had been in contact throughout Europe. These included people from his fact-finding tour in 1947 and those he had been in contact with or met since the family had moved to Europe. Fran had undoubtedly been prominent in his denomination prior to coming to Europe, and he was getting increasingly known and respected through the growing network of churches and groups within Europe that he was establishing. He would therefore be a key presence in the Geneva conference.

August opened with the Swiss national holiday, an event that reminded Edith of the American Independence Day. That day Champéry was full of Americans who would be attending the imminent Congress, joining in the exuberant celebrations. There were patriotic speeches and a parade, the events accompanied by a local band. Nightfall brought lanterns, sparklers, and other fireworks. The time for the Congress arrived, running August 16–23. A number of the delegates stayed with the Schaeffers in Chalet des Frênes, which allowed the renewal of friendships. Over twenty-five visitors joined the Schaeffers for tea in Chalet des Frênes just before the Congress opened to its more than four hundred delegates.

---

[23]Interview with Susan Schaeffer Macaulay. She recounts the event in her book, *How to be Your Own Selfish Pig* (Colorado Springs: Chariot/Victor, 1982).

In addition to his duties and making notes of the meetings, when he could Fran manned a booth publicizing Children for Christ International. He was helped by Priscilla, a very grown-up thirteen-year-old, and by Edith. Edith wrote soon afterwards:

> Fran was deeply engrossed in taking the Minutes of the meetings during all the business sessions. . . . That meant sitting on the platform and writing away through it all. . . . As for the children? Someone overheard Susan seriously complaining the second day, "I think I should be allowed to stay for the whole thing. Why, I'm getting so much out of it. This morning I listened to it all, every word of it—all in Portuguese!" . . . The little portable boxes with earphones were like a radio, and you could tune in on the meeting in French, Spanish, Dutch and Portuguese. Priscilla thought it was a fine thing to be able to help out with translation and errands at the Information Desk and listen to the meetings at the same time. She also helped out many hours in the Press Room. . . . As for Deborah, she went independently into the meetings, often sitting beside people she didn't even know, and usually listening to it all with her earphones tuned to French. Long after it was all over, we discovered that she had voted during one morning session, both by raising her hand and saying "aye" every time the Chairman called for a vote![24]

On the top of Fran's mind in the Congress was a paper he was due to give on "The New Modernism." The Congress had begun on a Wednesday, and his talk was due after the weekend. He had worked hard preparing the talk, which was dominated by an analysis and response to the theologian Karl Barth, who taught in nearby Basle. In fact, he had thought long and hard about Barth and "Barthianism," and "neo-Barthianism" since seminary days. He had written about Barth in a booklet that was published just before the Schaeffers left America in the summer of 1948 and that indicates his thinking as he prepared his paper for the Congress:

> Into this recognized need of "more vital religion" to offset the barrenness of Modernism there stepped a man. His name is Karl Barth. Karl Barth had an idea. In some ways it was the most stupendous idea that has ever come from the mind of man. It was a way to reconcile German

---
[24]Edith Schaeffer, *With Love, Edith*, 176.

Higher Criticism and this need of "more vital religion" in the barren Modernistic churches. . . . Karl Barth . . . stated that a thing can be false in history and yet religiously true. To Barth, history doesn't matter. . . . To Barth, the Bible is not the Word of God, it just contains the Word of God. What may be the Word of God in it to you may not be to me, and what may be the Word of God today to either of us, may not be at all tomorrow. . . .

Now in fairness, we have to say this. Barth seems to be coming more and more to the Christian position. He personally may be a saved man. It seems very definite that he is now nearer the Christian position concerning the Bible than he was ten years ago. . . . Some Bible-believing Christians in Switzerland who know him told me they believe he is. However, whether this is so or not, this weakness of his concerning history has loosed a flood upon the world.[25]

On the Saturday of the Congress, August 19, 1950, Schaeffer, with four others, had the opportunity to visit the great Swiss theologian, then in his mid-sixties. This gave Fran the chance to test out the judgments he had made of Barth, which he intended to present in his address to the Congress. Fran accompanied G. Douglas Young, dean of Shelton College, New York, J. Oliver Buswell, at that time president of that college and formerly president of Wheaton College, James E. Bennet, vice-president of Shelton, and Peter Stam. The morning had been kept free for sightseeing, which made possible a two-hour "chat" (as Buswell called it) with Karl Barth.[26] The five men traveled by train to Oberrieden, near Bergli, then (Buswell remembered) had to toil their way up "the steep road to the Pestalozzi cottage overlooking Lake Zurich where Barth spends the summer. He was waiting for us nearly a half mile down the road. . . . Nothing could have been more cordial than Barth's attitude during the two hour chat."[27] This cordiality was also remarked on by Fran: "He was most gracious and, of course, most stimulating."[28]

From Buswell's and Fran's memories and a subsequent letter from

---

[25]Francis A. Schaeffer, *Here We Stand* (Philadelphia: Independent Board for Presbyterian Foreign Missions, n.d.), 31–32.
[26]For Buswell's account of the encounter with Barth, see J. O. Buswell, "Geneva, for the Faith; Karl Barth Questions the Truth," in *The Bible Today*, 1950, 3–9.
[27]Ibid., 4.
[28]Francis A. Schaeffer, "The New Modernism (Neo-Orthodoxy) and the Bible," address given at the Second Plenary Congress of the International Council of Christian Churches, Geneva, Switzerland, 1950, 11.

Francis Schaeffer's father, Francis August III

Francis Schaeffer's mother, Bessie, April 1968

Edith's parents, George and Jessie Seville, Janet (10), Elsa (5), Edith (9 months)

Young Francis Schaeffer, Atlantic City

Francis (2)

Francis with pet dog, 1919

Francis Schaeffer as a young man

Elsa Seville (19) with her sister Edith (14)

Francis and Edith's wedding, July 6, 1936

Faith Seminary: Schaeffer at the end of the second row, right

Grove City: Rev. Schaeffer preaching

Edith, with Priscilla, 1940

Francis Schaeffer, pastor in St. Louis

St. Louis: Deborah (2), Susan (6), Priscilla (10)

St Louis: Summer Bible School, group photograph in front of church

Francis, Edith, baby Susan, and Priscilla, 1943

St Louis, 1948: Deborah, Priscilla, and Susan

Schaeffer family visiting Geneva, Edith pregnant with Frank, 1952

Edith typing letters during the early years of L'Abri

Champéry: Temple Protestant, where Schaeffer preached 1949–1975

Tampere, Finland: Francis and Edith, April 1950

At the front of Chalet Les Mélèzes: Francis and Edith, 1955

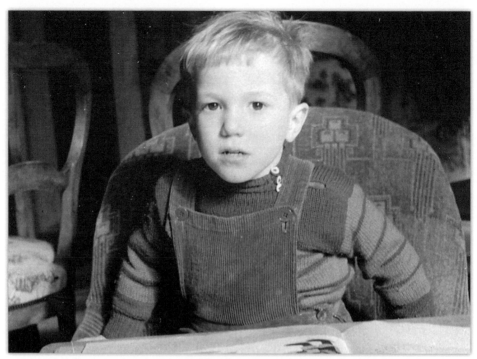

Frank Schaeffer (4)

Champéry: Susan, Priscilla, and Deborah inside Chalet Bijou

Schaeffer at a L'Abri discussion, clad in his hallmark breeches

Francis and Edith in the 1970s

Father and son working on a manuscript of *How Should We Then Live?*,0 1974

Edith and Francis typically together, around 1970

Barth to Schaeffer, we can glimpse some of the fascinating exchanges that took place, which were conducted in English. From the point of view of the five visitors, the meeting was satisfactory, as it confirmed their views of Barth's contribution to the "new modernism." From the accounts, however, there was much about it that was unsatisfactory: Barth was elusive, hesitant, uneasy, and apparently contradicted himself often; the five visitors appeared to shoot questions in an inquisitorial manner. They were systematic theologians through and through; he, technically speaking, was a biblical theologian wary of systems. The meeting on the road to Barth's cottage opened the conversations warmly enough. Buswell, from memory, records the gist of it:

> "I have read in the paper of I.C.C.C.," [Barth] said, "but what *kind* of Christian churches?"
> "We are called fundamentalists," I said.
> "Fundamentalists!" he exclaimed in somewhat broken English (far better than my poor German). "Fundamentalists, you would like to eat me!"
> "No," said Francis Schaeffer, "That would defeat our purpose; we wish to talk with you." And we all had a good laugh.[29]

According to Buswell, the ensuing discussion centered around four doctrines—the Trinity, time, truth, and the infallibility of the Bible. On the biblical doctrine of time, someone (reputedly Fran) asked Barth, "We seem to read in your writings that God created the world in the first century A.D. Did you mean that? Or did we misunderstand?" Buswell remembers him responding: "Certainly. God created the world in Christ in the first century A.D."[30] Fran took this to mean that theologically this world—the world examined by science and recorded by history— did not matter for Barth. There was a watertight dichotomy between matters of faith and the world of science and history. This impression was borne out by another reply Barth gave to a question. When Udo Middelmann studied at Covenant Theological Seminary in St. Louis he had a professor who had been among the group visiting Barth.

---

[29]Buswell, "Geneva, for the Faith; Karl Barth Questions the Truth," 5.
[30]Ibid., 6.

I remember him in class mentioning [a question was asked]: "Well, Dr. Barth, in your view, is the shortest distance between two points a straight line on earth as well as in heaven, or only on earth?" Barth said, "I don't know; perhaps yes, perhaps no." So what Schaeffer would later talk about—the upper and lower story—in a sense you can see here. There's not a continuity of truth. There are basically two truths—there's one for earth and one for the spiritual.[31]

Fran arrived home late that night. When his train from Geneva arrived in Aigle, where he connected to the branch line for the cog railway to Champéry, he discovered that he would have to wait three hours. Not realizing how far away home was, he started to walk. He was given a ride with a villager who spotted him walking. Over a warmed-up dinner he told Edith and the family about his visit with Karl Barth. He said that as a result of that meeting, he now knew that his paper for the Congress would give a true portrait of the New Modernism.

Fran's address to the Congress the next week was wide-ranging. It not only discussed Karl Barth and his followers (some of whom, "neo-Barthians" like Reinhold Niebuhr, had departed in important respects from him) but also similarities to the New Modernism across the whole sweep of culture, including the sciences, philosophy, modern art, and music, and the "general world tone" of relativism. On art, for example, he pointed out to the delegates:

Most Christians tend to laugh at modern art. This is quite a mistake. Modern art and modern music together are an expression of the same spirit we have seen embodied in modern science and modern philosophy. In studying the paintings of a man like Delvaux it is clear that, after we have made all allowances possible for modern art's struggle with the time and space problem, we must realize that the final message of modern art is the uncertainty and unrelatedness of all things.[32]

---

[31]Interview with Debby and Udo Middelmann.
[32]Schaeffer, "The New Modernism," 5. It is possible that Fran had discussed the work of Delvaux, a Belgium surrealist, with Hans Rookmaaker. In an undated review for *Trouw,* but almost certainly around this period, reproduced in *Art, Artists and Gauguin: The Complete Works of Hans Rookmaaker*, Vol. 1 (Carlisle, UK: Piquant 2002), 331, Rookmaaker comments: "Delvaux . . . is a Surrealist who, with real power and sometimes very convincingly presents us with his view that the world and our lives are meaningless, that 'the smell of death clings to them', that everything beautiful is past. He has not always scorned subjects that are popular and easy. The crucifixion with skeletons, for example, will appeal to certain snobbish viewers but is nevertheless, in every respect, of inferior quality. Other works, for example *Cyrialide*, are very effective. His characteristic work, *Penelope*, demonstrates how ridiculous and meaningless every beauty, every classic pose, is in these days of electric lights, with everything flat

In one section of his address Fran characterizes the New Modernism bluntly as cheating, self-contradictory, irrational, vague, "not interested in truth but manifestation," and non-historical.

During their meeting, Fran had told Karl Barth about his intention to give this address to the Congress and asked him if he would like a copy. When he said he would, Fran promised to send the theologian a copy. The address, which Fran revised slightly in light of the visit, contains these words: "If I have been unfair in any of the details of the presentation I am sorry. It is my hope, that after professor Barth has read it, that he will give me the privilege of another time with him to discuss these matters further."[33]

Karl Barth replied very negatively to Fran within days of receiving a copy of his address. The response was probably colored by the fact that he had also received a review from Buswell relating to his theology. This seems to have confirmed his impression that there was a fundamentalist consensus opposed to his views that had already made up its mind and was inflexible. Fran's depiction of his position and the links Fran made to the New Modernism evidently rankled:

Bergli, Oberrieden, Sept. 3, 1950
Rev. Francis A. Schaeffer
Châlet des Frênes, Champéry
Dear Mr. Schaeffer!

I acknowledge receipt of your letter from August 28, and of your paper "The new modernism". The same day your friend J. Oliver Buswell wrote to me from New York, enclosing a review (*The Bible Today* p. 261 s.) "Karl Barth's Theology". I see: the things you think of me are approximately of the same kind as those I found in the book of van Til on the same subject. And I see: you and your friends have chosen to cultivate a type of theology, who consists in a kind of criminology; you are living from the repudiation and discrimination of every and every fellow-creature, whose conception is not entirely (numerically!)[34] identical with your own views and statements. You are "walking on the solid rock of truth". We others, poor sinners, are not. I am not.

---

and without sparkle, robbed of all zest for life. Even the little flag hangs listlessly in the wind, not to mention the 'frozen flesh' of the female figure."
[33]Schaeffer, "The New Modernism," 11.
[34]A reference to their discussion of the oneness of the Trinity.

My case has been found out to be hopeless. The jury has spoken, the verdict is proclaimed, the accused has been hanged by the neck till he was dead this very morning.

Well, Well! Have it your way: it is your affair, and in doing, speaking, writing as you do, you may shoulder your own responsibilities. You may repudiate my life-work "as a whole". You may call me names (as: cheating, vague, non-historic, not interested in truth, and so on and on!). You may continue to do your "detective" work in America, in the Netherlands, in Finland and everywhere and decry me as the most dangerous heretic. Why not? Perhaps the Lord has told you to do so.

But why and to what purpose do you wish further conversation? The heretic has been burnt and buried for good. Why on earth will you waste your time (and his time!) with more talk between you and him? Dear sir, you said, that you are feeling your-selves nearer to the "old modernists" and to the Roman-catholics than to me and to men like me. Just as you like! But why then not try the effectiveness of your "apologetics" in some exercises with these "old-modernists" or with these Roman Catholics—both of whom you will find quite a lot here in Switzerland and everywhere? Why bother your-selves anymore about the man in Basle, whom you have finished off so splendidly and so totally?

Rejoice, dear Mr. Schaeffer (and you calling your-selves "fundamentalists" all over the world)! Rejoice and go on to believe in your "logics" (as in the fourth article of your creed!) and in your-selves as in the only true "bible-believing" people! Shout so loudly as you can! But, pray, allow me, to let you alone. "Conversations" are possible between *open*-minded people. Your paper and the review of your friend Buswell reveals the fact of your decision to close your window-shutters. I do not know how to deal with a man who comes to see and to speak to me in the quality of an detective-inspector or with the behaviour of a missionary who goes to convert a heathen. No, thanks!

Yours sincerely

Excuse my bad English. I am not accustomed to write in your language. I am sending a copy of this letter to Rev. Buswell!

Dear Mr. Buswell!
I have read your review together with the paper of Mr. Schaeffer. Every word in my letter refers also to you. Sorry, but it can not be helped!

Yours
(Signed) Karl Barth[35]

---

[35]Buswell, "Geneva, for the Faith; Karl Barth Questions the Truth," 8–9.

We have no record of Fran's response, but Oliver Buswell wrote to Barth expressing his concern at the letter, trying to reopen the lines of communication, and explaining why he thought this was important. We can only speculate, but this letter to Fran, full of implicit challenges, may have been a further catalyst in Fran's crisis, his renewed search for reality in his life, which followed soon after and which we explore more in the next chapter. Fran would continue for the rest of his life to feature Barth strongly in his analysis of the origins of contemporary culture, and the sorrow at its heart. While others he focused upon, such as Thomas Aquinas, George Frederick Hegel, and Søren Kierkegaard, could not return from the grave to comment on what he said about them, one of the most powerful cultural shapers of the twentieth century had communicated directly and forcefully to Schaeffer. As he questioned his life and his bedrock beliefs, it is inconceivable that the words of Karl Barth were not part of his soul-searching. He at some point around then made a decision that meant throwing open the shutters and facing up to whatever he found.

CRISIS AND CATALYST

(1951–1954)

ഌഌഌഌഌ

What is the secret of power and enjoyment of the Lord? Why
the need for both purity and love in the Christian life? These
questions are posed by the extensive title of an article that
Francis Schaeffer published in two parts in the *Sunday School Times* of
June 16 and June 23, 1951. Just after he sent it off to the periodical,
he told a friend in a letter, "I have been writing it for two years; it has
meant more to me than any article I have ever written."[1] The opening
words reflect deep spiritual struggle:

> What is the secret of power? Certainly, as we consider Christianity
> today—true, Bible-believing Christianity—we must be impressed by
> the fact that there is not the consistent power that there has been in cer-
> tain periods of the past. The same thing is also true of the enjoyment of
> the Lord. In our day, life is such that, while Christians do many things
> to serve the Lord, it is obvious from our faces and our conversations
> that few enjoy Him.[2]

The article concludes with what almost becomes Schaeffer's
manifesto:

> When we have purity leading to love and love leading to purity, and
> all because we love the Lord—then there will be lasting power and
> enjoyment of the One who is the dear Lamb of God, slain for us, our
> Saviour and our Lord.[3]

---

[1]*The Letters of Francis Schaeffer*, ed. Lane T. Dennis (Eastbourne, UK: Kingsway Publications,
1986), 33.
[2]Francis A. Schaeffer, "The Secret of Power and Enjoyment of the Lord: The Need for Both Purity and
Love in the Christian Life," in *The Sunday School Times*, Vol. 93, Nos. 24–25, June 16 and 23, 1951.
[3]Ibid.

These heartfelt words were rooted into his still ongoing struggle, which lasted for a long period, perhaps years. At its greatest intensity, for about two months, he paced up and down in his hayloft in the Swiss village of Champéry when the weather was wet and walked the countryside when it was dry, reexamining the basis of his faith and commitment to the Lord. His goal was a true evangelical foundation for life that was obedient to Scripture, convinced of God's sheer reality, and did not neglect the finished work of Christ and the present work of the Holy Spirit. "Finally the sun came out. I saw that my earlier decision to step from agnosticism to Bible-believing Christianity was right. . . ."[4] He emerged as committed as ever to a systematic biblical theology but was also convinced of the need for moment-by-moment dependence upon Christ—that is, a truly *existential* dimension to faith (to use a favorite adjective of his). Without a present reality, he felt, an orthodox theology does not lead to power and enjoyment of the Lord. What Jesus had accomplished in actual human history made a present reality possible—there could be a continuity in the real world between then and now. The phrase "the finished work of Christ" becomes a common refrain in his thinking and writing after his crisis. In practice, he knew there must be changes in his life. As he was to acknowledge twenty years later, "Refusal to consider change under the direction of the Holy Spirit is a spiritual problem, not an intellectual problem."[5]

Schaeffer's profound spiritual struggles in the early spring of 1951 led not only to the *Sunday School Times* articles but also to his book *True Spirituality*, which was not published until 1971 after many reworkings.[6] This volume was shaped from a series of talks originally given in 1953 at a Bible camp in the United States when the family,

---

[4]Francis A. Schaeffer, "Why and How I Write My Books," *Eternity*, March 24, 1973, 64.
[5]Francis A. Schaeffer, *The Church at the End of the Twentieth Century* (London: The Norfolk Press, 1970), 95.
[6]Francis A. Schaeffer, *True Spirituality* (Wheaton, IL: Tyndale House, 1971). Around late 1967 or early 1968, while I was studying at the University of Istanbul, Francis Schaeffer sent me a section of the manuscript so I could try my hand at editing it. This I did, but my study and other commitments at that time ruled out doing any more. Though that exposure was brief, the quality of thought in those pages of manuscript ranked with any I later edited professionally, such as books by John Stott, Alec Motyer, or Alister McGrath. I noticed a weakness in Schaeffer, however, in that he was overly reluctant to lose the oral character of the original when his work was edited. A good editor can turn such a manuscript into a written script without imposing him- or herself or "ghost-writing," provided there is quality of thought in the original. Schaeffer was blessed by having the talented editorial services of such men as David Winter, Lane Dennis, and James Sire at different times.

as missionaries with the International Board for Presbyterian Foreign Missions, was on furlough. The talks were honed and re-presented in Switzerland after L'Abri was started in 1955. They were given again in the United States in 1963 and at L'Abri in 1964, at which time they reached their final form. The book eventually was based on transcriptions of audiotapes of these L'Abri lectures, tapes that students at L'Abri were encouraged to listen to alongside their studies of Christianity and culture.

Many years later Fran's daughter Deborah reflected on her father's struggle for reality at that time and its aftermath:

> What came out of it were those lectures that became *True Spirituality*, but it wasn't a struggle over *spirituality*; I think sometimes it's been seen that way. It was really that he was rethinking what he had thought as an eighteen-year-old and that is, "Does this God exist?" "Is the Bible true?" and "Will I throw it out?" It wasn't, "What is spirituality?" What came out of it is the realization that, as he used to say, if it were not true, everyone would be going on doing their business in the church and the mission and so forth in the same way. In which case it pushed him, as an honest person, to say, "Well, maybe it's not true; maybe we've just invented this whole thing, and we're just pushing it on people as a program." So to him it was a really serious going back and rethinking everything he believed.[7]

Schaeffer always believed that without this deep struggle to find reality in the Christian and thus human life, the work of L'Abri would never have started.[8] What he had glimpsed was the fullness of the truth of Christianity, requiring a balance of truth and love. The reality behind reality, God himself in the high order of the Trinity, is both truth and love, and his image in human beings is meant to have both. Fran openly admitted he had failed to see this fullness, and he noticed that many of his fellow believers who were committed to the purity of doctrine and of the church failed to exhibit it. It was a failure that ran through the whole realm of human life. One of his most profound realizations was that without a true spirituality it was possible for a person to be doctrin-

---

[7]Interview with Debby and Udo Middelmann, 2007.
[8]Interview with Francis Schaeffer, 1980.

ally pure or to be genuinely loving to others but never both simultaneously.[9] He touched on his thinking at this period of crisis when I asked him in an interview, late in his life, "When you wrote *The God Who Is There*, you said the question of truth was the central one. Do you still feel that?"

> Of course. There is no reason to believe in Christianity if it isn't true. It is hard to put this into words, and yet I think it's crucial. I think there are many Christians—I mean, real Christians, real brothers and sisters in Christ, people I'm really fond of—who believe that certain things in the Christian faith are true, and yet, somehow or other, never relate this to *truth*. I don't know if it comes across, what I'm trying to say, but I believe it's truth—and not just religious truth, but the truth of what is. This gives you a different perspective. . . .
>
> I would say if Christianity is truth, it ought to touch on the whole of life. The modern drift in some evangelical circles toward being emotionally and experientially based is really very, very weak. The other side of the coin, though, is that Christianity must never be reduced merely to an intellectual system. It too has to touch the whole of life, which means the devotional and so on. . . . I think it fits into the concept of the fullness of truth. After all, if God is there, [if] it isn't just an answer to an intellectual question, then he's really there. We should love him, we're called upon to adore him, to be in relationship to him, and, incidentally, to obey him. . . . If God is really there, he is to be worshiped, he is to be adored, but he's also to be obeyed. . . . If you listen with care to a great deal of the emotional Christianity that's being put forth, it is always what God can do for you. You hear nothing about what we're supposed to do for God. This is a tremendous lack. The concept of Christianity as being truth and touching the fullness of life ought to contain all these elements. But then we would all have to say that none of us do it very well. We sure ought to struggle for it.[10]

It is noteworthy that with *The Sunday School Times* Fran departed from his usual procedure of publishing his articles in strictly separatist periodicals such as *The Bible Today* or *The Beacon*. In fact, the article, according to Lane Dennis, "set off a major controversy in the 'separated

---

[9]Francis A. Schaeffer, *The Church Before the Watching World* (London: Inter-Varsity Press, 1972), 54.
[10]Interview with Francis Schaeffer.

movement.'"[11] There is a discernible shift in content too in his writings during this period when the spiritual crisis intensified—a warm devotional edginess in some, an article about a visit to Rome on the occasion of the groundbreaking papal announcement of the Assumption of Mary that takes great pains to convey the atmosphere, or a whole article devoted to the importance of modern art. One might say that Schaeffer was developing a listening attitude, one of the most important gifts he offered to those who later studied under him. Though he would continue to suffer bouts of depression and to struggle with anger and frustration, he became far more integrated emotionally and intellectually as a result of his struggles. One of his daughters, Susan, noticed a marked difference in his attitudes. She recalled the time of crisis and its result:

> I remember when I was ten, in Champéry, that would be 1951, that winter when he went through the experience he wrote about in *True Spirituality*. I remember my mother was worried, and his walking back and forth, his footsteps at the top of the ceiling, in the chalet, as he worked things out. When he felt he'd found the key he shared it all with us first, and it made a huge impression on me. "You know you are not doing something, say, to witness to the villagers, but, quite honestly, you're doing it because it's right." The illustration he used to use to us [was], "You leave the towels all over the bathroom. Why do we pick them up and hang them up? So that people will know that Christians are good or something? No, you don't do it as a witness; you do it because it's right. It's the right thing to do. And you're kind to a person because it's the right thing to do, not because maybe you're going to have a little word to say to them about the Lord." It was a great shift. We are going to pray about things; we don't always have to do something. It was like a type of charismatic experience, and it made a huge difference. I saw the change in [him] . . . the flaws in his character really started to be worked on from then. You know, he really changed, considerably.[12]

This new way of seeing, Susan remembered, became his message. This is what he spoke about to the home churches when they were on furlough in 1953 and 1954. One incident has stuck in her mind, which

---

[11]*The Letters of Francis Schaeffer*, 31.
[12]Interview with Susan Macaulay, 2007.

was about his changing his attitude toward the behavior of separation among the fundamentalist churches of the time—a change in him that came when both truth and love were in the equation. It was the first time she saw her father have a drink of wine, during an annual vacation.

> We were having one of our hikes high up in the hills above Alassio in Italy. I must have been about ten years old, so it would have been about 1951. They were very poor up in the hills there, no electricity, no running water. It was rather like Champéry, poor Italians scraping a living out of a few olive trees, whatever they had. A sweating man invited us into this poor room—nothing but a hole for the window, and a table and a couple of chairs, literally nothing—and brought out a bottle of wine. I remember my father saying, "We have to drink it." . . . So we were brought up realizing the cultural influences and what mattered was *true* spirituality.[13]

The crisis period was not only a testing time for Fran. It was also enormously difficult for Edith. He had disclosed to her what he was doing. Much of this thinking and struggling he had to do in solitude. As he explained when *True Spirituality* was published, more than twenty years later:

> We were living in Champéry at that time, and I told Edith that for the sake of honesty I had to go all the way back to my agnosticism and think through the whole matter. I'm sure that this was a difficult time for her, and I'm sure that she prayed much for me in those days. I walked in the mountains when it was clear, and when it was rainy I walked backward and forward in the hayloft of the old chalet in which we lived. I walked, prayed, and thought through what the Scriptures taught, as well as reviewing my own reasons for being a Christian.[14]

Fran's intention, his absences in the mountains, and the constant sound of his footsteps in the hayloft of Chalet Bijou when the weather was bad panicked Edith. (It was very wet that spring.) She clearly remembered his warning to her, not long before they moved to Chalet Bijou from Chalet des Frênes in Champéry at the end of April 1951:

---

[13]Ibid.
[14]Preface to *True Spirituality*.

"Edith, I really feel torn to pieces by the lack of reality, the lack of seeing the results the Bible talks about, which should be seen in the Lord's people. I'm not talking only about people I'm working with in 'The Movement,' but I'm not satisfied with myself. It seems that the only honest thing to do is to rethink, re-examine the whole matter of Christianity. Is it true? I need to go back to my agnosticism and start at the beginning."[15] Edith was afraid of what was happening and the consequences. As Deborah remembers:

> I've heard her say that she was terrified. I've heard her use that word, because she, I think, knew my father well enough to know that if he concluded that he did not have enough evidence for the existence of God, and for the truth of it, he would throw it out, with just as much passion as he had accepted it originally. He always said that. I don't think many people think he meant it, but he did mean it. When people would say to him that they knew it [Christian faith] wasn't true, he would say, "If you can bring me the evidence that it is not true, I'll throw it out tomorrow." He meant that. He just wasn't being clever for the sake of a discussion. He really meant it. As he said from a platform at his last L'Abri conference before his death, when somebody asked him, "What is the reason to be a Christian, Dr. Schaeffer?": "There's one reason and only one reason to be a Christian, which is that you're convinced it is the truth of the universe." It's on tape. He really meant this. That was not just a good reason, but the only reason.[16]

After the crisis, in its intense phase, was over, and the sun came out again for Francis Schaeffer, his heart was lightened. He began to compose poetry again, poetry he rarely shared except with Edith, because he considered it technically poor. Songs of worship began welling up within him. He confided in a letter to Jeffrey, an American friend, when the struggle looked like it was beginning to be over, "I really feel lighter than I have for years. I do not know what all this means in my relation to the [separatist] movement, but I have come to this conclusion—that, God willing, I do not want to lose this joy I have before the Lord. There is nothing that would be worth getting back into the black humor I

---

[15]Edith Schaeffer, *The Tapestry*, 354–355.
[16]Interview with Debby and Udo Middelmann.

have been in."[17] He and Edith continued their traveling to speak of the dangers of the New Modernism and to encourage neighborhood children's classes. Outwardly it easily could have looked as if nothing had essentially changed as far as their work and ministry was concerned. This was true even after a unique preaching and pastoral opportunity opened up for Fran.

During the winter before their move to Chalet Bijou, an unanticipated development had taken place that would add a new dimension to their existing activities and contribute to the shaping of the future. A young Swiss pastor tracked them down who had been visiting the few Protestants in that Roman Catholic town. During a visit to a nearby girls' school, which remained open during the Christmas holiday season, he had heard that there was an American Protestant pastor living in Chalet des Frênes. He had come to tell Fran of a Protestant church building in the town that was usually empty. An Englishwoman who holidayed in Champéry had built it early in the century. At her death she had left the building in the hands of a Swiss committee, and it was available for a Christmas service.

As the family made their way to the church on a bitter cold Sunday morning, Christmas Eve, little Debby voiced their thoughts: "Who will come to the church to hear Daddy preach?" The answer came as they walked through the door. The Temple Protestant was full of people, many of them schoolchildren, about one hundred and fifty in all. Most were from Britain, including trimly uniformed girls from a London school and Scottish boys in kilts. There were groups on holiday trips and individuals from nearby hotels. It was the first of regular Christmas services led by Fran that would take place long after the family left Champéry. It has continued to this day, taken over by Udo Middelmann many years before Fran's death, as his associate pastor.

The Christmas service immediately led to the Schaeffers' being allowed to hold services weekly. These regular meetings soon put them in touch with a group of young women at a finishing school in Champéry who told the Schaeffers they would be there until March. International

---

[17]*The Letters of Francis Schaeffer*, 33. Letter dated April 14, 1951.

finishing schools were common at that time in Switzerland. Wealthy parents from throughout the world sent their daughters to learn social etiquette, partake in language and other courses, and enjoy character-developing sports such as skiing. Ages ranged from sixteen to the mid-twenties. Some came prior to university, some immediately after. The Schaeffers one Sunday invited some of them, as they stood chatting at the back of the church after the service, to "come to our chalet this Thursday night for an informal evening of conversation and tea. Bring any questions you might have concerning religion, or the Bible, or just anything that troubles you."[18] The director of the school initially stopped them from coming, but after meeting the Schaeffers, he allowed the invitation to extend to the whole school. Furthermore they were encouraged to come at any time.

On the first Thursday evening thirty-two tumbled into Chalet des Frênes, filling it with their voices. The young women represented many countries, ethnic groups, and religions from around the world. The evening began with Fran showing some of the slides he had taken on his European trip in 1947, after which Edith served cakes and tea, and then the serious questions began. Susan remembered the evenings vividly: "We were allowed to stay up and see the slides, and for the cake, and then we'd be sent to bed. They'd start to ask questions, and we wanted to stay up."[19]

These regular visits from the finishing school students brought the Schaeffers a new dimension of opportunity for mission. It was far more than their work with children and was a prelude to the not-too-distant future when Priscilla started to bring home students from the University of Lausanne. Prisca remembered:

> Daddy was asked to take the tourists' church service the first week, and there were two or three boarding schools that would come there for three months in the winter, and we had them on different nights for discussions, and that's where all of a sudden I saw my father in front of nineteen- and twenty-year-olds, answering their questions and relating it to the culture. Daddy loved that.[20]

---

[18]Edith Schaeffer, *L'Abri*, revised edition (Wheaton, IL: Crossway Books, 1992), 41.
[19]Interview with Susan Macaulay.
[20]Interview with Priscilla and John Sandri, 2007.

So it was that in those early years at Champéry, the seeds of the future work of L'Abri began to be sown.

The Children for Christ work, however, continued. It was brought home to them, literally, at the insistence of Susan, their middle daughter. She remembered with delight:

> I was the one who started the Children for Christ in our house, when I was nine years old. I said, "You're just frauds—you're hypocrites. You're all going around Europe telling everybody else to start these classes, and you won't even have one here in our house." "But it's a Catholic village, and that's not what we're here for." So I said, "Well, up on the Russian border you tell them to have one!" I can still remember it. He said, "But I don't speak French." I said, "Well, Priscilla could teach, and you could tell her what to do." So finally they said, "Well, if you get the children . . ." By three years later we had half the village there, between the two of us, and they loved it. There were parties; there were lovely stories and pictures. All along, as far as I was concerned, it was what we were doing, and would they please fit in with us?[21]

Ironically, having Children for Christ classes within a Roman Catholic town would contribute to the case against them when they were presented with a notice to leave Switzerland in 1955 for proselytizing.

When the family was forced to move out of their rented Chalet des Frênes because the property was sold, they were upset about losing somewhere that had become home for them amid the constant traveling and adapting the flux of their family experiences to a permanent life in Switzerland. They were overjoyed, however, with their new home, Chalet Bijou:

> It sat nestled down below the village, quite apart from other chalets, with a big field above it, between it and the village, a rushing torrent separating it from the path up to the village, and a wide field bordered by the torrent . . . going down to a steep cliff that dropped to the river below. There was a square balcony just outside the dining room, on the lower side of the chalet, which we called "the breakfast porch,"

---

[21]Interview with Susan Macaulay.

because it had an old rough wooden table where we ate in the morning sun.[22]

It also had a large loft, an original hayloft with hay still in it, which was to be an important sanctuary to Fran when he needed somewhere in which to move about and think when it was too wet to walk outside.

In all the bustle and activity Fran was constantly thinking. Some of his thinking he put into writing. Coinciding with the period of crisis and its immediate aftermath he composed two very significant articles, both of which reveal his growing insight into social and cultural trends.

The first was a journalistic account of one of the most significant developments in Roman Catholicism in the twentieth century—the proclamation of the Assumption of Mary on November 1, 1950. Fran visited Rome for the papal announcement and vividly recorded his impressions, in prose generally more elegant than much of his later writings (with the exception of more carefully crafted books such as *How Should We Then Live?*):

> When evening falls the spectacle continues; the whole city is illuminated. Standing upon Capital Hill, one has at his back and right the Palazzo Senatorio, now the city hall of Rome, which is built over the old Tabularium, erected in 78 B.C. Tonight the Palace has hundreds of blazing torches over its cornices, roof and cupola. These torches are shallow pans from which fire rises several feet into the air. Below us is the Mamertine Prison where Roman Catholic tradition says that Paul and Peter were imprisoned. In age it is old enough to have held Paul when he was in prison in Rome. Off to the left is a church completely outlined in electric lights, and with a huge electric "M" covering its entire high façade. In front of us is the ancient Roman Forum. Tonight these ruins, reaching back to the time of Christ and before, are all illumined. . . . Beyond [the Forum] is the Colosseum, finished by Titus in 80 A.D.; tonight it is lit with bluish-green flood lights and literally thousands of flaming torches. In an instant all time seems telescoped, and before us is a panorama of time. The centuries before Christ, the days of Paul, Pagan Rome fallen to be born phoenix-like in Roman Catholicism, the march of the Caesars and the march of the Popes, the

---

[22]Edith Schaeffer, *L'Abri*, 51.

worship of the old goddesses and tonight all this illuminated in honor
of a new.[23]

Schaeffer realized that dramatic changes were taking place within
the Roman Catholic Church, even though in 1950 Vatican II was still
in the undreamed future. It was not immune from the transformation
of ideas and culture sweeping the world. Its incipient "paganism" fitted well into the New Modernism he had discerned in theology. The
authority of Scripture, tradition, and history was being superseded by
the authority of the "living Church," which could declare that Mary
passed bodily into heaven, her flesh seeing no corruption caused by
the processes of death, even though this declaration had no biblical or
historical warrant, and even though this story of Mary's assumption
had been dismissed as heresy by the church in the fifth century. Part of
the papal declaration of a renewed veneration of the blessed Mary read:
"On the first of November, the feast of all saints, the radiant brow of the
queen of heaven and the beloved Mother of God will be wreathed with
a new splendor, when, under divine inspiration and assistance, we shall
solemnly define and decree her bodily assumption into heaven."[24]

Fran was to be proved right about radical change in Rome as the
decades unfolded. Even ten years or so later, someone as astute as
Harold O. J. Brown only learned from "the clarity of Schaeffer's analysis" that great change was coming, "that Roman Catholicism was on
the verge of doctrinal chaos and disciplinary collapse. . . . Who could
suspect that within a few years the Second Vatican Council would let the
fox into Catholicism's henhouse. . . . Schaeffer saw it coming."[25]

Even more radical in its insights than that article was a long piece
on "The Christian and Modern Art," published in *The Bible Today* in
March 1951. Its radicality is by no means as obvious as what was stated
about the failure of love among those who fought for doctrinal and
ecclesiastical purity in his *Sunday School Times* article published three
months later. Yet, in its way it is as much a manifesto essay and goes to

---

[23]Francis A. Schaeffer, "Rome," in *Biblical Missions*, February–March 1951. *Biblical Missions* was the
magazine of the Independent Board for Presbyterian Missions, for which Schaeffer was a missionary
at that time.
[24]Quoted in Edith Schaeffer, *The Tapestry*, 349.
[25]*Francis A. Schaeffer: Portraits of the Man and his Work*, ed. Lane T. Dennis (Wheaton, IL: Crossway
Books, 1986), 18.

the heart of Schaeffer's concerns as an evangelist to modern people for the rest of his life. It is stamped with insights that had come from his burgeoning friendship with Hans Rookmaaker, whom he acknowledges early in the article: "In writing on art, I acknowledge with pleasure the stimulating conversations I have had with a young Christian art critic of Amsterdam, H. R. Rookmaaker."[26] It is likely that some of the conversations came out of both men's viewing an exhibition of modern Belgian artists in Amsterdam, which included Delvaux, who is discussed at some length in the article. Fran mentions also looking at the artistic treatment of the medieval crucifix, where the figure of Christ is artistically elongated and of which he had himself found "clear examples all the way from Scandinavia through Germany and Holland into Southern Europe."[27]

Schaeffer amplifies on comments he made in his paper to the Geneva Congress the year before, on "The New Modernism." Carefully studying modern art, he says (preparing the reader for some searching analysis in the article), "tells us quickly and concisely the kind of a day in which we live. . . . Art not only speaks to us of the general world view of an age, or a people, but speaks to us of the religious thinking as well."[28] (He gives the example of Rembrandt for Protestant art, and Hans Baldung, from the century before Rembrandt, for Roman Catholic art.) In fact, he argues, "The New Modernism is to theology what Modern Art is to art." This is because they are both founded "upon a denial of the Bible, and therefore lack any fixed point. The only difference is that the modern artist and the modern musician have been far more honest in portraying this unrelatedness."[29]

The honesty of modern artists over what Schaeffer elsewhere called "the problem of reality," as propounded in this heartfelt article, makes it easy to see why his concern with understanding the arts and culture of the present time is intimately tied up with his own quest for reality in the hayloft of Chalet Bijou and in the surrounding hills that wet spring. It also explains why modern art and culture continued to be a predomi-

---

[26]Francis A. Schaeffer, "The Christian and Modern Art," in *The Bible Today*, March 1951, 163.
[27]Ibid., 164.
[28]Ibid., 163.
[29]Ibid., 168.

nant concern of his in his subsequent ministry. The honesty of the artist presented a doorway for communicating the hope for humanity that came from Christ's finished work on the cross. Not only that, the honesty resonated with him subjectively; he had discovered a deep affinity with those who were willing to face the outer darkness of a disrelated world, where all is relative. It further explains the bond between the prematurely wise Dutch art critic in bustling Amsterdam and the open-eyed American missionary in quiet Champéry.

Concluding his article, he broadened the picture of modern art that he had briefly but evocatively painted to take in the whole sweep of contemporary society and culture, a broad sweep that would eventually become his hallmark. It was inevitable that this was so, when modern culture and society is seen in the light of something as fundamental as "the problem of reality":

> Unsaved men of the past have kept from being washed into unrelatedness in theology, philosophy, art, etc. by various inconsistencies. Today it is as though God has released man and is allowing him in all the fields of life to go to his natural level.[30] This is true in the "practical" aspects such as government and morality, in the basic aspects such as theology and philosophy and in the expressional aspects such as art and music. This is one of the great signs of the times.
>
> Theology is not separated from life nor is art, and if we are to understand our day in a way which will enable us to be most on our guard against the drift of it, and to enable us to preach Christ to the men who are enveloped by the drift of our day, it is well not only to have some knowledge of modern theology but these other things as well. Such knowledge enables us to understand our day, and also provides a point of contact with those who are children of it. There are many people whom we can reach for Christ far better if we have an understanding of these things which exhibit the basic modern viewpoint, and therefore we can understand something of that by which today's men are bound, not only in spiritual darkness, but in intellectual and emotional darkness, which ultimately are rooted in and spring from that spiritual darkness.[31]

---

[30]Note the allusion here to Romans 1:18–32, particularly: God "gave them up . . . to impurity . . . dishonourable passions . . . a base mind and to improper conduct" (verses 24, 26, 28, RSV). The first eight chapters of Romans had become central to Schaeffer as he wrestled with the character of a proper spirituality and "the problem of reality."

[31]Francis A. Schaeffer, "The Christian and Modern Art," 169.

In writing his article on "The Christian and Modern Art" Fran was addressing an audience he knew and loved, through one of their vehicles, *The Bible Today* periodical. The audience was the nexus of separated churches and groups in the United States with whom he was so closely connected and within which he was highly regarded. He was soon effectively to lose the encouragement and support of this community as a whole that was so important to him, as a lifeline in fact, even though many individuals in it would continue to uphold him. In two more years he would have served five years as a missionary for the Independent Board, making his furlough due. He would then unleash his controversial message of true spirituality to his brethren across America.

In those two remaining years from the move to Chalet Bijou to the beginning of an extended furlough in the United States, the work of lecturing throughout Europe on the dangers of the New Modernism and maintaining and encouraging the Children for Christ outreach continued. Mingled into it, hospitality and question times for constant visitors to Chalet Bijou became a significant element in a slowly changing focus. Fran and Edith's perpetual activity on this "escalator" of events was punctuated in this period by a new and distinctive arrival in the family, following the disappointment and grief of a previous miscarriage. Franky, as he was known through much of his life (Francis August Schaeffer V), was born August 3, 1952. He is now well-known as the novelist Frank Schaeffer and is also a filmmaker and artist who wrote brash books in the eighties for an unwieldy evangelical constituency along the lines of his father's concerns, such as *Addicted to Mediocrity*, before converting to Eastern Orthodoxy. His Calvin Becker trilogy of novels (*Portofino*, 1996, *Saving Grandma*, 1997, and *Zermatt*, 2003) openly mocks a "fundamentalist" and pietistic lifestyle.

A vivid picture of the early hospitality offered by Fran and Edith in Chalet Bijou, and their somewhat narrow lifestyle at that time, is demonstrated by a ten-day visit by two unusual American women in 1951. They had been encouraged to visit Champéry by Madam Dumreicher, whom the Schaeffers had befriended when she vacationed in the village. She had omitted to tell Betty Carlson and Gea (her friend) that they were missionaries. Betty was a fast-witted writer who had tried her hand at a number of occupations. Her plainness was exaggerated in contrast to her friend, whose dark prettiness had won her the title of Miss Kansas the year before.[32] They had just arrived in Champéry on the cog railway from Monthey, being met at the station by Debby, the youngest of the Schaeffer daughters, and a pleasant friend of the family who was dressed in puritan clothes and wore her hair in a severe bun. This is because Fran and Edith had been called away that evening. From Marlise, the friend, Gea learned to her horror that the Schaeffers were missionaries, leaving her feeling trapped, as Betty recounts.

> We started down a steep hill, and we all helped with the wagon to hold it back, or to keep the luggage from going on ahead. Soon the path lev- elled off somewhat, and we were in a field of wild flowers. We crossed a wooden bridge over a fast-flowing stream, and as we approached the Schaeffer chalet, it was getting dark. . . .
>
> The old chalet was large, comfortable-looking, but icy cold inside. Debbie showed us to our room on the second floor, and the four of us carried up the luggage.
>
> "When you are refreshed," she said politely, "come down to the dining room, and we'll have supper. Susan and Priscilla, they're my sisters, are *supposed to* be fixing it."
>
> The way she said, "supposed to," led us to suspect Debbie did not have supreme confidence in her sisters' ability to fix supper. Marlise had already gone down to help out.
>
> "If you need anything," Debbie added, as she handed us towels, "let me know."
>
> "She's amazing," I said to Gea, when our young hostess gently shut the door and went out. . . .[33]

At which point Gea told Betty her discovery about the Schaeffers. For the first few days the unnerving fact that Fran and Edith were mis- sionaries dominated the perceptions of the two young women.

The Schaeffers were missionaries all right. Missionaries of the worst sort. They started all meals with long prayers. They talked about

---

[32]According to Edith Schaeffer, Gea was the title holder the year before she visited. This would mean Gea's proper name is Anabel Baker, Miss Kansas 1950.
[33]Betty Carlson, *The Unhurried Chase* (Wheaton, IL: Tyndale House, 1970), 124.

spiritual matters from morning until night, and often, far into the night. Whenever Gea and I mentioned a good musical we had seen in Lausanne, or told about the latest French or Swedish movie, some-how the conversation always worked back to Methuselah, Moses or Mephibosheth, or Shadrach, Meshach, and Abednego.[34]

They hoped they might influence the Schaeffers for the better, how-ever, as the missionaries were definitely human!

> Gea and I had quickly observed what a wonderful family spirit the Schaeffers had. They thoroughly enjoyed one another; but not in any way that shuts out others, and they had such good times together over simple pleasures. We remained convinced that they were "off" in their religious conviction and their narrow-minded insistence that the Bible is the final truth of the universe; but we were hopeful that *our* influence on *them* would be rewarding, and that they would come to adopt a broader concept of truth. But there was no denying it, they were delightful people, interesting and interested in many of the same things we were. It surprised us greatly to discover how fond we were of them.[35]

When the two of them left at the end of their short visit, their atti-tudes had changed so much that, to their surprise, they had come to share the Schaeffers' faith. Many years later Betty would come to live and work in Switzerland, right in the middle of the L'Abri community. There was a similar response of faith from some of the girls and young women from the finishing schools who visited Chalet Bijou. A variety of other visitors descended on the Schaeffers. The visit of Betty and Gea was the shape of things to come. Betty Carlson observed many years later:

> In less than a year after Gea and I cluttered up the Schaeffer chalet, there has scarcely been one weekend that the Schaeffers haven't been overrun with swarms of young people seeking fuller, deeper, richer answers than the ones they are hearing on TV, or in their universities and in many churches.[36]

---

[34]Ibid., 127.
[35]Ibid., 129.
[36]Ibid., 146–147.

One result of the ties that developed between the finishing schools and the Schaeffers was that the director of *Le Grande Verger* ("the great orchard"), Monsieur Fonjallaz, offered Prisca free tuition at his finishing school so her education could proceed more satisfactorily than it was doing at the nearby boys' boarding school. While they were on furlough and based in Philadelphia, another unexpected provision came up for Prisca's education—she along with Susan and Deborah, was given a place at the prestigious Stevens School. The three had previously studied there in the period leading up to the family's departure from the United States in 1948, using money provided for Edith's secretarial training—the ever-resourceful woman had taken a correspondence course instead. This meant that by the time they returned to Switzerland Priscilla was fully prepared to enter the University of Lausanne.

The furlough itself was extensive, lasting eighteen months rather than the usual one year. It marked a watershed in the lives of the family members. Because of the controversy Fran had stirred up in his denomination and the fact that their missionary work now included "hospitality" and not just obvious activity, their very return to Switzerland was for a time in doubt.

Throughout the furlough the Schaeffer family, enlarged considerably by a demanding infant, lived in a tiny house at 6117 Lensen Street, Philadelphia, belonging to Fran's widowed Uncle Harrison. It was empty for that period as he was living for a while with his brother and sister-in-law as he came to terms with his bereavement. "Empty" is not a precise term—in fact, the house was crammed full with Uncle Harrison's furniture and possessions, creating challenges for Fran and Edith as they tried to establish living space for the family. Susan remembered the Philadelphia house well:

> When we were on furlough, we lived in a funny little house, my father's uncle's house, a terraced house (a row house), stuffed with Victorian furniture and a little like [one you find] in Liverpool or somewhere—little front room, dark dining room, tiny little kitchen, and a scullery to do the laundry in, with [a] mangle. I used to do my brother's nappies [diapers] and hang them out on the line at the back.[37]

---

[37]Interview with Susan Macaulay.

It was not easy living in such a cramped habitat. Many nights Edith forced herself to stay awake so she could pat baby Franky in his cot beside their bed, so he would not cry. His cries would disturb not only the family's sleep but that of neighbors on the other side of the thin dividing wall of the terraced house.

Fran taught for the academic year 1953–1954 at his alma mater. It was easily accessed, since they had moved the year before to Elkins Park, just north of Philadelphia. At Faith Theological Seminary he taught pastoral theology. His duties there were necessarily light because of his responsibilities as a missionary on furlough for the International Board for Presbyterian Foreign Missions. The speaking engagements were legion. Edith records that he spoke 346 times in 515 days.[38] The venues were scattered across America and included a nearby church in Willow Grove, Pennsylvania, Carl McIntire's Collingwood Church in New Jersey, Shelton College, where Oliver Buswell was still president at that time, and places as far afield as California. As was his custom, Fran reworked talks and sermons, some of them going back to his ten years as a pastor before 1948. (Many of the sermons in *No Little People* were preached in earlier forms.) His talks included the subject of modern art and the history of Europe. His main message, however, was that which had been born in his "hayloft crisis" in Champéry. A series on the message of truth and love that he often preached was most fully delivered in a summer camp July 5–12, 1953—fittingly, in an old barn. His meticulously kept notebook simply records the series as "Sanctification I, II, III, IV, V." It was only later that the title "true spirituality" was conceived.

It was when the message was focused into a graduation message in 1954 at Faith Seminary that an increasing rift with his denomination became apparent. The pivotal talk was entitled "Tongues of Fire," on the equal necessity of holding out for truth and of doing this only in the power of the Lord. It included the challenge, "There is no source of power for God's people—for preaching or teaching or anything else— except Christ himself. Apart from Christ anything which seems to be

---

[38]Edith Schaeffer, *The Tapestry*, 387.

spiritual power is actually the power of the flesh."[39] Afterwards a grim-faced wife of one of the denominational leaders approached Edith with the warning, "Edith, there's going to be a split in our denomination."[40]

The split did not occur in its final form until 1956, when the Bible Presbyterian Church fractured into two Synods and Covenant College was established, Covenant Seminary being formed the following year. Oliver Buswell sided with the larger Synod[41] and Carl McIntire with the other (named Collingswood Synod). The McIntire wing in the meantime accused Fran of dubious motives for his message of balance; he was, they said, trying to take over the leadership of the denomination. This paranoia reflected deeper tensions within the denomination at that time. Suspicion of Schaeffer must have been enhanced when Robert Rayburn, on behalf of Highland College, presented him with an honorary Doctor of Divinity degree on May 28, 1954. That same year Rayburn led several younger ministers in the denomination to challenge the "oligarchical" direction of McIntire's crusading separatism. As a result Rayburn, President Buswell (who defended the critical ministers), and others were removed from positions of leadership in the denominational institutions, such as the Independent Board for Presbyterian Foreign Missions, under McIntire's influence. Susan, who reached her early teens at the time, was only dimly aware of what was happening, as she happily attended a very different church's young people's service in Philadelphia. What the furlough meant for her was the long absences of her father, not denominational politics.

> I don't know too much about the whole McIntire era. All I remember, it was in the McCarthy era and there were Communists under every single little inch of space. In the end I think McIntire said my Dad was a Communist—that was [his] problem. Dad was dealing with a great big idea, the denominational idea. I hardly saw him that year. He was off preaching.

---

[39]"The Lord's Work in the Lord's Way," in *No Little People, The Complete Works of Francis A. Schaeffer*, Vol. 3, second edition (Wheaton, IL: Crossway Books, 1985), 42. The graduation message provided the substance of this later L'Abri sermon. Edith, who was present, quotes this sentence in *The Tapestry* (388) as from the graduation message.

[40]Edith Schaeffer, *The Tapestry*, 388.

[41]It later, in 1965, became the Reformed Presbyterian Church, Evangelical Synod, after merging with another, like-minded, denomination and adopting a more open eschatological position. In 1982 it merged with the Presbyterian Church in America (PCA), a national church, the second largest Presbyterian denomination in the USA.

I took exception to American Christians at twelve years old! It came from my parents and my father's preaching [in Champéry]. They did lovely Sunday evening things and they would read out loud to us—my mother called it "Young People's." We would do all these family type of [things]. I was twelve when we went to a Presbyterian church, imagining it a real church. It was actually a tin shack; it was terrible. Dreadful. There were trolley cars in Philadelphia. As we rode on one to go to school I saw a lovely gray, "proper" church—it turned out to be [Reformed] Episcopalian. The [sign] said "Young people's." I trotted along. Then I started going to the morning services and that's when I found the liturgy and Communion—going to the rail. Right away, I felt at home there.[42]

The girls very much missed Switzerland and were appalled when the mission board hesitated over their return. It became clear that the family needed to raise its own support for the return to Europe, even when, finally, it was agreed that they return. The older girls came up with an idea. Edith recorded soon afterward:

> During the middle of our furlough Priscilla and Susan made a fat thermometer to put up on our kitchen wall—"To show how the money is coming in for our passage back." We contemplated sending out a letter informing people of this need, but kept deciding against it—"Let's just pray about it for the time being." And so it went on this way. Very little red crayon was needed as the weeks and months went on, for the thermometer was very low! "What is the Lord saying to us? If He wants us to go, He will send it in; let's just keep praying."[43]

Working out a timetable with their travel agent, they settled for a departure date of September 1, which meant that they would need to post a check for the full amount by July 29.

> That was the date the children and I began "praying towards." "If you want us to keep these reservations and get back to the work then, dear Lord, please send in the needed passage money by that date."[44]

---

[42]Interview with Susan Macaulay.
[43]Edith Schaeffer, *With Love, Edith: The L'Abri Family Letters 1948–1960* (San Francisco: Harper & Row, 1988), 290–291.
[44]Ibid., 291.

It was already the end of June. After another week nothing more had come in. But by July 29 all that was needed came through the mail, checks coming in daily over the last three weeks. The final amount needed came on the last possible day. Trusting the Lord to provide, and having this as affirmation that they return to Europe, did not make that period of uncertainty easy.

Fran and Edith passed through much greater testing as they voyaged back over the Atlantic. Their little son, full of life and mischief, succumbed to polio, leading to permanent damage to one leg. They were not able to get proper treatment for him until their arrival in Switzerland, Edith flying ahead with the children from Paris instead of taking the train. A whole period of testing lay ahead.

Although in a way this made the times of difficulty no easier, both Fran and Edith were prepared to face trouble. This made them more resilient to discouragement. As they headed back to Switzerland, they knew that nothing could be the same again. Fran's crisis back in 1951 had not only changed him but would continue changing him. The message he received from those struggles simply had to be the main burden of what he preached and spoke about in the year and a half of furlough in America. The new way of seeing had also had a life-changing impact on Edith.

> We had done quite a lot of thinking and self-examining over the previous few years. It seemed to us that so much of Christianity was being spread by advertising designed to "put across" something, that there was very little genuine recognition of the existence of the supernatural work of the Holy Spirit. One morning at Chalet Bijou's breakfast table, Fran had said to me, "Supposing we had awakened today to find everything concerning the Holy Spirit and prayer removed from the Bible—that is, not removed the way liberals would remove it, but that God had somehow really removed everything about prayer and the Holy Spirit from the Bible. What difference would it make practically between the way we work yesterday and the way we would work today, and tomorrow? What difference would it make in the majority of Christians' practical work and plans? Aren't most plans laid out ahead of time? Isn't much work done by human talent, energy and clever ideas? Where does the supernatural power of God have a real place?" Challenged by this, we began to think and look over our own

lives and work . . . and, we asked God to give us something more real in our work of the future.[45]

Their prayer was being answered. They increasingly saw that this was why they were experiencing such testing times. There was a cost to facing the reality of a mission that was done in the Lord's way rather than in the wisdom of human effort and state-of-the art mission methods. This is not to say that they would not be required to work unrelentingly. Somehow, though, they were servants, not masters, in their endeavor; the initiative came from the Lord, and they were cast upon the possibilities of his infinite imagination. The situations they encountered required what Fran called an "active passivity."[46] His engineering metaphor still applied: they were on a sometimes dizzying "escalator," taking them onward and upward.

---

[45]Edith Schaeffer, *L'Abri*, revised edition (Wheaton, IL: Crossway Books, 1992), 64–65.
[46]Francis Schaeffer, *True Spirituality*, in *The Complete Works of Francis A. Schaeffer*, Vol. 3, 247, 252–253, 281, etc.

THE SHELTER

(1955–1960)

ᗏ ᗏ ᗏ ᗏ ᗏ

dith has told the story of the beginning and development of
L'Abri many times in many places, eventually putting her narrative into a book called simply *L'Abri*. Appropriately she begins
her account with a winter avalanche that nearly wiped away their chalet
in Champéry early in 1955, within months of the family's return from
the USA and baby Frank's affliction with polio. It is a fitting metaphor
for what was to come soon after that year—a sequence of overwhelming
events that required all the courage and faith that Fran and Edith could
muster. The avalanche of events was to be a supreme test of seeking a
new reality in the way they worked and planned. Fran starkly jotted
down in his heavily annotated Bible, not long after the spiritual avalanche began, "Jan. 1955—Edith felt a promise concerning our coming
work. Feb. 14 told to leave."

The promise that was perceived by Edith had come about while she
was reading from the book of Isaiah in her devotions.[1]

> *It shall come to pass in the latter days that the mountain of the house
> of the LORD shall be established as the highest of the mountains, and
> shall be lifted up above the hills; and all the nations shall flow to it.*
> *(2:2)*

Edith penciled into the margin of her Bible page, "Jan. '55, promise
. . . Yes, L'Abri." She later reflected upon her excited jotting:

For I had the tremendous surge of assurance that although this [pas-
sage of Isaiah] had another basic meaning, it was being used by God

---

[1]Edith Schaeffer, *L'Abri*, revised edition (Wheaton, IL: Crossway Books, 1992), 76.

to tell me something. I did not feel that "all nations" were literally going to come to our home for help, but I did feel that it spoke of people from many different nations coming to a house that God would establish for the purpose of making "His ways" known to them. I felt these people would tell others, and would say in effect, "Come . . . let us go up the mountain . . . to the house of the God of Jacob; and He will teach us of His ways, and we will walk in His paths." It seemed to me that God was putting His hand on my shoulder in a very real way and that He was saying that there would be a work which would be His work, not ours, which man could not stop. I felt that this work was going to be L'Abri.[2]

"L'Abri" was a name that Fran had come up with that would be suitable for their chalet in Champéry as he and Edith imagined its work in a future full of possibilities. Edith explained its meaning in a Family Letter written soon after they received the catastrophic notice to quit: "L'Abri is what we feel the Lord would have us add to the work He had given us here in Switzerland. L'Abri means 'shelter' in French, and our thought is to have a spiritual shelter for any who have spiritual need."[3]

Now, following the terrifying landslide of mud and ice in January 1955, a spiritual avalanche threatened that seemingly frail spiritual shelter. The same letter from Edith that explained the meaning of the Shelter went on to describe both the real and the spiritual avalanches. The spiritual is alluded to in Fran's comment in his Bible margin that on February 14 they had been ordered to leave. What they had been told was not only that they had to leave the chalet they loved in Champéry, their hoped-for Shelter, and their Roman Catholic canton of Valais, but also Switzerland itself, all within six weeks, that is, by March 31.

The Schaeffers, however, were convinced that the verses from Isaiah were a direct "promise" or "sign" from God himself, notwithstanding the seeming impossibility of annulling the edict. The ruling appeared as immovable as the great mountains around them. With Isaiah's words in mind they were convinced that they must attempt to get it annulled.

---

[2]Ibid., 75–76.
[3]Edith Schaeffer, *With Love, Edith: The L'Abri Family Letters 1948–1960* (San Francisco: Harper & Row, 1988), 308; letter of March 7–9, 1955.

"As I see it," Fran said, "there are two courses of action open to us. We could hurry to send telegrams to Christian organizations, our Senator in Washington, and so on, trying to get all the human help we could possibly get; or we could simply get down on our knees, and ask God to help us."[4] Rather than going into a frenzy of telegramming, they chose the way that acknowledged dependence upon a God who acted and responded in a personal way, which for them did not rule out making their own efforts in conjunction with prayer. They felt, however, that they should acknowledge that a sign had been given that pointed out that more was going on than could be responded to adequately by even their best efforts. Though a deeply prayerful woman, Edith in fact was more convinced about practical effort to change the situation in conjunction with prayer than Fran and took the initiative in much that was to go on in the ensuing weeks.

The reason given by the Swiss authorities for their expulsion was, "having had a religious influence in the village of Champéry."[5] Five years later Jane Stuart Smith, an opera singer who joined the work of L'Abri, reflected at an annual meeting of senior staff, "Not one of us would be here if it hadn't been for Mr. [Georges] Exhenry and his salvation, leading to the Schaeffers' being put out. . . ."[6]

Exhenry was a leading figure in Champéry village life who became friendly with the Schaeffers in the summer of 1951 and was soon asking questions about the differences between Roman Catholicism and Protestantism. His conversion to an evangelical faith and baptism caused quite a stir in the village. The year before their expulsion from Champéry, Exhenry became a founding elder of a church that was part of a new Presbyterian denomination especially set up by Fran called the International Church. The purpose of its foundation was to formalize the church meetings in Champéry. Exhenry's high-profile conversion, together with the popularity of the Children for Christ classes in Champéry, led to the charge against the Schaeffers of having had "a religious influence" on the village, a stronghold of Roman Catholicism. Another important local person who came under the influence of the

[4]Edith Schaeffer, *L'Abri*, 78.
[5]Ibid., 313.
[6]Annual members' meeting, Wednesday, March 23, from ibid., 454.

Schaeffers' message was the area physician, Dr. Otten, for whom Fran wrote a series of systematic Bible notes later published as *25 Basic Bible Studies*.

Deborah, the youngest daughter, vividly remembered the doctor and his quest for faith:

> Dr. Otten, our medical doctor for Champéry, took care of the whole valley—the only doctor from Monthey all the way up. He had to hike to all the far-flung chalets and take care of people. He would have long conversations with my parents. Other people in the village were all peasants, so when he would come to our house he would always stand around and talk for a couple of hours. He said to my father, "I would like to know what Christianity is, but I really do not have time to read the entire Bible" (which is what my father felt you needed to do if you were going to consider Christianity, as he had done with Georges Exhenry. Instead of saying to Georges Exhenry, "Here is the gospel; believe it," he gave him a Bible and said, "Read the entire thing and keep coming and we'll discuss it." It was at the end of an entire year that Mr. Exhenry decided to become a Christian and accept this as the truth. But Dr. Otten said, "I don't have time to do this.") So my father said, "I'll work out studies for you." The doctor would come once a week and get the next page.
>
> My father really was confident that when he challenged people to take the Bible seriously, to look at it—[his view was that] if you honestly look, you'll find out this is the truth. (As he always used to say, we don't have the luxury not to look: we've been born without being asked, here we are, we have the questions, we have to find the answers.) That's how he gave the twenty-five Bible studies to Doctor Otten, page by page, so he was able to know what the Bible was.[7]

Far from forcing his message on the village, Fran was working in a context of friendship and care, with the conviction that it was the Bible that was true, and that its claims were worthy of the attention of even the busiest person—indeed, that they demand our attention.

In a sequence of events that reads rather like a new chapter of the book of Acts, the catastrophic order to quit Switzerland was annulled, although the Schaeffers were nevertheless forced to move into the

---

[7]Interview with Debby and Udo Middelmann, 2007.

adjoining Protestant canton of Vaud on the other side of the great Rhône Valley. They were required to buy a property as part of their appeal against deportation and chose a chalet called Les Mélèzes ("the Larches") in the tiny village of Huémoz.

Edith makes it clear when she tells the story of the purchase of Chalet les Mélèzes there were three critical points before the transaction could be completed. These in themselves represented important further signs or trail-markers. The first was in Edith's prayer that very night: "Please show us Thy will about this house tomorrow, and if we are to buy it, send us a sign that will be clear enough to convince Fran as well as me; send us one thousand dollars before ten o'clock tomorrow morning."[8] In the mail the next morning there was a letter that included the momentous words: "Tonight we have come to a definite decision, and both of us feel certain that we are meant to send you this money . . . to buy a house somewhere that will always be open to young people."[9] That letter contained a check for exactly one thousand dollars! The second critical point involved having enough money for a "promissory payment" of eight thousand Swiss francs (a considerable amount of money). For this the various gifts accrued to 8,011 francs. The remaining critical point involved asking God for the exact amount to cover the down payment and closing costs of more than seven thousand dollars. The amount in hand at the time for finalizing the purchase of the house on May 30 turned out to be about three francs more than what was needed.

With the house effectively purchased with the promissory payment of March 4, the way ahead looked clear from the markers, which Fran and Edith saw as personal signs from God. They had the place for the Shelter, to which people from all parts of the world, they believed, would come. However, the edict was still in place requiring them to leave Switzerland by March 31. It was at this point that one of the most dramatic markers was established, with the neighbors of their new home in Huémoz contacting their brother, one of the Swiss Federal Council of Seven. Paul Chaudet duly checked into the matter and was able to secure

[8]Ibid., 97.
[9]Ibid., 95.

the permission for the Schaeffers to remain in Switzerland, specifically in the Canton of Vaud.

Events continued to move rapidly, even when the edict was annulled. On June 5 Fran resigned from the Independent Board for Presbyterian Foreign Missions, convinced that a new chapter had started in the work, one which would center on providing a "Shelter," demonstrating the reality of God's existence in throwing themselves upon his care: ". . . both Edith and I have felt," he wrote some years later, "that this work here is not first of all called of the Lord to be an evangelistic one in any sense, but rather to be a demonstration in a small way of [the existence and character of the God who does exist]."[10]

He spelled out the momentous implications of the decision to resign in a letter nearly three months later to a friend and supporter of the new L'Abri:

> Incidentally you should know that when Edith and I stepped out of the Independent Board we really did not have any promise of support—nor had we asked for any. He has cared for us these first two months in a way that overwhelms us. . . . [W]e would bear our testimony that although the decisions we have made on principle have cost us everything into which we had put twenty years of interest and work, still he has given us a quietness of heart. And in these hearts which He has prepared and sent to us, we have seen the Holy Spirit working in a new way. And we have lacked neither bread nor friends.[11]

The resignation, in other words, was far more than a break with an organization; it marked an end of Francis Schaeffer's separatism. In the North American perception, he was now an evangelical rather than identified with Reformed fundamentalist groups. A year later he affirmed in a letter, "The process is still continuing, but at this time [1956] I no longer have connections with any of the large organizations which have been known as 'the separated movement.'"[12]

---

[10]Letter to a close friend, Jim, March 2, 1959. Text in square brackets was added by Lane T. Dennis. Lane T. Dennis, editor, *The Letters of Francis Schaeffer* (Eastbourne, UK: Kingsway, 1986), 79.
[11]From a letter to someone revealed only as Garrett, August 27, 1955. Ibid., 60–61.
[12]Letter to a Mr. Lohmann, August 19, 1956, in *The Letters of Francis Schaeffer*, ed. Lane T. Dennis (Eastbourne, UK: Kingsway Publications, 1986), 65.

Overwhelmed by the way the events unfolded, Fran wrote the timetable of significant moments in his Bible, the place where, in his annotations, he saw his thoughts and actions integrate into the ancient message:

> Told to leave Champéry—Feb. 14, 1955 (to be out by end of March)
> Promissory money paid on Mélèzes—c. March 4, 1955
> Moved to Huémoz—March 31, 1955
> Rest of money on Mélèzes—May 30, 1955
> Resignation from I.[ndependent] B.[oard]—June 5, 1955
> Permit de Séjour came—June 21, 1955
> First prayer letter sent on July 9, called for day of prayer and fasting on July 30, 1955

In keeping with their vision of a Shelter, Fran and Edith clarified the founding principles of L'Abri:

> 1. We make our financial and material needs known to God alone, in prayer, rather than sending out pleas for money. We believe that He can put it into the minds of the people of His choice the share that they should have in the work.
> 2. We pray that God will bring the people of His choice to us, and keep all others away. There are no advertising leaflets. . . .
> 3. We pray that God will plan the work, and then unfold His plan to us (guide us, lead us) day by day, rather than planning the future in some clever or efficient way in committee meetings.
> 4. We pray that God will send the workers of His choice to us, rather than pleading for workers in the usual channels.[13]

Edith later spelled out the ethos of L'Abri in more concrete terms:

> We who want to live in the light of the existence of God, and who want to lead balanced lives on the basis of the truth of what exists and also of who we are, need to be aware that the atmosphere or environment has been polluted and that we need some kind of discernment, perhaps seen as a "gas mask," to sift ideas and understanding so that we don't become either warped or stifled.

---

[13]Edith Schaeffer, *L'Abri*, 16.

We need to consider what "sense" rather than "senselessness" has to do with our own day-by-day living, what "wisdom" rather than "foolishness" has to do with our own day-by-day thinking.[14]

In place of their much-loved chalet in Champéry, Bijou, the Shelter was to be Chalet les Mélèzes, almost a character in the story, which would become familiar to thousands of pilgrims and sojourners who made their way up there in the next years and decades. Their new home, well over three thousand feet above sea level, had a dramatic impact on Susan, the Schaeffers' middle daughter, who was very much caught up in the escalating events:

> Here I was, not fourteen. I was sent to Chalet les Mélèzes the day before the family moved, with Madame Fleischman, the German lady who had been my piano teacher—she had been a refugee from Germany. She was very aristocratic, an unlikely person [for the task]. We went the night before to get the house ready. It was March, and horribly dark and damp, and the furnace broke that night. There were little woodstoves on both floors, and I built fires, warming it up and getting it ready for the family. I couldn't see anything. The next morning I woke up early and went on the balcony. It was all clear and blue sky; the mountains were glistening with snow. It was a very beautiful panorama, very different from Champéry, where there was still fog below. I skipped up and down. It sounds terribly holy, but I was saying, "Hallelujah! Thank the Lord. This is what you've given us!"[15]

Susan in fact was the first to see the view, as it had been hidden when first Edith, then Fran and Edith together had examined the property. Edith first saw it the morning after the family moved in.

> We could look right across the Rhône Valley, counting fourteen villages and towns hugging the mountainsides, or dotted on one side or another of the Rhône river below. Looking up and beyond the inhabited parts of the mountainside, we could see the rocky, snow-covered tops of the Dents du Midi (our old friends!), a gleaming, glistening glacier, and many, many other peaks. Keeping our eyes at the upper peak level we could see jagged snow-covered granite peaks mingling

---

[14]Edith Schaeffer, *Common Sense Christian Living* (Nashville: Thomas Nelson, 1983), 22–23.
[15]Interview with Susan Macaulay, 2007.

together, in the soft blue sky, with fleecy puffs of white clouds on three sides of us. Behind the chalet we saw there were no peaks, but steep grassy fields that disappeared in thick, dark pine woods. Just below the front hedge bordering the lawn there was a twenty-foot drop to the road, so that when the morning bus stopped, we could only see its roof from the breakfast table. That bus connects with the train, and from Aigle a person can go straight on to Lausanne, Geneva, and on to London, Paris, etc., directly . . . or if going in the other direction the train in Aigle also goes straight to Milan, and points south![16]

The landscapes surrounding Chalet les Mélèzes were to be captured vividly by a student at L'Abri in the 1960s, the photographer Sylvester Jacobs, upon whose life Francis Schaeffer had a dramatic impact.[17]

The chalet rose up three floors, with the ground behind rising steeply to a dirt road. In fact, at the rear of the chalet, the ground was level with the middle floor, due to the mountain slope. On the upper floors there were full-length balconies, and all the windows, as usual, had shutters. The building had been converted into apartments and had twelve rooms in all, but no proper living room at that time. Much work needed doing to Les Mélèzes in order for it to serve properly as the home of L'Abri, the Shelter.

Less than two weeks after moving to Huémoz, and just after Easter weekend, Priscilla enrolled at the University of Lausanne. Immediately she was inviting student friends to visit "the Chalet" in Huémoz, and even the friends invited other friends. With this influx of students on weekends, a recognizable L'Abri work began, which has carried on uninterrupted from that time onward, though the seeds of it lay in the earlier visits by young women from finishing schools to Chalet Bijou in Champéry. From those earlier visitors Priscilla had realized just how much her father enjoyed talking with them and fielding their questions, and it gave her pleasure to know that she could invite new friends from the university to stay with her family as guests.

In Champéry all of a sudden I saw my father in front of nineteen- and twenty-year-olds, answering their questions and relating it to the cul-

---

[16]Edith Schaeffer, *L'Abri,* 106–107.
[17]Sylvester Jacobs, *Portrait of a Shelter* (Downers Grove, IL: InterVarsity Press, 1973).

ture. Daddy loved that. At the same time that we arrived [in Huémoz]
I went to university. The first weekend I brought home a girl, and then
the next weekend she brought home John, [who became] my husband.
The whole thing snowballed. It took a couple of years before Farel
House really started and people started paying. At first it was just free
[with some] sleeping on the kitchen floor. As it went on, it got more
and more orderly and organized. What was so wonderful was that
for the first time in those early days I saw my father not reading all
his religious Presbyterian magazines or whatever; he was interested in
his *Newsweek* and his *Time* magazine, and spending all the hours he
had talking to students, my friends, which was my joy. There wasn't
anybody that I couldn't bring home—no matter how eccentric, how
rebellious, how blasphemous—as long as they had an interest, liked
talking. I didn't have to be ashamed.[18]

John Sandri does not remember much of his initial visit on the
second weekend that students traveled from Lausanne. However, he
remembers first seeing his future wife, Priscilla, as she boarded the bus
to go up to Villars as he alighted from it at the steps below Chalet les
Mélèzes. Prisca, however, recalls a comment he made that became part
of family lore. Along with another visitor, a GI from Germany named
Karl Woodson,[19] known to the Schaeffers from St. Louis days, John set
off for an afternoon hike with Fran. As they started off John innocently
remarked, "I don't think Christianity has a leg to stand on intellectually,
do you, Mr. Schaeffer?"[20]

What John does remember vividly is Fran's answer to that question
as it unfolded in the ensuing months.

The first time I came up it was an overnight kind of a thing. I don't
remember that much of what occurred. I know what impression I was
given over the next couple of weeks and months. Basically it was a
presentation of Christianity as a worldview that could measure up to
any other worldview, any other religion, or any other philosophy—it
could be compared to and measured by other points of view. I had
had a good friend in high school who was into philosophy and was

[18]Interview with Priscilla and John Sandri, 2007.
[19]Brother of Hurvey Woodson.
[20]Edith Schaeffer, *With Love, Edith: The L'Abri Family Letters 1948–1960* (San Francisco: Harper &
Row, 1988), 337; interview with Priscilla and John Sandri, 2007.

a rebel at heart. He was an intelligent guy. We talked a lot, and I remember one of the things he said was, "Santayana[21] had this point of view that you have to dream with one eye open; this is the only way to live. You've got to pretend that there are ideals, but you know very well with the other eye that there are none." At the same time I was going to a Congregational church on Sunday, and we had youth group and so forth, and there was a total chasm between the two worlds—talk about philosophy, and then church religion. They just didn't relate. One was for Sunday and the other for [the other] six days of the week. That's what got integrated when I came to L'Abri and to Schaeffer—realizing that Christianity properly understood is an intellectually respectable thing. It deals with all of reality and gives you a worldview on everything. You now are in a position to be able to appreciate other points of view, to evaluate them, and to see their weaknesses and strengths.[22]

The weekend before John's first visit, the Schaeffer household was swollen not only by the presence of Priscilla's student friend, Grace (who would invite John), but also by the visit of two American university graduates hitchhiking around Europe and staying in youth hostels. One of them was to play an important part in the next years of L'Abri's life—Dorothy ("Dot") Jamison, a psychology graduate student from California. Her friend Ruth Abrahamson, from Minnesota, had graduated in mathematics. The Saturday evening conversation was unusually dramatic as it took place in flickering candlelight—a storm had taken out the electrical supply. Dorothy only intended to stay for a couple of months as a kind of au pair—there was talk of her helping to look after the lively and irrepressible Franky, now nearly three. As it turned out, she stayed two years helping at L'Abri and was not called upon to care for the child, much to her relief.

The tiny "fellowship" of L'Abri to which Dorothy had committed herself was at that time made up of the Schaeffer family and a very small network of supporters. There were 350 people on the Family Letter list, and twenty-seven were committed to regular prayer for L'Abri, known as "The Praying Family." The fellowship had a rudimentary

---

[21]George Santayana (1863–1952), leading philosopher, poet, and novelist.
[22]Interview with Priscilla and John Sandri.

board, "The Members": Fran and Edith, Georges Exhenry, and Fran's
father-in-law, George Seville. Its first "Worker" was established on
July 1, 1955: this was Priscilla, who juggled her help with her studies
at Lausanne. A second Worker was added shortly after, on the 18th of
that month—Dorothy Jamison. Workers proved to be the backbone
of L'Abri as a mission that served people in need, providing the infrastructure of practical help and upkeep of the chalet and its gardens that
was essential in its being a Shelter. As the work opened up, they were to
augment the teaching and leadership offered by Fran in many ways. At
first, however, the emphasis was on infrastructure as L'Abri struggled to
survive the demands of its fledgling years.

Even after the "hayloft experience" in the early fifties, Francis
and Edith Schaeffer had been prepared to continue their dual work of
reaching post-Christian children—European children who had had no
opportunity to hear the gospel—and of alerting evangelical churches
throughout Europe to the dangers of theological liberalism and neo-
orthodoxy. Over the seven years between their arrival in Switzerland as
nomads and their settling in the Alpine village of Huémoz-sur-Ollon,
where L'Abri became based, a new factor had gradually entered their
lives. Boarding-school children and young women attending finishing
schools, of many nationalities, came to attend their worship services
in the Temple Protestant in Champéry and, more importantly, to raise
questions about the Christian faith in their chalet home. The discussions and an attendant hospitality took on increasing importance,
leading to a realization of the need for a work like L'Abri, even though
buried in the rural Alps. Years later Fran confessed, "I was amazed in
those discussions to find that I could answer those girls' questions in
a way that a lot of them actually became interested."[23] With students
from Lausanne and elsewhere, and GIs from Germany, descending
upon them in 1955 and the following years, the shift to meeting the
spiritual needs of visitors to their home became their central work. In
the early years this was focused upon weekends, and Fran led Bible
studies in various localities, including Milan in Italy, as an extension of

---

[23]Quoted in Philip Yancey, *Open Windows* (Wheaton, IL: Crossway Books, 1982), 105.

the International Church he had planted. "Children for Christ" classes continued locally.

Deborah Middelmann remembered how the initial Bible class in Lausanne began.

> We didn't think of it as starting a work in that sense, like an organization, a work. It was very much that the people just were coming. They were coming on the weekends, staying as guests of the family, and then they left on Sunday evening on the bus and went down to university. After a while they had said that as there were ten or twelve of them, [they couldn't] all come every weekend. They asked, "Why can't you come once a week and we'll keep on the discussions down there?"[24]

Soon a pattern to the Schaeffers' "L'Abri" lives was established to the satisfaction of both Fran and Edith at that time, though Fran was to feel increasingly cut off and isolated, having broken the links with his former separatist network. At this time guests would visit for weekends rather than for extended periods. By autumn 1956 a daily schedule, essential to Fran's organized makeup and to the success of the work, was established.

> *Sunday*
> 11:30 A.M. church service
> Late afternoon, high tea and "conversation" [According to Edith Schaeffer, this refers to answering honest questions with honest answers on a broad range of subjects.]
> *Monday*
> 8:30 P.M. Bible class for local people (translation into French).
> *Tuesday*
> Fortnightly Milan Bible class, 8:45 P.M. to 11:45 P.M; in-between week, Bible study in Madame Avanthey's home in Champéry.
> *Wednesday*
> Children for Christ class at Chalet les Mélèzes for English-speaking children from Ecole Beau Soleil.
> *Thursday*
> Lausanne Café Bible class, 11 A.M. to 2 P.M

---

[24]Interview with Debby and Udo Middelmann, 2007.

Friday
A "weekend crowd" arrives for dinner; evening of "conversation" and Bible study.
Saturday
Walks and "conversations" with "weekend crowd"; evening hot dog roast by fireplace—family prayers and "conversations" throughout the evening.[25]

Both the Milan and Lausanne Bible classes were to become very significant to the work of L'Abri. The former was to turn into the first L'Abri institution outside of Switzerland, led by Hurvey and Dorothy Woodson (née Jamison) from 1959. The Lausanne class was to result in a related and lively student discussion group and was to be the setting for Fran's formative studies on Romans 1–8 (later to be published as *The Finished Work of Christ*). The Bible studies helped Fran work out in a systematic way the biblical principles undergirding his vision for L'Abri. One person who attended those Bible studies was Marte Herrell, an American student.

> My first encounter with Francis Schaeffer was in the autumn of 1958. I was a student at the University of Lausanne and a nonbeliever, perhaps unconsciously seeking truth. I was conned into going to a Bible study held in a small cafe near the university. The teacher was Dr. Schaeffer, the text, the book of Romans. I was fascinated and exasperated that such an intelligent man as Schaeffer could believe that the Bible was true.[26]

Susan, at that time studying in Lausanne, invited Marte to Huémoz. She visited weekend after weekend for three months before becoming a believer. When she did, the Schaeffers played Handel's "Hallelujah Chorus" from *The Messiah* on their record player, as was their habit at moments worth celebrating.

Hurvey and Dorothy had arrived at the Schaeffers' home in Huémoz within a year of each other and lived with them, intimately sharing their home life. The two eventually fell in love and married—the first of many L'Abri romances. Dorothy had arrived during the spiritual crisis of the threatened expulsion of the Schaeffers from Switzerland. She

---

[25] Adapted from Edith Schaeffer, *With Love, Edith*, 375.
[26] *World Magazine*, March 26, 2005, Vol. 20, No. 12.

initially stayed on to help as an au pair for a couple of months, which became two years, the point at which she married Hurvey. She returned with him to the USA so he could finish his studies, after which the two settled in Milan to run a L'Abri work there, building upon the years of Bible studies Fran had given in that northern Italian city. Hurvey Woodson was well-known to Fran and Edith. He was a boy when they ran the summer camps in St. Louis, and he and his family attended their church. While at Faith Seminary he became convinced that he should interrupt his studies for a year to help in the fledgling work of L'Abri in Switzerland. Both Hurvey and Dorothy thus experienced the very first years of L'Abri and had vivid memories of the period. They also had the rare experience of living with the Schaeffers in this transitional period in which the pattern of L'Abri was established.

Dorothy was very struck by the necessity to make do with very little, especially as winter approached.

> I was planning just to stay for a couple of months, and I ended up staying almost two years. When I went there, there wasn't anybody else there. It was me and the family, and so it was a very unique kind of an experience. L'Abri was very poor, and if anybody says otherwise, they are mistaken. I mean, we prayed for money and I'm telling you, there were times when we just really didn't have anything. And I remember Mr. Schaeffer going through the dead ashes to get out the pieces of coal that might still be remaining, so that we could use those again. That place was *cold*.[27]

Hurvey had joined the family later, in 1956, and he took over many practical tasks, including the low-budget heating. He remembered, "Wood was always a premium in Switzerland, and so my job was to sit near the fireplace and guard that wood block, so they [visitors and others] wouldn't put too much wood on that fire!"

Desperate measures were called for, Dorothy pointed out. "If Mr. Schaeffer would be away for whatever reason, well, the mice would play. So the house would get maybe one degree warmer. Nobody minded much. When Hurvey came, he was on our side."

---

[27]Interview with Hurvey and Dorothy Woodson, 1998.

Hurvey remembered the situation vividly.

> They would try and entice me with nice bakery things to make that
> furnace a little hotter! I would try to gauge it, knowing when Mr.
> Schaeffer would come back on that yellow bus. Sometimes he would
> get there a little bit too soon, and he'd walk in that door and the first
> thing he would do was to yell my name, because it was too warm! He
> would want to know what was I doing with that furnace. In all serious-
> ness, it was a very tight situation. We ate a lot of cornflakes, and we
> didn't have much, we really didn't.[28]

The cold very much dominated their lives, underlining the shortage of funds in those early days of L'Abri. That, and the hard-working
nature of the Schaeffers, stuck in Hurvey's memories of the time.

> In those early days it was really cold, and Mrs. Schaeffer would often sit
> in that little office in Les Mélèzes right inside the door, with a thermos
> bottle on her hand—I don't know how she typed, it was so cold. That's
> how she kept typing. Then later on things got very, very busy, and I
> always was impressed with the amount of endurance she had, because
> there were times when she would not go to bed for a couple of days.
> Yes, she would not sleep but work right through the night. She had an
> enormous amount of stamina and drive. She just worked constantly.[29]

Hurvey's decision to take a year out from seminary in order to be
of service to the Schaeffers was in response to a strong compulsion that
he should do this, even though many people advised him against it. This
is how he came to be sharing in the Schaeffer family life in those early
years of L'Abri, along with his future wife.

> Dorothy and I really had an unusual time—that is, we literally lived
> with the family, right in their home, and there was no one else there.
> So we really got to know the family—maybe too well! But it was a very
> positive experience. Our task, in those early days, was to do all the
> physical work. We had to clean bathrooms, all the floors, do all those
> things. We tried to take care of the kitchen. I worked in the gardens
> along with Mr. and Mrs. Schaeffer. Mrs. Schaeffer loved garden work,

---

[28]Ibid.
[29]Ibid.

and we planted as many gardens as we could because we needed food; we had to get the gardens going. We tried to do everything to relieve them so they could talk with guests and spend their time on other things.[30]

One task that Hurvey took very seriously was to help with Franky, who was rapidly overcoming the debilitating effects of polio, the marks of which he would always live with.

He was only four or five years old when I was there. I was really his kind of playmate. I would play games with him all the time, because he didn't really have any friends. I mean, he didn't have any kids his age. One of the things I always remember was that both Mr. and Mrs. Schaeffer wanted him to be a real boy, but, I'm not sure why, they didn't want him to play with guns. Guns were a no no, which, knowing them, was kind of strange. So Franky would make his little simple swords and spears and things like that, which were quite dangerous. He was pretty aggressive, to put it mildly, throwing those things, so I had to watch him on that. I had a pretty close relationship with him at that time. Because he really didn't have any playmates at all, I had to do things with him all the time, and that was a challenge.[31]

Part of being very much in the family was that Dorothy, and then Hurvey, joined the Schaeffers on their annual vacation to Italy. Even on those occasions the family had to scrimp. Hurvey recollected, "In the early days they went down to Alassio on the Italian Riviera, and they stayed in this hotel called Hotel Spiaggia.[32] Mr. Schaeffer would ration out the mineral water. That was a really big treat for them, the mineral water. He'd pour that bottle out, and it had to really go a long ways! And Parmesan cheese, the same way."[33]

Hurvey and Dorothy were able to witness tensions in the Schaeffers' family life under the pressures of living by faith and enormous pastoral commitments. Fran and Edith had an intensely close relationship for such very different personalities, and sometimes Fran's temper would

---

[30]Ibid.
[31]Ibid.
[32]Via Roma 78, Alassio, Italy, on the Western Riviera. Though he fictionalizes people and events, Frank Schaeffer captures the setting in his novel, *Portofino*.
[33]Interview with Hurvey and Dorothy Woodson.

fray over Edith's thoughtlessness. Hurvey and Dorothy regularly witnessed a situation that many who in later years knew the Schaeffers intimately would immediately recognize.

> The class started in Lausanne, and also they would take trips. Sometimes Dorothy and I would be there alone, and they would be off somewhere. They never had an automobile. They always took the buses. Mr. Schaeffer was always out there on time for the bus, you know, but Mrs. Schaeffer was always late. I knew this was happening, so I'd go way out, and I'd be looking way up toward Chèsieres, trying to listen for that bus coming down. And I would yell, "It's coming," hoping to give her as much time as possible. Mr. Schaeffer would be going, "EDITH, EDITH!" Finally she would make it. We'd hold the bus, and she'd come running down, her hair down, and everything in her arms. She'd go down those steps, and she would get on the bus. Dorothy and I would just stand there. "Ah, they made it!" What took place after that, on the bus, we didn't care! That happened time and time again; it was just like clockwork. But it was very humorous to us. I'm sure it wasn't so humorous to them.[34]

Fran was not averse to turning the tables on Edith, making her wait. Dorothy remembered feeling uncomfortable at dinnertime.

> To give a picture of the atmosphere at home, we would fix dinner, and we would let everyone know that dinner was ready. Mr. Schaeffer was always the last one to arrive. Anybody else who was late, it was not good news. We would have rushed around. The way we served dinner in those days (no one would do it now) was that the soup was already served. We always had soup because of financial reasons. Then he would come, and he would sit and start talking or do something else. My feeling was, Please let's get on with it because the soup's getting cold. But no one would dare say this. So we would all just sit there while Mr. Schaeffer would do his thing, and then we would pray. I remember that as one of my feelings of tension as far as he was concerned.[35]

Despite all the hardships and the tensions at times, and knowing the Schaeffers so intimately, both Hurvey and Dorothy were deeply

---

[34]Ibid.
[35]Ibid.

impressed by Fran. Dorothy articulated an impression of the man that many in subsequent years gained, myself included:

> When Mr. Schaeffer would talk to you, there was nothing else in the world that was going on. He was totally focused on you and what you were talking about and was very involved, very interested. It wouldn't matter who the person was. It could be from the most simple person to the most intellectual—that focus and interest and involvement was the same. I saw it time and time again. I experienced it myself, and it wasn't anything false. He was really interested in people, and it was something that was very, very striking. I'd never seen that degree of concentration and having that kind of attention, I don't think, with anybody else. That enormous personality that he had, it would be all focused on you. And he never forgot anything that you ever told him. For instance, he went way back with my family. He would remember all the little details of the family and my brother and my sister—various things over the years that he had learned. It was part, obviously, of that phenomenal memory he had for everything. But it was his memory for these personal details that made his talking with people enormously effective.[36]

After Hurvey and Dorothy Woodson went to Milan in 1959 to build upon the several years that Fran had held Bible classes there, he would visit from time to time, as Dorothy revealed.

> We were in Milan, working in Italian with Italians, and formed a church. So it was more of a missionary-type activity, church planting, rather than a typical L'Abri branch. We had our apartment, and Mr. Schaeffer would come down and speak to our little group occasionally, and he would stay with us. That was another pretty unique time; we had one-on-one time with him that was really quite special. He took great interest in all of our people, almost none of whom would you consider really intellectuals, although they were educated. He was very interested in all of their lives and in everything that we were doing.[37]

Hurvey and Dorothy looked forward to these occasions, which gave them a unique time with Fran. Hurvey particularly benefited from them. Schaeffer would be relaxed and share his thoughts and concerns

---

[36]Ibid.
[37]Ibid.

with the young man as they sometimes traveled in Italy together to conferences. (This sharing was very significant, as Schaeffer was quite isolated in Switzerland; he had only a few close friends, such as Hans Rookmaaker. Italy was for him a place where he could relax, away from the incessant demands of Huémoz.) Hurvey remembers:

> I would meet him at the train station in Milan. The first thing he always wanted to get was his espresso, and we'd go over to the espresso bar. He liked that very much, with lots of sugar in it. He liked to stay up late at night sometime. [He was all wound up after having a Bible class and couldn't just go to bed then.] We would finish around twelve o'clock, midnight, and then usually we [Hurvey and Fran] would go out and walk the streets. That was very interesting for me because Mr. Schaeffer in those days was writing articles and getting involved in a lot of things, controversy and things of this sort. He would always tell me what he was doing, articles he was in the process of writing, and would bounce things off me. I would say, "Oh, I see, I see," or "How's that?"—very brief answers. We would walk and talk for an hour, or an hour and a half, through the city of Milan, which he enjoyed a lot. It was very interesting. Then, two or three weeks or a month later, I would see the things we talked about in an article in *Christianity Today* or some other evangelical magazine. Or he'd be getting ready to speak at some conference, and he would go over some of his talk. I would be a kind of sounding board for him.
>
> When we went down to a missionary conference, a couple of times, in Italy, he was quite a character. After the evening was over, he was all wound up and wanted to talk. We would go to a little restaurant—trattoria—with a garden and a little music playing; he liked that a lot. Sometimes the Italians got all wound up, and they'd take their wine bottles and start beating them on the table. Mr. Schaeffer always got a Coke. He'd sit there with a Coca-Cola bottle, doing the same thing, and I'd sit and watch. I just laughed—he was having such a good time. We would stay there for a long, long time. He wanted to be one of them and join in. That relaxed him; it took his mind away from everything else.[38]

There was plenty to keep Fran's mind occupied. By word of mouth, the news spread to college and university students that there was a

---

[38]Ibid.

place in the Alps where one could get honest answers to life's deepest questions. Schaeffer was basically content to continue carefully and compassionately listening and then give answers to the small groups of guests who became, during their stay, part of the Schaeffers' home. At that period they were not classified as students, and no charge was made. Their stay, usually on weekends, was an extension of what the Schaeffers felt should be normal hospitality on the part of Christians. Though sometimes he felt deeply frustrated, Fran believed that God would work on the seeds that he and Edith planted. They took pleasure in seeing some guests, such as John Sandri, praying to Christ for salvation. In the early days there was no thought of books or films or even audiotapes of conversations and discussions. The development from tapes to books to films was a gradual, almost reluctant process that did not start to take off until the sixties.

With the growth of L'Abri, pressures on their family life increased, particularly with the intense pastoral demands of so many visitors. The youngest children, Franky and Debby, were most affected by the demands on their parents. Susan, the second oldest, was prey to long illnesses—rheumatic fever kept her bed-bound for years. Priscilla was vulnerable to demands placed upon her, ironically because of her pleasure and delight in inviting university friends to Huémoz. Fran's French was poor, and Edith's only somewhat better, so Priscilla assumed the role of translator late into the night at weekends and during the Bible study classes in Lausanne. This was on top of the requirements of her studies.

> Because they were my friends, from the very early days we had a lot of Swiss, French-speaking students come up. Then I translated, instantaneous translation, at the table. We'd talk for three or four hours, and I translated what Daddy said, what they said, back and forth. One of the things I remember was having my exams and doing this. I was sitting at the table translating, and John was there. Suddenly I couldn't remember the sentence that Daddy had just said. My mind went blank. It was the first of my three nervous breakdowns.[39]

In later years, as L'Abri expanded and several families were involved

---

[39]Interview with Priscilla and John Sandri.

in leading its work, provisions were built in to protect family life and to build in time off.

Fran and Edith knew, when L'Abri began, the risk of opening up one's home. It was a risk they were prepared to take, but this did not mean that the consequences did not hurt. Francis Schaeffer recalled:

> In about the first three years of L'Abri all our wedding presents were wiped out. Our sheets were torn. Holes were burned in our rugs. Indeed once a whole curtain almost burned up from somebody smoking in our living room. . . . Drugs came to our place. People vomited in our rooms.[40]

They saw gritty hospitality as part of the meaning of providing a shelter. They and their family experienced the personal costliness of this.

A turning point in the development of L'Abri was the beginning of a similar work in England in 1958 after Francis had given lectures in Oxford, Cambridge, and elsewhere in Britain. That work was eventually to be led by Ranald Macaulay and Susan, the Schaeffers' second daughter, whom he married. The beginning and later establishment of an English L'Abri was symbolic of the deep influence Schaeffer was to have on a generation of British evangelicals. In particular, he was to forge warm and significant links with Inter-Varsity Fellowship (the British equivalent of Inter-Varsity Christian Fellowship). He also began to take a deep interest in what was happening both on the British theological scene and in British culture, an interest that developed rapidly in the sixties when its rock music began to have a worldwide influence. In the visits in the late fifties Fran was fascinated to see Teddy Boys, with their Edwardian-style clothes and interest in American rock and roll. As the first self-aware "teenagers," they were an augury of things to come.

An influx of guests over the summer period became an established part of L'Abri life. As far back as 1956 guests had included Hans and

---

[40]Quoted in Michael S. Hamilton, "The Dissatisfaction of Francis Schaeffer," in *Christianity Today*, March 3, 1997; http://www.christianitytoday.com/ct/1997/march3/7t322a.html. Original source unknown.

Anky Rookmaaker and their young children, Hans Junior, Kees, and Marleen. The visit was a turning point particularly for Anky, regarding the place of prayer in the Christian's life. She confessed:

> I didn't like the church I was in; it was very strict. So we wrote to the Schaeffers—that was the first time that we went to Huémoz in Switzerland. We were there for three weeks, and that meant a lot to us for all our lives. It's very strange, you become a Christian, and you go to a church, and you don't like it. Then you go to Switzerland, and Dr. Schaeffer explains all these things, all my questions. Then when you go back, you hear the same things in your own church. It seems that I needed to be with the Schaeffers. [L'Abri had] just started. We were almost the first people who came to Huémoz. Because there were many students coming then, that made a big impression on us. What I remember most was that the Schaeffers prayed, prayed actually much more than the Dutch churches, and the prayers were answered. That you see the prayers answered helps a lot, I think, in your belief. I think [Mrs. Schaeffer's] a wonderful woman; I learned a lot from her. I came from a non-Christian background. She took time to teach me. She'd teach me about praying, because I didn't know very much. I'm very grateful for that. From that time on we [were friends and] always had regular contact. Dr. Schaeffer preached about [prayer], I think especially for me to understand it. Without the Schaeffers I wouldn't be here, a Christian now, I think.[41]

By visiting L'Abri Hans was simply continuing his meetings with his friend. They had met together on a number of occasions over the previous years. Sometimes they had found themselves in the same foreign city, where Hans might be attending a conference or visiting art galleries. In later years he would take his art history students abroad and sometimes meet up with Fran. It eventually became a pattern for the Rookmaaker family to vacation near Huémoz in the summers and frequently visit L'Abri.

The numbers of guests (soon called "students") attending over the summers gradually grew. Edith records in one of her Family Letters, written September 1, 1959:

---

[41]Interview with Anky Rookmaaker, 1998.

Since writing to you on June 9th, 185 different people of 16 different nationalities have been here (some of them several times over, of course, as students have returned several times)—and in addition to the 16 nationalities, there have been missionaries from five other countries. Would it be dull to list the countries? There have been: Argentinian, Dutch, Swiss, American, South African, English, Malaysian, French, Greek, Italian, El Salvadoran, New Zealander, Australian, Belgian, Hungarian, German, and missionaries from Japan, India, Africa, Belgium, and the Congo.[42]

The social diversity and quantity of those attending meant that the reputation of L'Abri spread widely by word of mouth. Eventually it came to the attention of an alert journalist whose daughter was at high school with Deborah Schaeffer. He tipped off a friend at *Time* magazine about a potential story. On Monday, November 30, 1959 the *Time* journalist arrived in the tiny village high above the Rhône valley and interviewed Fran and Edith for four hours. They failed to convince him not to write a story, and next day a *Time* photographer arrived, who took a number of photos and, recorded Edith, "became interested in what was being taught."[43]

The January 11, 1960 *Time* article entitled "Mission to Intellectuals" characterized the Schaeffers' chalet as the venue of "one of the most unusual missions in the Western world." Describing Fran as sandy-haired and "sad-faced," the article briefly told the history of L'Abri, from the expulsion from Champéry. It sketched what was happening when the journalist visited: "The 20-odd guests this week include an Oxford don, an engineer from El Salvador, a ballet dancer and an opera singer. The one thing they have in common is that they are intellectuals. And the European intellectual is the single object of the Schaeffers' mission in the mountains." The article quoted extensively from the long interview that had taken place the previous November, including a seminal comment from Fran on those who visited L'Abri:

These people are not reached by Protestantism today. . . . Protestantism has become bourgeois. It reaches middle-class people, but not the

---

[42]*With Love, Edith*, 439.
[43]Ibid., 447.

workers or the intellectuals. What we need is a presentation of the Bible's historical truth in such a way that it is acceptable to today's intellectuals. Now as before, the Bible can be acted upon, even in the intellectual morass of the 20th century.[44]

I read this article some years later when I first visited L'Abri in the summer of 1967 as a young university student sharing cramped sleeping quarters, meals, and study with a hundred or more visitors comprised of some of the most interesting people I had ever met. If I remember correctly, it was pinned to the small bulletin board in the corridor of Les Mélèzes, which usually sported stimulating items. The *Time* article appeared on the cusp of a worldwide expansion of Fran's influence, an impact undreamed of either by him or by Edith.

---

[44]"Mission to Intellectuals," *Time*, January, 11, 1960. Note Schaeffer's use of the term "Protestantism" rather than "the Church" or "Christianity," reflecting perhaps his narrower focus at that time.

CHAPTER SEVEN

THE PILGRIMAGE TO L'ABRI

(1960–1976)

෧෧෧෧෧

A decade, like any label for a period of history, is a human construction, and it may or may not capture the essence of the period. In the case of the 1960s, it does appear that was a defining decade of great changes and events. Francis Schaeffer certainly came to think so, chronicling the 1964 free speech movement on the Berkeley campus of the University of California as a decisive moment when what had hitherto been discussed as theory by academics and others was put into practice by young people who discovered themselves to be outsiders. Berkeley started a chain reaction. When scientists were developing the first atomic bomb in the 1940s, there was some brief speculation that splitting the atom might ignite the atmosphere. For Schaeffer, the Berkeley protests ignited youth culture in the sixties throughout the world. In some ways the impact of a changed youth culture and student unrest in the sixties had similarities with that of the French Revolution near the end of the eighteenth century, of which it is a child. At Berkeley, Schaeffer observed,

> . . . the Free Speech Movement arose simultaneously with the hippie world of drugs. At first it was politically neither left nor right, but rather a call for the freedom to express any political views on Sproul Plaza. Then soon the Free Speech Movement became the Dirty-Speech Movement, in which freedom was seen as shouting four-letter words into a mike. Soon after, it became the platform for the political New Left. . . . For some time, young people were fighting against their parents' impoverished values of personal peace and affluence—whether

their way of fighting was through Marcuse's New Left or through taking drugs as an ideology. . . . They were right in their analysis of the problem, but they were mistaken in their solutions.[1]

Changes in youth culture were mirrored by developments at L'Abri that were so far-reaching that the ideas and vision of a small man in a quiet high-alpine village would touch the world. Indeed, Schaeffer was almost unique as an individual Christian in being close to the pulse of cultural change, both in interpreting it and in speaking effectively to it. As Frank Schaeffer remarks in his memoir, *Crazy for God*:

> Dad . . . got interested in the secular culture, not as a means to an end but for its own sake. . . . In evangelical circles, if you wanted to know what Bob Dylan's songs meant, Francis Schaeffer was the man to ask. In the early '60s, he was probably the only fundamentalist who had even heard of Bob Dylan.[2]

The sixties was an exciting time for the pilgrimage to L'Abri. I visited in 1967 and 1968 and then again at the beginning of the seventies, in all spending several months studying under Francis Schaeffer. I listened to hours of tapes, read his books as they appeared, heard his tabletop and Saturday night discussions, and read out two papers prepared under his tutelage, one on Islam and the other on imagination in Tolkien. I found his teaching challenging and painful as he forced me to see so much from another point of view. In my university studies in English literature and philosophy I rarely if ever quoted him (that did not seem appropriate), but my approach and thinking were transformed.

Looking back I find him a curiously modern thinker. In the first place he was in the style of modern art and culture because he defamiliarized the familiar. In place of abstract shapes or surrealistic images of artists like Henry Moore or Salvador Dali he deliberately used a quirky vocabulary and his own visualization of the development of ideas that he felt had transformed the West into a post-Christian culture. Thus he spoke of "true truth," "mysticism with nobody there," the "infinite-

---

[1]Francis A. Schaeffer, *How Should We Then Live?* (Grand Rapids, MI: Revell, 1976), 208.
[2]Frank Schaeffer, *Crazy for God: How I Grew Up as One of the Elect, Helped Found the Religious Right, and Lived to Take All (or Almost All) of It Back* (New York: Carroll & Graf, 2007), 118.

personal God," and the "line of despair." Such terminology could not be employed in university essays—he forced you to think through this new way of seeing for yourself and to find your own language for deconstructing modern culture, or indeed demystifying patterns of thought in the history of art, literature, philosophy, and even science. Schaeffer was like the boy who cried that the emperor was not wearing any clothes.

In the second place, he employed a structuralist approach in his analysis of culture that was state-of-the-art at the time. Hearing Schaeffer I naturally went on to read Jean Piaget, Claude Levi-Strauss, Noam Chomsky, and similar thinkers. In the third place, he anticipated postmodernism. In fact, most of what he was saying applied to postmodernism rather than to "old-fashioned modernism," if I might use such a term, Schaeffer-style. Through his wide reading of popular (as opposed to academic) writing, he picked up on Michel Foucault long before most people.[3] In the fourth place, as a result of his intellectual struggles in the early fifties, he expressed an existential type of evangelicalism. He encouraged students to listen to his tapes on "True Spirituality," later published, and constantly spoke of the importance of living in the moment, dependent upon the finished work of Christ and the power of the Holy Spirit. I heard him say several times that when he went to bed with his wife, it was a different woman with him each night.

There was a causal development in the growth of Schaeffer's influence. The origin lay in word-of-mouth recommendation on the part of those who visited L'Abri in the fifties and afterward, picked up in the *Time* article in 1960. Then Schaeffer's talks began to be captured on audiotape and widely disseminated. This in turn led to more and more speaking engagements across the UK and North America, which then resulted in the first books, transcribed and written from series of lectures honed by being presented in many locations, often given to thoughtful and questioning audiences. Schaeffer had always paid particular attention to movies as so many university students converged on L'Abri. He recognized cinema as a major twentieth-century art form embraced by the young. He was eventually persuaded to use that medium himself,

---

[3]In *Escape from Reason*. See *Francis A. Schaeffer Trilogy* (Wheaton, IL: Crossway Books, 1990), 253–254.

escalating his audience. At each stage Schaeffer was reluctant to make the next step into a wider medium. By nature he was introverted and self-doubting. He was at his best with a group of people, no matter how small (or large), to whom he could relate, preferably as teacher to student, but always with a pastoral concern.

In the first three or four years of L'Abri there were no tape recordings of Fran's lectures or question-and-answer sessions. Teaching centered around live Bible studies, such as going through the first eight chapters of Romans in Lausanne and answering the questions of visitors to the Schaeffers' chalet in Huémoz. What led to the fact that by 1968—the zenith of the pre-Schaeffer-book *L'Abri*—over one thousand hours of audiotape had been recorded, covering such themes as true spirituality, the books of Romans and Revelation, the Westminster Confession, and various pressing cultural issues?

Fran himself explained in 1980 when I put this question to him:

> When I was working at L'Abri in the early days, I really expected just to be talking one to one. I never intended even to make tapes, and the tape program just opened up. It's rather ironic now.
>
> Somebody sent us a tape recorder, and I said, "I'll never use it. It'll kill the spontaneity of the conversation." The tape recorder must have been in our office for at least six months. Then, one Saturday night, down in Les Mélèzes living room, we had a really bang-up conversation going with some Smith College girls. One of our workers came up and said to Edith, "It's a shame this isn't being recorded; it'll be lost. If you'll just make a lot of noise serving tea, I'll hide the microphone in the flowers." I noticed some kind of confusion and wondered what was going on. When I found out later that the conversation had been recorded, I must say I was furious. I felt this was unfair to those girls; they thought it was a private conversation. Then to my amazement every one of the girls was delighted and bought copies of the tape to take home, not only for themselves but for their friends. This opened the tape program: it was as simple as that.[4]

Fran and Edith were soon able to see the benefits of recordings, not least in their impact on the fledgling "Farel house," at first a very

---

[4]Interview with Francis Schaeffer, 1980.

small studying program based in the rented neighboring chalet of Beau Site, now vacated by the Chaudet sisters. The first students were Ranald Macaulay, recently of Cambridge University, by then engaged to Susan Schaeffer, and Richard and Deidre Ducker. Deidre had become a Christian through the Schaeffers in Champéry before L'Abri began, while at finishing school. Farel House was named after the Swiss Protestant Reformer William Farel, who was associated with the Canton of Vaud in which the Schaeffers now lived and who was much admired by Fran. Udo Middelmann, son of a luminary in the United Nations who would marry Debby Schaeffer, became a Farel House student soon after its inception. In her Family Letter of July 21, 1961, Edith observes:

> If you had been a bird looking down at the chalets, you would have seen Udo [Middelmann] listening to the Romans studies on tapes, taking notes hour after hour. The sound from the window would have made you think Fran was tirelessly teaching Romans without rest for days! We began to see in the three weeks Udo was with us what the tapes could mean to the various ones coming back for deeper Bible study, in giving them opportunity to go ahead at their own speed. . . . Jeremy Jackson has also moved in as a L'Abri Worker full time, taking over the copying of tapes which is proving an almost full-time job. The Lord put it on the hearts of two "L'Abri spiritual children" to sacrificially give gifts of tape recorders so that we now have four, almost always in use. Two are for making copies of tapes, two for playing them back.[5]

The giant open-reel recorders could record four tracks, two playable from the upper half of the tape and two on the lower, as the tape was turned over, allowing many hours of storage on one reel. Some students in later years (myself included) often speeded up the tape to access the content more quickly—Fran's already high-pitched voice became even shriller. One exception was a taped lecture by the youthful Franky Schaeffer on the Beatles' newly released *Sergeant Pepper's Lonely Hearts Club Band*. Students tended to skip the commentary and listen to the tracks in awe.

By the second half of the sixties, the tape library had grown enor-

---

[5]Edith Schaeffer, *Dear Family*, 16. Letter of July 21, 1961.

mously both in variety and quantity. An annotated list from 1968, which all students at L'Abri were given, included the following:[6]

The intellectual climate of the New Theology. (14 lectures, 20 hours.)
Senghor: Review of his *African Socialism* and *Selected Poems.*
Apologetics: A summary exposition of Dr Schaeffer's basic apologetic method.
Christian Apologetics: communicating to the 20th century.
Eastern thinking in Western theology.
Music: Traces the underlying philosophic expressions from Bach to Beethoven, Schoenberg, musique concrete and some Zen poems.
Our real enemy: Relativism.
Marshall McLuhan and the New Communication.
Review of Bishop Robinson's *Honest to God.*
The later Heidegger and the new hermeneutics.
The Christian artist and modern techniques.
Art forms and the loss of the Human.
The possible answers to the basic philosophical questions and a consideration of the Christian answers to those questions.
Modern man's predicament. Exhibited in W[illiam] Golding, the movie "High Wind in Jamaica," A. Schoenberg's "Moses and Aaron," James Baldwin, J.[oan] Littlewood's "Oh, What a Lovely War," and the Irish play-wright Brendan Behan.
Framework for the Christian life.
Our monolithic culture.
Speaking the historic Christian position into the 20th century. A series of lectures given at Wheaton in Sept. 1965 [the foundation of the book, *The God Who Is There*, 1968].
The problem of the dating of the early chapters of the Book of Genesis.
Open Pornography in Modern Art.
Romans: Chapter 1-8 (20 hours)
The Doctrines of the Bible.
True Spirituality, or The Christian Life. (18 hours.)
Principles of the Exegesis of the Prophetic Portions of Scripture.
Review of the Vatican Council II. (3 lectures, 4 hours.)
Florence trip. Morning sight-seeing in museums, and evening lectures. (14 hours.)

[6]Four-sided mimeographed handout entitled "The New List of L'Abri Tapes," dated "as of February, 1968."

Students selected from this list with the help of Francis Schaeffer ("Dr. Schaeffer" as he was known to students and staff alike) or a "Worker," a more senior staff member, usually responsible for running a chalet and providing hospitality.[7]

The breadth of the L'Abri "syllabus" by 1968 reflected Fran's own awareness that he could make a contribution to the evangelical world that was much more comprehensive and radical than the necessarily brief (though sometimes twenty minutes or half an hour long) and piecemeal responses to questions posed by visitors to L'Abri. His reading and lectures in the early sixties gradually reflected a very broad analysis of contemporary culture and its origins, as well as a realistic rather than ivory-tower apologetic response. It was astonishingly broad and comprehensive. With limited resources, and isolated from major libraries and scholars (with the exception of Hans Rookmaaker, with whom he kept in constant touch), Schaeffer extended his earlier thinking on the arts and created a unique and radical take on the development and decline of Western culture and Christian cultural and political involvement. In the process he felt more and more frustrated, both with himself and with the lack of understanding in the Christian world of the great changes and the speed of those changes in Western culture.

This growing awareness and frustration coincided with a related period of "spiritual struggle," as she put it, on Edith's part. In *The Tapestry* she expressed the long-lasting struggle like this: "In the early part of the 1960s, I had been going through a time that could only be described as one of self-pity. I had begun to look away from 'willingness for anything' to a desire for 'something for myself,' and this filled far too much of my thoughts and prayer times. It was an elusive thing that could be rationalized as something I 'deserved.'"[8] Edith does not tell us anything more about her longing, and we must leave it there. Her self-absorption ended abruptly one evening in the fall of 1964 as she watched the faces of non-Christian friends of a Christian flight attendant in Zurich as they listened to Fran answering their questions. Edith describes her sudden realization.

---

[7]By February 1968 seven chalets were owned or rented to L'Abri or were informally affiliated with the work (as in the case of Jane Stuart Smith and Betty Carlson's Chalet le Chesalet).
[8]Edith Schaeffer, *The Tapestry* (Nashville: Word, 1981), 520.

Before the evening had come to an end, something happened to me. I silently talked to the Lord, "Oh, Lord," I said, "please forgive me if I have been a piece of dirt in the water-pipe. Forgive me if I have hindered the work of Your Spirit in any way. If *You* want Fran to do a much wider work, if You want what happened here in this room tonight to happen on a much larger scale, if You have people in other parts of the world who should hear what Fran has said tonight . . . then I am willing for whatever it takes on my part. Forgive me for my selfish prayers for a different life. I promise I'll go on, as You give me strength, to do whatever my part requires."[9]

Within a short while after what Edith called "that struggle, and that victory," Fran with her blessing crossed the Atlantic with speaking engagements, five years after his last visit to the USA in 1960. As he presented, adapted, and reworked series of talks between 1965 and 1967 on trips to the US and the UK, the material became the foundation for the earliest of many books, *Escape from Reason* (1968), *The God Who Is There* (1968), and *Death in the City* (1969).[10] Of his publications he considered the core to be *Escape from Reason, The God Who Is There*, and *He Is There and He Is Not Silent* (1972). His many other books, he said, are "the spokes radiating out from them," which apply "this unified Christian system to various areas" and depend on the three core books.[11]

On Fran's first speaking engagement—twelve days of lecturing and discussions in Boston in February 1965—Edith traveled with him to care for his mother, Bessie, who had had a stroke. Because Bessie now needed twenty-four-hour care, Edith and Fran brought her back from Germantown to live with them in Chalet les Mélèzes at the end of the visit. About 350 to 400 students attended three main lectures in Boston from colleges and universities in the area, including Harvard, MIT, Wellesley, Radcliffe, Smith, Mount Holyoke, and Barrington. There was also an exhausting schedule of discussion groups, as well as many personal conversations. Harold O. J. Brown, then working with college

---

[9]Ibid.
[10]These were the earliest commercially produced books. He had self-published *Empire Builders for Boys* (1946), *Empire Builders for Girls* (1946), and *25 Basic Bible Studies*, n.d.
[11]Francis Schaeffer, "How I Have Come to Write My Books," in Inter-Varsity Christian Fellowship, *Introduction to Francis Schaeffer: Study Guide to a Trilogy* (London: Hodder and Stoughton, 1975), 58.

students in Boston, arranged the events. The lectures were more or less repeated in familiar Wilmington, for the Philadelphia area, in three seminars and a public meeting.

On September 23 that year Fran and Edith again set off for America, this time in answer to a cry of "help" that for them was reminiscent of the call to Paul in the book of Acts: "Come over to Macedonia and help us" (16:9). The trip included a momentous lecture series at Wheaton College and a concentrated course of teaching at Covenant Seminary, St. Louis. Greg Jesson commented:

> When Francis August Schaeffer . . . first burst onto the American evangelical stage in the mid-1960s, the reaction within that community was similar to the reaction of Americans to the appearance of Sputnik streaking across the autumn sky—no one had ever seen anything quite like it before and it was difficult to discern what it all meant. There was great concern over his long hair, and why did he wear those funny knickers, knee socks, and hiking shoes? . . . All in all, evangelical Protestants were, for the most part, at a complete loss.
>
> When Schaeffer lectured at Wheaton College and frequently referred to the existentialist films of Ingmar Bergman and Federico Fellini, the students were in the midst of fighting with the administration for the right to show films like *Bambi* and *Herbie the Love Bug* on campus.[12]

The lectures had a profound impact on many faculty members and students who heard them. Francis Schaeffer explained to me how the response at Wheaton College to the lecture series led to his initial venture into deliberate publication. He had been as reluctant about going into print as he had been about being recorded on audiotape:

> As I lectured in very many places, in Britain, Germany, and the USA, I gradually developed a basic lecture, "Speaking Historic Christianity into the Twentieth-Century World." When I gave it at Wheaton College, Illinois, they asked if they could put it out as a small xeroxed book. I said, "Well, only for your students, because I don't want published books." When I saw that, however, and read

---

[12]Greg Jesson, "Beyond Ideological Impasses: Francis Schaeffer on Truth, Community, and the Life of Discussion," Witherspoon Lecture, Family Research Council, November 17, 2004; http://www.frc.org/get.cfm?i=WT05B01.

it over, I realized I had a responsibility to publish. It became *The God Who Is There*.[13]

Soon afterward Fran and Edith traveled to California, where he gave a week of lectures at Westmont College in Santa Barbara on "Historic Christianity and Twentieth-Century Man." In the process, Greg Jesson revealed, the guest lecturer made good use of his hiking boots. He heard that "a band of young vagabonds had been living in the hills above the campus for several years. Schaeffer inquired what their philosophic views were, but nobody had ever even thought of talking to them. Schaeffer . . . climbed up the steep California hills and spent several hours discussing with the counterculture campers their views of reality and truth."[14] When he returned to the West Coast in 1968 to speak, it was just as typical for Fran to join a throng of hippies at Fillmore West to hear one of the leading bands of the San Francisco sound, the Jefferson Airplane. This time Franky, now sixteen, had accompanied Fran and Edith on their "American trip." They heard iconic songs like "White Rabbit" and "Somebody to Love." Grace Slick crooned the words:

> *When logic and proportion*
> *Have fallen sloppy dead . . .*
> *Remember what the dormouse said:*
> *"Feed your head, feed your head."*

Frank recalls after nearly forty years:

Dad loved the concert and stayed the whole night. . . . The next day, Dad bought several Airplane albums. After that, once in a while he played them at top volume in his bedroom. He was the coolest dad anyone I knew had, and the only one who knew the words to "White Rabbit."[15]

Edith also recorded the occasion:

---

[13]Interview with Francis Schaeffer, 1980.
[14]Jesson, "Beyond Ideological Impasses: Francis Schaeffer on Truth, Community, and the Life of Discussion."
[15]Frank Schaeffer, *Crazy for God*, 210–211.

> In Berkeley . . . we not only sat and talked about the problems of the
> '60s, but after a discussion one night, went to Fillmore West. There we
> mulled around with the hippies and druggies. . . . We watched the light
> show, breathed the heavy air, and sorrowed over . . . the glassy-eyed
> young people. . . . Our brains whirled not only with the music, which
> threatened in volume to break the eardrums, and the dizzying effect of
> the light show, but with the lostness of humanity in search of "peace"
> where there is no peace. . . . A time of listening is needed—listening to
> what the next generation is saying, listening to the words of the music
> they are listening to, listening to the meaning behind the words. If true
> communication is to continue, there is a language to be learned.[16]

Edith was transposing the vision of the China Inland Mission
of her childhood to the new world being created by sixties youth.
Hudson Taylor had enjoined and demonstrated the central importance
of learning the Chinese language, dressing in the style of the people,
and adopting indigenous cultural habits in order to communicate
effectively. Fran wholeheartedly took on the Taylor model ingrained
in his wife.

The California visit was the culmination of popular lectures in
fourteen locations in the USA that fall, a highlight of which was an
enthusiastic reception at Harvard. As well as Christian students wearing "Schaeffer is not a beer" buttons to create a stir, their committee
prepared a simple flier explaining what a mystery Schaeffer in fact was,
even though in its excitement it anticipated an unfortunate American
evangelical tendency to hype up the streetwise pastor-intellectual:

> Dr. Francis Schaeffer: philosopher-critic-theologian-organizer of a
> community in Switzerland where scholars and students gather to ana-
> lyze and discuss topics of major contemporary importance—frequent
> lecturer at major universities of Europe and Britain. His field is the
> analysis of contemporary thought and culture from a specifically
> Christian viewpoint, but directed beyond the Christian community.
> He is concerned about the world in which we live and is sensitive
> to the despair which blights our achievements. He argues that only
> historic Christianity, rightly understood and fearlessly applied, can
> solve the dilemma of modern man. His answers may not be the ones

---

[16]Edith Schaeffer, *The Tapestry*, 527–528.

modern man expects, or even welcomes. But clearly they cannot be ignored.[17]

Some of the brightest minds in the nation were there to hear Schaeffer, not a beer but nevertheless exceedingly difficult to sum up, and their expectations raised by the flier were not dashed when he spoke. It is hard to imagine Harvard, Yale, Oxford, or Cambridge officially inviting him to lecture at that time, but it is equally difficult to envision an official academic speaker drawing and holding captive the large and intelligent audiences that Schaeffer attracted. His quirky attire and high-register voice, if anything, deepened the interest. His easy knowledge of Bob Dylan, Salvador Dali, and Federico Fellini spoke the language of Harvard's Schaefer-drinking students. Budweiser later superseded Schaefer beer in popularity, but the man Schaeffer has never been replaced, not even by what appeared to be a different Schaeffer in his final years. Edith recorded not long afterward:

> The final lecture at Harvard found Lowell lecture hall jammed with people sitting on the floor in the aisles, and standing at the back, after all the downstairs seats were full. Os [Guinness] reported that one could feel almost an electric charge in the air, the interest was so keen, and at the conclusion of the lecture, "The God Who Is There," there was a burst of applause that lasted 10 minutes, although many of the audience were agnostics or atheists.[18]

It was in London, England, in the fall of 1966 two years before those Harvard lectures, that I first heard Francis Schaeffer. Rapidly sketching diagrams on a chalkboard, he spoke compassionately of the development of the modern person's "line of despair" as classical philosophy had come to a dead end. The choice was between taking a leap of faith and viewing the human condition as futile or seriously considering the Christian claims, which are radical in our day. His American voice, his sorrowful expression, and his unusual attire engaged my attention. The content of his lectures, full of unfamiliar references

---

[17]Quoted in ibid., 527.
[18]Edith Schaeffer, *Dear Family*, 127. Letter dated January 14, 1969. Os Guinness at this time had become a close associate of the Schaeffers.

and concepts, gripped my heart and mind. Those lectures, repeated in January 1967 for an Inter-Varsity conference in Loughborough in the English Midlands, were the heart of his *Escape from Reason* (1968), which traces from the time of Thomas Aquinas and his medieval natural theology what Schaeffer's associate Hans Rookmaaker called "the death of a culture."

After Schaeffer left the Inter-Varsity conference early in the new year, one of the leaders, John Paterson,[19] found Schaeffer's box of chalks and dubbed it "cosmic chalk," leading to the expression "Francis Schaeffer's cosmic chalk and talk." In a sense this captures the man. In his passionate concern for truth—no, not just truth, but "true truth"— he ranged not only through the world today and yesterday but also through the universe.

I was a gawky teenager, just out of high school, reading C. S. Lewis's *Miracles* and his autobiography, *Surprised by Joy*, like someone parched in the desert who finds cool water. As I was adjusting to Lewis's deliriously exciting and bookish way of seeing the world, Schaeffer's lectures offered me his unique overview of Western history and the roots of radical change taking place right then in London, Liverpool, San Francisco, and wherever the Beatles, the Rolling Stones, and Bob Dylan were being heard—in other words (Marshall McLuhan's in fact), throughout the new "global village."

Another person experiencing Schaeffer at that fall conference had just become my friend. Sylvester Jacobs was a black man born in Oklahoma, a sensitive, loyal man forced to don a thick skin and conditioned to put up with the prejudices of even well-meaning whites. While I eagerly sat near the front of the audience to hear Schaeffer, Syl sat near the back. He recalls:

> I sat back in my seat and looked him over. The American twang was plain enough, though he pronounced some words in a funny way. I guessed that was because he had lived so long in Europe. It must also

---

[19]John Paterson was an active supporter of the Inter-Varsity Fellowship (later named Universities and Colleges Christian Fellowship) and took on the Chair of Geography at Leicester University, with a special interest in North America. He and his wife, the poet Evangeline Paterson, were both deeply influenced and inspired by Francis Schaeffer, and he was responsible for getting Schaeffer to speak at the conference.

explain his clothes. He had on grey corduroy knee breeches with bright red socks and a red shirt to match, and an enormous wide-necked pullover with knitted patterns all over the front. Running stags, I think they were.

"The direction of thought goes: Barth—Brunner—Niebuhr—Tillich. And by the time we get to—"

He kept drawing circles on the blackboard, then crossing them out again. In between he'd stand in the middle of the platform, his red socks crossed at the ankles while he swung his glasses round and round in the air between finger and thumb. Now and then he'd lean his cheek against his free hand as if he needed a good sleep.[20]

Afterward Sylvester was taken by surprise when the speaker stepped out of the gaggle of "clever people" assailing him with questions and comments and walked briskly to him, introducing himself as "Mr. Schaeffer" and awaiting Syl's response. After Syl gave his name, Fran asked him where he was from and other questions. The black man was bemused as to why he was spending time talking to him and leaving the others waiting. Fran concluded by inviting him to stay at L'Abri for a while. As Fran walked back to the eager group, Syl's impression was clear: "So that was the great Francis Schaeffer. Philosophic talk and un-American clothes and sad brown eyes. What I remembered most was that he'd been kind to me."[21] When Syl did eventually study at L'Abri for a few months, he said it gave him back his life, freeing him to resume his craft of photography and to formulate his own well-thought-out approach to living as a Christian in the contemporary world, not being misshaped by the prejudices that buffeted him. His work became known and admired through his books and exhibitions, appreciated, for instance, by writer and photographer Val Wilmer. Syl lived in England for many years, where he was an educator as well as photographer, with an enthusiasm for teaching basketball to British schoolchildren.[22]

Apart from a few homegrown productions—*Basic Bible Studies* (date unknown), *Empire Builders for Boys* (1946), and *Empire Builders for Girls* (1946)—Francis Schaeffer's first commercially published book

---

[20]Sylvester Jacobs with Linette Martin, *Born Black* (London: Hodder and Stoughton, 1977), 100.
[21]Ibid., 104.
[22]Some of Jacobs's photographs of L'Abri in Switzerland may be seen at www.flickr.com/photos/22440028@N06.

was *Escape from Reason* (1968).[23] Like the tape program, the book program came into being not because of conscious planning but because of demand. In fact, most of Schaeffer's voluminous writings are based on transcripts of talks captured on audiotape. The evolution of *Escape from Reason* is typical.

> *Fall 1966. London, England.* Lectures tracing the despair of modern humanity from a medieval dualism of nature and grace are given to a large and international group of young people embarking on a mission program under Operation Mobilization. The same series of lectures, which has already been given at the Free University of Amsterdam and elsewhere, is filmed by a lecturer at Indiana University for use with students in the United States.[24]

> *New Year 1967. The Midlands, England.* Schaeffer is guest speaker at the annual conference of the Graduates Fellowship, which is part of Inter-Varsity Fellowship and is geared to Christians in the professions and to postgraduates.[25] He gives three talks that overrun his allotted time by a half hour or more. He is asked to give one more talk to give him the chance to say what he has to say, the chairman, Dr. John Marsh, a pediatrician, being given orders to get him to finish on time for the meal that follows—in vain. The talks, however, make an indelible impact on the audience, including a number of future evangelical leaders.

> *April 1967.* Oliver Barclay, the general secretary of Inter-Varsity Fellowship, hands over to Geraint Fielder, one of the staff workers, a transcript of the tapes of the lectures Schaeffer gave at the conference. Fielder agrees to consider whether the material warrants publication. He spends the next two weeks editing it and then meets with Schaeffer at the English L'Abri (then in Ealing, London) to discuss the project.

> *June 15, 1967.* Schaeffer writes to Fielder, thanking him for all the work he has put into editing. An even more appreciative letter, dated August 14, whimsically wishes that Fielder was at L'Abri in Switzerland to work on more taped material.

> *March 1968.* Publication of *Escape from Reason.*

---

[23]Francis A. Schaeffer, *Escape from Reason* (London and Downers Grove, IL: Inter-Varsity Press, 1968).

[24]I have been unable to find out what happened to those recordings, which would be of great interest.

[25]In the UK, Christians in postgraduate studies, including those pursuing doctorates, are in secular universities, with the exception of some theology students. After World War II a large number of evangelicals taught in secular universities in both humanities and sciences, and many became heads of faculties.

Upon revising *Escape from Reason* not long before his death from cancer, Schaeffer reaffirmed its continuing topicality. In fact, he felt that it was more topical in 1980 than when it was first published.

The preface to *Escape from Reason* explains why Schaeffer, in analyzing the trends in modern thought, begins deep in the Middle Ages with St. Thomas Aquinas. Such an analysis, he points out, should be concerned with both philosophy and history. By investigating the historical background, we can discover the "unchanging truth in a changing world."

Because of Aquinas's accommodation to the intellectual tradition of Greece and Rome, asserts Schaeffer, Christian thinking was to become seriously weakened. In particular, Aquinas allowed human thinking a fatal autonomy from the guiding pattern of biblical revelation. This autonomy was not in the proper sense of free, dignified human thought but in the sense of "rationalism" (that is, humanism as a form of idolatry, in this case, idolatry of the mind). As a result, in some areas of reality, knowledge was viewed as beginning with the human mind as final authority rather than depending for its orientation upon biblical revelation. The Word of God is the ultimate authority, Schaeffer argues, both in the sciences and in the humanities.[26]

When Thomas allowed the human mind to begin from its own authority, albeit in a limited way, believed Schaeffer, there were eventually serious consequences for the positioning of nature and grace, which was a dualistic frame of reference throughout the Middle Ages and beyond. "Nature," in Schaeffer's words, "began to eat up grace." Grace was seen as the realm of universals and of absolute principles. In the Greco-Roman scheme universals determined reality, and nature was relatively unimportant. In biblical Christian thinking, however, nature exists in its own right and does not need to be forced into a dialectical tension with the spiritual world. Observing rightly that it is glorifying to God to explore nature in intellectual freedom, Aquinas helped the pro-

---

[26]In an important appendix to his later book *The Church Before the Watching World* (1972), "Some Absolute Limits," Schaeffer gives examples of how Scripture sets guiding boundaries in areas such as right and wrong in dogmatic systems, objectivity and subjectivity in history, and justification and sanctification. Within those boundaries, as they are obeyed, there is great freedom, he argues. Another book, *Genesis in Space and Time* (1972), demonstrates the proper freedom of the sciences that in fact is guaranteed by obeying biblical boundaries (e.g., freedom in exploring the age of the universe and humanity on the planet).

cess that led to modern science. However, the new emphasis on nature in conjunction with even a limited autonomy of the human mind (as rationalism) had the result that knowledge now focused inordinately on particulars and eventually was unable to attain universals.[27] The classical world exalted universals at the expense of particulars (form over matter), whereas the post-Aquinas world gradually saw universals fading in favor of particulars (nature over grace), a process that is embodied in the history of art, thought, and culture.

Schaeffer graphically and movingly demonstrates this new dilemma of the demise of the universal in the work of Leonardo da Vinci. Unlike the distinctively modern person, says Schaeffer, Leonardo never relinquished the hope of a unified field of knowledge encompassing nature and grace, particulars and universals, quantities and qualities, fact and meaning.

The next stage in the development of modern consciousness, according to Schaeffer, was a paradigm shift from the nature and grace dualism to one of nature and freedom. Between these worlds of discourse there was still continuity, however. Most importantly, philosophers, scientists, and artists continued to seek a unified field of knowledge. On the negative side, they also worked within the framework let in by Aquinas: instead of depending on the biblical revelation, where God discloses truth about both himself and his creation, including the identity of the human being, knowledge began with the human mind as primary authority. In addition, there was increasing tension between human freedom and the conception of the human being as a mechanism describable in terms of natural laws.

Parallel to this period was the Protestant Reformation.[28] This development was in principle free of the dualistic dilemmas of the nature-freedom paradigm, even though its dependence on biblical revelation was far from perfect. Nevertheless, it introduced into society and culture insights about nature and the human being that resulted in

---

[27]Michael Polanyi, *Personal Knowledge* (Chicago: University of Chicago Press, 1974) points out the dramatic consequences of this kind of reductionism. He argues that to avoid loss of meaning, particulars should be indwelt rather than focused on. Particulars, if respected, allow us to participate in higher levels of meaning—that is, more general and universal meaning.

[28]For a more extensive discussion see Francis A. Schaeffer, *How Should We Then Live?* (Grand Rapids, MI: Revell, 1976).

tangible blessings that reverberate to our day: the principles of democratic government, the growth of scientific knowledge and technology,
enormous advances in health care, a strong legal base that protects the
weak and powerless, a richness in the arts and language, and so on.

Schaeffer then describes the final step in the development of the
modern world. This represents an absolute discontinuity with the past.
There was a paradigm shift like no other (except perhaps in the East
millennia ago). Here the vanguard thinkers abandoned the defining
human quest for a unified field of knowledge. The transcendent realm
that in the past had been labeled grace or freedom was put beyond the
categories of rationality. All that gives meaning to the world and to the
human being was seen as lying outside of rational investigation, now
identified with scientific knowledge. Universals no longer obeyed what
Schaeffer called "classical rationality." They were no longer subject to
basic logic such as the law of non-contradiction, nor were they to be
understood in causal terms.

There was, however, at the same time a significant continuity with
the past, he argued. This is because modern consciousness was still
humanistic in the sense of believing that humans begin totally from
themselves in knowing and in defining reality. Thus there was now open
revolt against the idea that true knowledge is inevitably dependent upon
biblical revelation.

The leap into nonrational meaning centered, for Schaeffer, in the
giant figures of the philosophers Georg Hegel and, more controversially, Søren Kierkegaard. The remainder of *Escape from Reason* traces
the chronological, geographical, and social spread of the new way of
thinking, a way of thinking that, in C. S. Lewis's phrase, divides modern
people from "Old Western Man."[29]

Schaeffer describes the "methodology" of the old rationality as
antithesis: A is true in contrast to non-A. God is there in contrast to his
not being there. Beauty exists in contrast to ugliness. Evil and cruelty

---

[29]See C. S. Lewis, *"De Descriptione Temporum,"* in C. S. Lewis, *Selected Literary Essays*, ed. Walter
Hooper (New York: Cambridge University Press, 1969), 1–14. Lewis identified the shift into modern
consciousness with the rise of the "machine archetype," which was associated with a myth of progress.
Lewis's emphasis is on the social context of knowledge and world models rather than on ideas. Schaeffer
tends to focus on the individual ideas of key players, even though much of his analysis is structural and
cultural.

are in contrast to goodness. Murder, theft, and similar deeds are wrong as opposed to right. The deliberate killing of an unborn child is an evil, and ignoring such an act is a sin of omission. Such judgments are foreign to the new way of thinking, taken to its logical conclusion.

Escape from Reason provides the frame for much of Schaeffer's lifework as a pastor, apologist, evangelist, and, in the closing years of his life, a campaigner for several human rights. His work should be seen in this context rather than that of academic philosophy, theology, or even the politics of the American Christian Right. Not surprisingly, his little book, which reads like an intellectual slide show, has provoked criticisms that also apply to some of his other publications. Some have disputed his thumbnail sketches of great historical figures. This is particularly true of his portrayals of St. Thomas Aquinas and Kierkegaard.[30] It should be borne in mind that there is room for honest differences of interpretation of such figures. It is plausible to see, as Schaeffer does, Kierkegaard as the father of both religious and secular existentialism even if it is unfair to blame, as he did (though with some later qualification), the godly Dane for modern fragmentation of knowledge. Numerous other thinkers, e.g., Nietzsche and Freud, contributed in a deeply significant way to modernist and postmodernist worldviews. Schaeffer's interpretation of Aquinas is also plausible, especially as the nature-grace framework so basic to Thomas's thought arguably did transform into a dualistic paradigm of nature-freedom.[31] Even if it were granted that Aquinas did open the door to rationalistic knowledge, and eventually the Enlightenment, we need not conclude that much or even most of his work is not valuable nor distinctly Christian.

The key issue here perhaps is the causal relationship between significant individuals and historical changes. It may be that figures like Aquinas and Kierkegaard, as Schaeffer understood them, were not first movers, so to speak, but articulated the spirit of their times, their

---

[30]See Ronald Ruegsegger, *Reflections on Francis Schaeffer* (Grand Rapids, MI: Zondervan, 1986), 112–115, 118–120; and Norman L. Geisler, *Thomas Aquinas: An Evangelical Appraisal* (Grand Rapids, MI: Baker, 1991), 61.

[31]C. S. Lewis, for instance, as a medieval scholar, had misgivings about Aquinas's contribution to a later dualism in thought, leading to qualities being stripped out of the natural world (see C. S. Lewis, *The Allegory of Love* [New York: Oxford University Press, 1958], 88; also C. S. Lewis, *English Literature in the Sixteenth Century* [Oxford: Clarendon Press, 1954], 3–4). Dooyeweerd was also concerned about his accommodation to Aristotle (Herman Dooyeweerd, *A New Critique of Theoretical Thought*, 4 vols. [Philadelphia: P&R, 1953–1958], 1:179ff.).

thinking and creativity patterned by a paradigm or world model that was either dominant or coming into existence. Numerous thinkers and cultural shapers, major and minor, contribute to a dominant worldview. If this is so, we should be able to cite philosophers of the times whose thinking was similar in many ways to that of Aquinas or Kierkegaard, and perhaps who may have been more formative. It may also be that hindsight leads us to see meanings in their work of which they themselves were not fully conscious and from which they may even have recoiled had they been. What is important is that Schaeffer credibly identified dualistic patterns to worldviews that were held for very long periods, shaping thought, belief, and culture.

Schaeffer is in line with many scholars in seeing Aquinas and Kierkegaard as radically innovative, even though his interpretations of their culpability in the decline of Western thought are disputed, especially his portrayal of Kierkegaard. Schaeffer himself showed signs of qualifying his understanding of Kierkegaard when he revised his books, not always consistently, for the edition of *The Complete Works* that appeared in 1982. Furthermore, his book *How Should We Then Live?* is often more nuanced than *Escape from Reason*. The philosopher Herman Dooyeweerd's structural analysis of the "ground-motives" of form-matter, nature-grace, and nature-freedom backs up Schaeffer's impressionistic sketches of Aquinas and other primary thinkers.[32] Schaeffer's portrait of Thomas's radical dualism fits, in spirit, with C. S. Lewis's generalization of the period, just as his view of a radical discontinuity in the recent West that ushered in a post-Christian culture fits with Lewis's view of the end of the "Old West" in the early nineteenth century:[33]

> The recovery of Aristotle's text dates from the second half of the twelfth century: the dominance of his doctrine soon followed. Aristotle is, before all, the philosopher of divisions. His effect on his greatest disciple [Aquinas], as M. Gilson has traced it, was to dig new chasms between God and the world, between human knowledge and reality,

---

[32]Herman Dooyeweerd, *A New Critique of Theoretical Thought*, 4 vols. (Philadelphia: Presbyterian & Reformed, 1953–1958), 1:36, 180–181; Dooyeweerd, *The Roots of Western Culture* (Toronto: Wedge, 1979), chap. 5; and L. Kalsbeek, *Contours of a Christian Philosophy* (Toronto: Wedge, 1975), 144.
[33]See his *De Descriptione Temporum*.

between faith and reason. Heaven began, under this dispensation, to seem farther off. The danger of Pantheism grew less: the danger of mechanical Deism came a step nearer. It is almost as if the first, faint shadow of Descartes, or even of "our present discontents" had fallen across the scene.[34]

Schaeffer's broadbrush picture of the development of Western thought is full of vitality and, very significantly, encourages further work on worldviews, structures, and paradigms held by intellectual, artistic, and other cultural communities at distinctive moments in history. Furthermore he, courageously, I think, tries to establish causal links between earlier and later dominant worldviews, which is at the center of understanding histories of science, art, ideas, and similar subjects. He wrote *Escape from Reason* in the context of a radical fragmentation of knowledge that he felt lies at the heart of the sorrow of modern thinkers and artists. It came fully out of a pastoral concern, not from a pretension to be considered a great thinker.

Because of striking similarities between Schaeffer's structural patterns of change in the development of Western thought and Dooyeweerd's, Schaeffer has been charged with employing Dooyeweerd's analysis without acknowledgment. However, Schaeffer considered that he owed no debt to Dooyeweerd, an outstanding twentieth-century philosopher, except for a single unnamed article on nature and grace. I was in the habit of sending him pieces I had written, on which he would comment. After sending him an article on Dooyeweerd's thought, tentatively suggesting affinities with Schaeffer's, he responded:

I am really not sure that I have much relationship to Dooyeweerd. Most of my thought was developed prior to my detailed contacts with Hans Rookmaaker and in our detailed contacts I do not think that what we exchanged had so much to do with Dooyeweerd at all, but simply our own thoughts which undoubtedly we have shared backwards and forwards to our mutual advantage for the 20 years. As for Van Til, I do not think he would appreciate being linked with Dooyeweerd at all. Van Til was helpful to me simply with his empha-

---

[34]C. S. Lewis, *The Allegory of Love* (New York: Oxford University Press, 1958), 88. For more on the medieval world model see Lewis, *The Discarded Image* (New York: Cambridge University Press, 1964).

sis on presuppositions as such rather than anything detailed from his work. I think this is clear because he really does not seem to[35] agree with the thrust of my apologetic[36] work, although I know he is thankful for L'Abri and its work among the young people of our generation. Dooyeweerd did write one thing which was helpful to me. It was a very short article with a very clear exposition of nature and grace. When I read this it was helpful as I was already working in these areas in my own thinking. . . . Let me quickly say that I am not minimizing his work, or even saying that I do or do not agree with it (that would be another matter to write about), but rather that his work and mine really have very little contact.

I increasing[ly] realize that really I have very little interest in theoretical apologetics at all. Recently someone wrote a rather lengthy and involved study of my books and asked me to comment on it and I could only write back and say that really I had no interest in doing so because to me apologetics only had value in so far as it was related to evangelism. Of course I was thinking of evangelism in the wide sense here and not in a narrow one. In this same direction I have no interest ever in writing another book on philosophy after *He Is There and He Is Not Silent*. I might write short things, but the reason I do not expect to write another book after the trilogy of *The God Who Is There*, *Escape from Reason* and *He Is There and He Is Not Silent* is because from this point on it would become a more abstract apologetic and abstract philosophy and while I believe others may be called to this I am quite sure it is not my calling from the Lord.[37]

In the letter Schaeffer's reference to Rookmaaker is significant, as the latter believed that there were affinities between his friend's thinking and that of Dooyeweerd's. In a L'Abri lecture, published after his death, Rookmaaker says:

> Dooyeweerd himself wrote a good and short introduction to his work called [*In*] *The Twilight of Western Thought*. In the first part of that book he asks the question how Western thought is to be approached. Is it really Christian and if not, what is it? *Escape from Reason* is Schaeffer's version of what Dooyeweerd develops in those chapters. They both talk for instance about nature and grace and about the

---

[35]Schaeffer added "seem to" in a copy of excerpts from the letter to me that he sent the next day to Hans Rookmaaker.
[36]Schaeffer similarly added "apologetic" to the copy for Rookmaaker.
[37]Francis A. Schaeffer, unpublished letter to Colin Duriez, June 16, 1972.

influence of Greek concepts. Dooyeweerd tries to trace the various ways of thinking in Western history to their starting points. A starting point can be defined as the basic answers that are given to basic questions like: What is the world? Who is God? or What is the source of this world? The answers given to those questions color the answers that are given to all other questions. The second part of Dooyeweerd's book deals with a truly Christian approach to reality. Firstly it is basic to such an approach that we begin with a world that is created. Secondly we hold that this world is fallen, it is not perfect. But thirdly we say that this is not the end, there is redemption as Christ came to redeem this world. On the basis of these truths we can try to grasp reality and analyze how this world is made. Dooyeweerd then proceeds to give such an analysis.[38]

This apparent contradiction between the views of Schaeffer and Rookmaaker on the influence of Dooyeweerd is fascinating, and this book is not the place to discuss it, but only to point it out as part of the complex origins of Schaeffer's thinking. It is certainly true that Schaeffer's work does not resemble at all the usual writings of those who follow Dooyeweerd. While Rookmaaker was a self-confessed pupil of Dooyeweerd's, he developed his ideas selectively and in his own way (for example, in his emphasis upon meaning). He also drew on other Dutch scholars, such as Groen Van Prinsterer, J. P. A. Mekkes, and Abraham Kuyper. These represent a family of thinkers. For those within the family, the differences look great, while for those outside the similarities seem obvious. In my view Schaeffer was influenced by this family of thinkers, for example, through Van Til and Rookmaaker, rather than by Dooyeweerd's epic system of thought. In Schaeffer, for instance, there is no discussion of ordinary, pre-theoretical knowledge, so pivotal to Dooyeweerd's thought.

The God Who Is There is the second book in Schaeffer's core trilogy, which was in preparation before and published soon after *Escape from Reason*. This seminal book was originally released in what the British publisher informally described to Schaeffer as their "egghead series." Though the initial press run of the large paperback was low, the book

---

[38]Hans Rookmaaker, "A Dutch Christian View of Philosophy," in *Our Calling and God's Hand in History: The Complete Works of Hans Rookmaaker*, Vol. 6 (Carlisle: Piquant, 2003), 179.

was soon reprinted several times and was later issued in a more popular format. Hodder and Stoughton, represented by its religious publisher Edward England, was nervous at first about the book, expecting it to be a failure, and requested several hundred pounds to underwrite it. The money was not required, as it turned out.

The God Who Is There picks up on the thesis of *Escape from Reason*, tracing the origins of modern relativism in knowledge and morals to an abandonment of the perennial human search for a unified field of knowledge. All that gives meaning to human beings and their society and culture is relegated to the realm of the mystical and nonrational. Schaeffer continues to ascribe to Hegel and Kierkegaard the origins of the notion that a blind leap of faith is necessary if we are to find any meaning in human life. He then traces the steps by which a mentality that has lost objective absolutes eventually spread to every part of society and culture. He emphasizes as well the role that modern theology has played in promoting relativism and the mystical leap. The problem is particularly insidious because the new theology uses orthodox Christian terminology, conveying the impression of rational content and categories that in fact are increasingly absent. Friedrich Nietzsche's declaration of the death of God has proven to be prophetic.

Because the modern person is typically "below the line of despair," we have to rethink Christian apologetics and evangelism, according to Schaeffer. Classical apologetics fails to communicate because it is built on the old methodology of antithesis. It was once meaningful to speak of God's existing (as opposed to his not existing), of sin, of the finished work of Christ; this, however, is no longer the case. We must now begin by recognizing that Christian belief is in fact radical in our day and how it differs from the new theology. If, for example, we say that the Bible is true even though its portrayal of historical events is full of errors of fact, we are speaking with the voice of the new theology, of modernity, not of biblical Christianity. Schaeffer goes on to demonstrate a person-centered apologetics that will have bite in our day. We have to combine obedience to the written words of Scripture with a demonstrable godly reality in our own lives and in our relations with others. Focus on personality and the value of the person is the ultimate apologetic for the

Christian faith. Each human being is confronted with the form of the
real universe and the reality of one's own humanness. Only Christian
faith is at home with these fundamental realities. Non-Christian systems
actually divide the person internally, because they pull one away from
these basic realities.

Schaeffer's unshakable realism allows him to steer a path between
extreme presuppositionalism and evidentialism or foundationalism in
apologetics, a course he had decided upon since the days of his pastorate in St. Louis. Although Christianity is a system, a fact for which no
apologies need be made, it is also a historic faith. It is therefore in this
respect open to verification. If Christ did not rise from the dead at an
actual time in history, our faith is in vain. But what, then, is the role of
presuppositions? Schaeffer explained in 1980: "I do believe [that pre-
suppositions] are crucial. . . . From my way of looking at them, presuppositions are not accepted by you unconsciously, as a prior condition to
your first move of thought. For me, the proper way to get at it is that,
if you are a thinking person, you decide what set of presuppositions are
going to lead to the answers to the questions."[39] For Schaeffer, a worldview is articulated in response to questioning life and the world on the
basis of one's presuppositions.

In that same interview, made weeks before he revised *The God Who
Is There* for inclusion in *The Complete Works*, he spoke more of the
apologetics that are at the heart of the book.

> I'm only interested in an apologetic that leads in two directions, and
> the one is to lead people to Christ, as Savior, and the other is that after
> they are Christians, for them to realize the lordship of Christ in the
> whole of life. I don't believe there is any one apologetic that meets all
> the needs any more than I believe there is one form of evangelism that
> meets all the needs. . . . So therefore, if I were in the Philippian jail
> with Paul and Silas, and the jailer says, "Sirs, what must I do to be
> saved?" this is no place to talk about apologetics, as it usually is con-
> ceived of. You say what Paul said: "Believe on the Lord Jesus Christ,
> and thou shalt be saved." On the other hand, if in your empathy and
> love—because now, I think, that's really the key, that you ought to
> approach every individual and lovingly try to find out where he is

---

[39] Interview with Francis Schaeffer, 1980.

or she is—if in your empathy you find out that he or she is a person who still believes in truth, which is not the mark of our age, but there are still people who live there, and they're really troubled, let us say, about the historic evidences, the physical resurrection, then I think you ought to talk to them on that level. So this would then be what's usually called "evidences." But what I tried to show in *The God Who Is There*—and I must say when I rewrite it in these next few weeks [for *The Complete Works*], I realize I didn't make myself clear—all I tried to do and show there was not that what I was presenting was to be used with everybody, but even if people are twentieth-century people, there's still a way to talk to them, and then that's all. As I said, I don't think there's one form of apologetics for all people.

Underlying both *Escape from Reason* and *The God Who Is There* is a concern for the issue of knowledge. Schaeffer had demonstrated that shifting approaches to knowledge in the recent and far-off history of the West had had dramatic consequences for how we live (and die). He turned once again to this matter in *He Is There and He Is Not Silent* (1972), arguing that only the historic Christian faith gives adequate answers in the fundamental areas of metaphysics, morals, and epistemology.[40] In each of these areas he posits that God's existence and communication to us are "necessary." If he is not there, or if he is there but is silent, then there are no answers to the big human questions in these areas. These questions are particularly acute for modern people, which is why Schaeffer was so concerned, as a pastor and apologist, to express the exciting answers to be found in a biblical Christianity.

He Is There and He Is Not Silent, inevitably, is popular philosophy as well as popular theology. Yet Schaeffer does not write as a philosopher. That is not his intention. In fact, this book is the furthest he went in philosophical debate, and he had no wish to go further. Consequently, there may be difficulties for the reader. For instance, Schaeffer's use of the term *necessity* is not the standard philosophical use (i.e., the opposite of *contingency*). By the "necessity" of historic Christianity he means that without God's existence and communication there are no answers to the fundamental human questions. His analysis of Western cultural themes in previous books had demonstrated the lack of answers out-

---

[40]Francis A. Schaeffer, *He Is There and He Is Not Silent* (Wheaton, IL: Tyndale House, 1972).

side of biblical Christianity, resulting in the despair of modern humans. Though God's existence and communication answer these questions, Christianity stands or falls as truth on the basis of actual historical events such as the death and resurrection of a first-century Palestinian called Jesus.

By 1984, when his life ended, Francis Schaeffer was the author of over twenty books and booklets in total. The first of them, entitled *Escape from Reason*, was not published until he was fifty-six. Two of them were coauthored, one with Edith and the other with the distinguished pediatric surgeon C. Everett Koop.[41] There is some overlap in material, but all the publications (except for *Everybody Can Know*) have been usefully gathered together and thematically arranged in *The Complete Works of Francis A. Schaeffer*.[42] Though ill from cancer, he was able to revise his books for this compilation. Most importantly, he rewrote a section on his apologetic method for the new edition of *The God Who Is There* (Appendix A). It is essential, however, to read *True Spirituality* in connection with his core trilogy to get to the pulse of his thinking. A slim volume, *Pollution and the Death of Man*, is a pioneering statement of proper evangelical concern for the environment, for nature, our "fair sister."[43] It is a characteristic example of Fran's unexpectedness. Just as he wrote on anti-Semitism in wartime and the importance of the arts at the end of the forties, he prophetically wrote on one of the overriding concerns of the beginning of the new millennium. He can now be seen as a prophet—a weeping prophet—in many areas, including the devaluing of human life in an escalation of abortion and euthanasia. The books representing the other "spokes" he mentioned, radiating out of the central core of his work, must await another chapter.

---

[41]Francis and Edith Schaeffer, *Everybody Can Know* (Wheaton, IL: Tyndale House, 1975); Francis A. Schaeffer and C. Everett Koop, *Whatever Happened to the Human Race?* (Old Tappan, NJ: Revell, 1979).
[42]Francis A. Schaeffer, *The Complete Works of Francis A. Schaeffer*, 5 vols. (Wheaton, IL: Crossway Books, 1982).
[43]Francis A. Schaeffer, *Pollution and the Death of Man* (Wheaton, IL: Tyndale House, 1970).

CHAPTER EIGHT

THE LAST BATTLES

(1977–1984)

ග ග ග ග ග

O ver a decade after Francis Schaeffer's death, Inter-Varsity Christian Fellowship worker Gordon Govier remarked that he "may have done more to shape the culture of American evangelicals at the end of the 20th century than any one person outside of C.S. Lewis or Billy Graham. A 1997 article in *Christianity Today* referred to Schaeffer as 'evangelicalism's most important public intellectual' who 'prodded evangelicals out of their cultural ghetto.'"[1]

In the first twenty years of L'Abri's existence, when he was in his early forties to early sixties, Francis Schaeffer's priority was the established work of L'Abri, particularly in Europe, including the United Kingdom. In this work he steadfastly followed the principle of not having a program (unlike even Fran and Edith's mentors Hudson Taylor or Amy Carmichael) but simply pastoring those who came along to L'Abri. He had, however, done speaking trips on a number of occasions in the USA, at first sounding out developing material that, unknown to him, would become books, and best-selling ones at that, and then later speaking as a result of increasing opportunities created by the popularity of his publications. It was in the final phase of his life, taking up less than a decade, however, that his impact upon America became colossal, causing conclusions such as that of *Christianity Today* magazine cited by Gordon Govier of IVCF. For most of those last years he was fighting a particularly virulent form of cancer.

The escalation of Schaeffer's impact upon America was firmly founded upon the reputation of his iconoclastic early books, such as the trilogy of *Escape from Reason*, *The God Who Is There*, and *He Is*

---

[1]March 9, 2005; http://www.intervarsity.org/news/francis-schaeffer-changed-the-landscape.

There and He Is Not Silent. It was directly and more immediately caused by his embrace of what he saw as a new communication tool, the powerful medium of film. There was another factor, however, that, when combined with that medium, became dynamic. This was the explicit extension of his emphasis upon the lordship of Christ into the social and political realm—an idea many fundamentalists and evangelicals in America had become ready for once their quietism, cultural separatism, and pietism had been challenged by the message of Schaeffer and others such as Carl F. H. Henry, Charles Colson, and C. S. Lewis.[2] This message emphasized the cultural impact of ideas and worldviews (with their dramatic consequences on the arts and morality), the decline of the West, the rise of a new darkness, and the fact that we now live in a post-Christian culture.

Schaeffer's ever-present realism—his concern for the practice of truth in his generation—led him to defend the rights of unborn children, the weak, and the elderly. In principle, this defense applied to any of the innocent who suffer.[3] He was convinced that a worldview that had no basis for valuing human beings as human was now shaping and distorting Western society and would inevitably devalue them. Humanity itself was threatened. Writing during the Second World War, C. S. Lewis came to a similar conclusion, writing a powerful philosophical tract, *The Abolition of Man* (1943), and embodying its thesis in his science fiction story, *That Hideous Strength* (1945). It was not a new Schaeffer that was emerging. His theology, honed over many decades since the passionate articles of the later forties and early fifties, was that of the lordship of Christ over every area of life—the womb as well as the university seminar room. His slowly developing political pro-life stance received special emphasis only after his move into filmmaking, into what he would have called general culture. Whereas his previous books were based on many years or even decades of thought, the emphasis

---

[2]On the impact of Schaeffer, Colson, and Henry see, for example, Wyman Richardson, "Francis Schaeffer and the Pro-Life Movement"; http://walkingtogether.typepad.com/walking_together/2007/09/francis-schaeff.html. On C. S. Lewis's views on post-Christianity and the importance of worldviews, see, for example, my *Tolkien and C. S. Lewis* (Mahwah, NJ: Paulist Press, 2003) and *The C. S. Lewis Encyclopedia* (Wheaton, IL: Crossway Books, 2000; London: Azure, 2003).

[3]For instance, in 1983, as he was dying, Fran fully endorsed and supported his son-in-law Udo Middelmann's decision to work with the humanitarian organization Food for the Hungry. Furthermore, he and Edith applauded Anky Rookmaaker's work in India with Save a Child (*Red een Kind*).

on abortion, infanticide, and euthanasia was quite new. Just as he had been persuaded first to record talks and discussions and then to publish books, so was he eventually persuaded of the value of creating movies. The idea sprang from his son Franky. Schaeffer explained to me how the first film series, *How Should We Then Live?* came about:

> As the books came out and sold so well—millions, in 25 languages— the next thing was that Franky came to me and said, "Dad, you're saying something that most people aren't saying. In order to give what you're saying a wide hearing, would you do a film?" This was a brand- new idea, and I was very reticent. The more I thought and prayed about it, the more I realized that, rather than being a discontinuity, a film is very much a continuity with writing books. Quite frankly, also, I had seen Kenneth Clark's *Civilisation* and felt that he was totally unfair, especially in the "Reformation" episode, so I wanted to counter that in some way. I remember one night in Carmel, California, when I was there for a week's vacation I happened to see this episode, and I said to Edith, "If I ever get a chance to hit that I want to hit it." So when this [opportunity to film] came along it just naturally dropped into place.[4]

Fran mentioned his hesitation and doubts over doing movies. But Franky, like his father, was very persuasive. He also had in his favor a feeling of guilt on Fran's part that all parents will recognize. The prospect of working with his son no doubt had great appeal to Fran, conscious of neglecting Franky under the unremitting pressures of the L'Abri work and the more recent further demands of speaking tours gen- erated by interest in the best-selling books. In his memoir, not intended as a factually accurate biography in every detail, Franky admits in words that ring true (though with a strong hint of projection):

> No one has more power over a loving father (especially if that father feels a bit guilty for neglecting his children) than a beloved son. I would know! Years later, I practically followed my youngest son John into the Marine Corps and dedicated almost seven years to writing about military service out of solidarity with his choice to volunteer.[5]

---

[4]Interview with Francis Schaeffer, 1980.
[5]Frank Schaeffer, *Crazy for God: How I Grew Up as One of the Elect, Helped Found the Religious Right, and Lived to Take All (or Almost All) of It Back* (New York: Carroll & Graf, 2007), 267.

Fran's susceptibility to his son's arguments probably went right back to Franky's polio as an infant, an affliction in a child that has complex effects on a parent's attitude to that child henceforward. In any event, Fran gave in, just as he had over the tapes and then the books, from family persuasion. Not long into production, twenty-three-year-old Franky was made producer of the movie series by Billy Zeoli, president of Gospel Films, who financed and promoted the movies. Zeoli took Franky under his wing. By a happenstance that appealed to Fran and Edith, he was the son of the evangelist Fran heard speaking in a tent in Germantown in 1930. A Dutch public television company, the Christian station Evangelische Omroep, helped to support the project from early on.

Parallel to the film series Fran wrote a large-format hardback book of the same name, drawing on the work of researchers also used rather unevenly for the film, including his friend Hans Rookmaaker. Especially written rather than based upon taped lectures, *How Should We Then Live?* is one of Schaeffer's finest books, and far more nuanced than his earliest books, *Escape from Reason* and *The God Who Is There*, in portraying the decline of Western culture.[6] Its portrayal of the history of art (necessarily selective) particularly was written in consultation with Hans Rookmaaker. He wrote, for instance, to Hans in February 1975: "I would appreciate a bit of help. When I am talking about the Vatican *Pietà* showing humanism in Michelangelo's early work, in contrast to the later *Pietà* in Milano what would you add in a bit more detail indicating the marks of humanism in the early *Pietà*?"[7] Lacking ready reference books, Fran sent notes to Hans for the exact dates of artists such as Van Gogh. Various consultants were used for other areas—for example, Jane Stuart Smith for music.

The basic thesis of *Escape from Reason* was expanded, with the historical sweep now going right back to Roman times. Edith records Fran's working on the ambitious book in November 1974, then with the working title of *The Rise and Decline of Western Thought and*

---

[6]An example of the book's more nuanced approach is its portrayal of Hegel and Kierkegaard—see, for instance, page 163 in Francis A. Schaeffer, *How Should We Then Live?* (Grand Rapids, MI: Revell, 1976).

[7]Unpublished letter to H. R. R. Rookmaaker, February 21, 1975, from Hotel Excelsior, Montreux.

Culture (this ended up being the book's subtitle), and being concerned with "tracing history, art, music, science, philosophy, theology, political thought, etc., from the fall of the Romans until the present time."[8] As a series consciously made in response to Kenneth Clark's *Civilisation*, it suffers in comparison with the beautifully made BBC production and lacks an open subtitle like Clark's—"A Personal View." It does have a certain freshness and vitality, however, which ties in with Schaeffer's deconstruction of the familiar humanist definition of reality expounded by Kenneth Clark. Though the authenticity of Schaeffer's message is carried by his convictions—in the movie he is the quietly spoken and "sad-faced" prophet with fire in his voice—he sometimes appears tired and searching for words. This very human Schaeffer, however, deeply appealed to the movie's large audiences, even though it failed to be tele-vised in Clark's Britain. Schaeffer's message of how Western civilization for all its greatness sowed the wind and reaped the whirlwind contrasts with the optimistic Clark's humanist tract, evidenced in the words emblazoned on the back cover of his companion book: "A personal view of how Western Europe evolved after the collapse of the Roman Empire and produced the ideas, books, buildings, works of art and great individuals that make up a Civilisation."

Filming meant great changes in the lives of Fran and Edith. It signi-fied the end of a persistent presence at Swiss L'Abri that had marked the first twenty years of "the Shelter." Looking back after several months into the filming Edith observed:

> Starting at the end of August [1975], Fran and I have lived very dif-ferent lives, or have worked very differently from any other period of our lives. It has been in many ways the most difficult period of our lives thus far! We have been introduced to what it means to "shoot" a documentary film, traveling by car from town to town, country to country, sleeping in a variety of places for one-night "stands," often getting up for "dawn shots" and staying up for "night shots," and being involved in the grouping of a "crew" all involved in the same thing for a period of time. It is all-consuming in time, energy and con-centration, and does not leave room for correspondence or dipping in

---

[8]Edith Schaeffer, *Dear Family*, 225. Letter dated November 26, 1974.

to other areas of life. For Fran "pasting up" the next day's lines from
the script, studying them, packing and unpacking, constantly washing
his hair before breakfast to keep the continuity of looks for cutting
together various parts of any one episode, taken of course in different
places at different times, caring for a deluge of physical difficulties,
actual speaking for the camera in a tremendous variety of places (top
of scaffolding, on the ledge of a dam, walking through a field of cows,
in museums, churches, on an empty beach, etc., etc.), the long hours of
waiting, the retakes, took more than a "normal day" compared even
to L'Abri work.[9]

Schaeffer spoke at seminars across North America where the film
series was shown, attended by vast audiences. In an initial speaking
tour of eighteen cities in 1977, there was an enthusiastic response to the
screening of the ten half-hour episodes. In Oakland around 4,500 people attended, in Chicago 3,900, in Los Angeles 6,600, and in Toronto
4,400. The film series was also shown around Europe, including local
screenings set up by churches and Christian groups in the United
Kingdom. The response was unprecedented for Gospel Films, rewarding
their commitment to the ambitious and untried project.[10] The prospect
of a large-screen presentation perhaps removed people's fears of being
lost, as when hearing or reading Schaeffer undiluted. The seminar pattern, with a lecture by Fran and a showing of an episode followed by his
taking questions from the audience, anticipated the more controversial
series *Whatever Happened to the Human Race?* which, however, had
smaller audiences. Not only were the movie-centered events great hits.
The substantial companion book sold forty thousand copies in the first
three months and even three years later, in 1979, was selling around
1,500 copies a month.[11]

The tour in February and March 1977 coincided with three bitter
blows to Fran and Edith. Two were the deaths of members of L'Abri.
Edith's father, George Seville, attained the magisterial age of 101 before
his death. In contrast, at not much more than half Seville's age, Hans
Rookmaaker was taken at merely fifty-five from many innovative writ-

[9]Edith Schaeffer, *Dear Family*, 240–241. Letter dated February 23, 1976.
[10]Richardson, "Francis Schaeffer and the Pro-Life Movement."
[11]Ibid.

ing and scholarly projects, as well as his international and home-based work with L'Abri. His heart stopped suddenly one Sunday afternoon in March. At a memorial service held at the beginning of a three-day annual members' meeting held early in May that year, Fran remembered his close friend of many years, commencing, recorded Edith, "by telling a little history of each of the two men. It was hard for him to use the past tense concerning his friend Hans Rookmaaker, who was ten years younger than Fran and had been a friend and coworker for so many years. Tears flowed unashamedly."[12] The third loss was a fire that gutted the L'Abri chapel and Farel House study area in Huémoz.

Francis Schaeffer's essential analysis of Western civilization, focused in *How Should We Then Live?* had underlying it his threefold emphasis upon the lordship of Christ, the reliability and inerrancy of the Bible, and the necessity for a coherent Christian worldview. Each of the three elements within this emphasis is dynamically interrelated. Many who criticize Schaeffer or who have failed to understand his nuances do not realize this interrelationship. A biography is not the place for an exposition and analysis of Schaeffer's thought, but it can and should point to its development and integrity as an important part of the person. The interrelationship is implicit in the following quotations from *How Should We Then Live?*

> To the Reformation thinkers, authority was not divided between the Bible and the church. The church was *under* the teaching of the Bible—not above it and not equal to it. (82)

> As Christians we are not only to *know* the right world view, the world view that tells us the truth of what *is*, but consciously to *act* upon that world view so as to influence society in all its parts and facets across the whole spectrum of life, as much as we can to the extent of our individual and collective ability. (256)

> This book is written in the hope that this generation may turn from that greatest of wickedness, the placing of any created thing in the place of the Creator, and that this generation may get its feet out of the paths of death and may live. (258)

---

[12]Edith Schaeffer, *Dear Family*, 257. Letter dated May 1, 1977.

A Christian worldview, for Schaeffer, is one that steers us from idolatry and rather centers upon the God "who is there and is not silent," to use Schaefferian terminology. It is not merely theoretical and abstract but necessarily is also existential. We live and do the truth as well as think it and are obliged not to be selective in practicing it. Christ's rule over us is total, demanding that we think and act authentically as well as obediently. The authority of a Christian worldview is derived from the Bible—it is under Scripture rather than equal to it. Elsewhere in his writings, lectures, and biblical expositions, Schaeffer did a great deal of work that concerned the complex relationship between the truth of a Christian worldview and the truth of Scripture. He focuses on the relationship particularly clearly in his appendix to *The Church Before the Watching World*, "Some Absolute Limits," where he gives examples of scriptural boundaries[13] or borders within which there is great freedom of movement—a principle of having both form and freedom. Because of this necessity of scriptural control over thinking, a control that allows proper freedom for our humanity, it was important to defend biblical authority (hence Schaeffer's long-standing concern with inerrancy as a concomitant of working out the lordship of Christ in a Christian worldview). Significantly when he prepared the five volumes of his *Complete Works* in 1981, he subtitled them "A Christian Worldview." Just before he started the revision he told me:

> [The move into filmmaking was] a very natural extension, because back in the earlier books I've got a tremendous emphasis, as you know, upon the lordship of Christ in the whole of life. I was one of the first evangelical writers to speak of the meaning of Christianity in music and art and philosophy and these things. But as time went on, and I emphasized increasingly the lordship of Christ, it became obvious that the battlegrounds were not only the cultural ones and the intellectual ones but in the area of law. So with *How Should We Then Live?* I used the Supreme Court ruling in the United States on abortion as an illustration of arbitrary law and arbitrary medicine, and then in *Whatever Happened to the Human Race?* we really extended that. So there's never been any great decision, just each thing has followed after

---

[13]Schaeffer sometimes employed the term "boundary conditions" when referring to the "form" of Scripture, a term he borrowed from the sciences.

the other. . . . I'm only interested in an apologetic that leads in two directions, and the one is to lead people to Christ, as Savior, and the other is that after they are Christians, for them to realize the lordship of Christ in the whole of life.[14]

In the context of the debate about biblical inerrancy at that time among evangelicals he commented:

It is hard to put this into words, and yet I think it is crucial. I think there are many Christians—I mean, real Christians, real brothers and sisters in Christ, people I'm really fond of—who believe that certain things in the Christian faith are true, and yet, somehow or other, never relate this to *truth*. I don't know if it comes across, what I'm trying to say, but I believe it's truth—and not just religious truth, but the truth of what is. This gives you a different perspective.[15]

With Franky's persuasion, the final episode of *How Should We Then Live?* discussed the pivotal decision in January 1973 by the Supreme Court to assign the right of abortion in the first three months of pregnancy to every woman in the United States. Fran discussed this as an example of an "arbitrary absolute" of increasingly authoritarian government. It marked for him a speedy devaluation of the human being. The same being who after birth is seen in wholly materialistic terms is ruled to be only fetal tissue in the earliest stages of life. The three-month line was drawn arbitrarily he felt, both in medical and legal terms, by the elitist Supreme Court.[16]

The question of abortion, up to then seen by evangelicals largely as a Roman Catholic issue, was about to enter their consciousness in a big way. The process, begun in *How Should We Then Live?*, escalated with a visit by Fran's old friend C. Everett "Chick" Koop to Huémoz in 1977. Koop was a leading pediatric surgeon who later under President Ronald Reagan became Surgeon General. He had become known internationally for his pioneering surgery separating Siamese twins. He had become opposed to abortion, infanticide, and euthanasia as a matter of conscience and had written on the subject, *The Right*

---

[14]Interview with Francis Schaeffer, 1980.
[15]Ibid.
[16]Francis Schaeffer, *How Should We Then Live?*, 218ff.

to Live, Right to Die (1976). In the early days of the Schaeffers' move
to Switzerland he had helped arrange medical care for the children,
especially that of Franky after he had been partially crippled by polio.
Many years later, during a visit to Huémoz, he addressed L'Abri students about his concerns, and Franky involved him in the new movie
project. Koop remembers:

> An elegantly moustached young man standing at the door introduced
> himself to me as Frankie. I could hardly believe that my patient from
> long ago, the little boy whose foot had been so seriously hobbled by
> polio, had become a young man with barely a trace of his earlier dis-
> ability. He said something rather cryptic, which I did not appreciate
> at the time: "If you can talk as well as you can write, I think there are
> some things we can do together."
>
> After I had addressed the students Frankie and I walked up the
> Alpine paths to the next village and then back to Huémoz, stopping
> briefly for hot chocolate at a roadside stand, discussing all the while
> the possibilities of doing something significant about the issues of abor-
> tion, infanticide, and euthanasia. Late that evening we sat in front of
> his fireplace and scribbled down the scenario for five motion pictures
> and the outline for a book, the entire project to be known as *Whatever
> Happened to the Human Race?* Together, the Schaeffers—father and
> son—and I determined to awaken the evangelical world—and anyone
> else who would listen—to the Christian imperative to do something
> to reverse the perilous realignment of American values on these life-
> and-death issues.[17]

Unlike the first film series, which was funded by Gospel Films, the
second series was the responsibility of a new company set up by Franky,
in conjunction with Jim Buchfuehrer, a talented producer. It was called
Franky Schaeffer V Productions, Inc. Jim and Frank raised all the
money, forming a dependence upon a rapidly growing and cohering
Christian Right. In *Crazy for God* Frank paints an acerbic picture of the
unusual bedfellows they acquired in the fund-raising. Gospel Films was
signed up as the distributor. Frank neatly summed up the impact of the
movies on the evangelical world in *Crazy for God*:

---

[17]C. Everett Koop, M.D., *Koop: The Memoirs of America's Family Doctor* (New York: Random
House, 1991).

The impact of our two film series, as well as their companion books, was to give the evangelical community a frame of reference through which to understand the secularization of American culture, and to point to the "human life issue" as the watershed between a "Christian society" and a utilitarian relativistic "post-Christian" future stripped of compassion and beauty.[18]

Its appeal was wider than the evangelicals. Appealing to a less defined "Moral Majority," the second series particularly was designed to encourage action from like-minded groups or "co-belligerents" (they might be Mormon as well as fundamentalist, Reformed evangelical as well as Roman Catholic) prepared not to be motivated by "personal peace and affluence"—a deadly and widespread mentality identified by Schaeffer that would, he was convinced, tolerate authoritarian government, even where it legislated abortion and, in all likelihood, euthanasia and infanticide. Some concerned citizens might even be willing to practice civil disobedience, as enjoined by a follow-up book, *A Christian Manifesto* (1981). Schaeffer commented in *How Should We Then Live?*: "To make no decision in regard to the growth of authoritarian government is already a decision for it."[19]

Whatever Happened to the Human Race?, *How Should We Then Live?*, and *A Christian Manifesto* substantially helped create a new Evangelical Right in America. Certainly, joining the pro-life lobby identified Schaeffer with America's Religious Right, which was able to exercise considerable political clout during the Reagan era. The German magazine *Der Spiegel* described him in a major feature in 1983 as "the philosopher of the Moral Majority,"[20] an ayatollah of the Scriptures, an uncanny saint who had a cult-like following. Fran saw the books and movies as in continuity with his earlier vision (see the 1980 interview in Appendix A), even when he strongly attacked the "middle-class church."[21] His views on the "death of the West" earlier and during his last years of political activism were not in his thinking an abandon-

---

[18]Frank Schaeffer, *Crazy for God*, 273.
[19]Francis Schaeffer, *How Should We Then Live?*, 257.
[20]Peter Brügge, "'Wie Besitz zu teilen ware, sagt die Bibel nicht': Peter Brügge über Francis A. Schaeffer, den Philosophen von Amerikas 'Moralischer Mehrheit,'" in *Der Spiegel*, May 16, 1983, 192–199.
[21]See Francis A. Schaeffer, "The Problem of the Middle-class Church in the Latter Half of the Twentieth Century," in *The Francis Schaeffer Trilogy* (Wheaton, IL: Crossway Books, 1990), 189–193.

ment of cultural participation in favor of a Christian subculture or the takeover of a society by a theocracy. He lived in hope of real change in mainstream culture. In his *Whatever Happened to the Human Race?* the opening analogy of the fall of Rome—paralleling the decline of the West—referred to a culture that eventually returned to life. It was not a doomsday scenario. At the time, he may have felt, the new Right was a co-belligerent, not an ally in the battle for the human, though he saw many in the Right as allies. In the context of siding with Roman Catholics over the abortion issue, Schaeffer commented in an interview with two British journalists:

> I have two words which I would recommend to anybody . . . and they are "ally" and "co-belligerent." An ally is a person who is a born-again Christian with whom I can go a long way down the road . . . now I don't say to the very end, because I'm a Presbyterian and I might not be able to form a church with a strong Baptist . . . but we can go a long way down the road—and that's an ally. A co-belligerent is a person who may not have any sufficient basis for taking the right position but takes the right position on a single issue. And I can join with him without any danger as long as I realize that he is not an ally and all we're talking about is a single issue.[22]

In answer to a question of clarification Schaeffer agreed "absolutely" that this meant he could be working with co-belligerents against his allies.[23]

Schaeffer saw the 1980 election of Ronald Reagan, with his openly pro-life views, as a unique opportunity for political change, with an ultimate purpose of rehabilitating a human-friendly worldview.

> With this [the conservative swing] there is at this moment a unique window open in the United States. . . . And let us hope that the window stays open, and not just one issue, even one as important as human life. . . . [A]s we work and pray . . . we should be struggling and praying that this whole other total entity—the material-energy, chance world view—can be rolled back with all its results across all of life.[24]

---

[22]Martin Wroe and Dave Roberts, "Dr Francis Schaeffer," in Stewart Henderson, ed. and comp., *Adrift in the 80's: the Strait Interviews* (Basingstoke, UK: Marshall Morgan and Scott, 1986), 31.
[23]Ibid.
[24]Francis Schaeffer, *A Christian Manifesto*, in *Complete Works*, Vol. 5: *A Christian View of the West*

He had always been a Republican voter, but here he was not making a party political point, even though it has been taken as such. For one thing, he knew from his experience at L'Abri and long exposure to European culture that the American political system was just one of a variety of robust democracies across Western nations. Like the British Empire, it may not last forever. Furthermore, he believed that the principles set out in *A Christian Manifesto*, although written specifically for Americans, could be transposed into many different political situations. He felt a responsibility, for instance, for Christians in the then USSR who might act on the principle of civil disobedience that he propounded and have to bear the cost of such action. He also worried that Christians with a "socialistic" political approach might wrongly apply the principles: "we should clearly recognize that those who do confuse the Kingdom of God with a socialistic program could misuse this book."[25] He furthermore clearly warned his fellow Americans, "We must not confuse the Kingdom of God with our country. To say it another way: 'We should not wrap Christianity in our national flag.'"[26]

Daymon Johnson, a historian at Bakersfield College, California, has analyzed Francis Schaeffer's enormous impact upon the New Christian Right in the 1980s. He focused particularly upon Schaeffer's impact upon Christian fundamentalists.

> While Schaeffer shared with the separatists a fundamentalistic theology, he came to differ from them in a number of important respects. . . . He believed salvation was dependent not only on accepting the fundamentals as true, but on a "life of love" as well. He rejected the idea that the Bible forbade cooperation with unbelievers in a common cause, and he was a severe critic of the pietistic tendencies of many separatists. As a result . . . Francis A. Schaeffer became one of the major intellectual and spiritual forces behind the New Christian Right during [the] 1980s.[27]

(Wheaton, IL: Crossway Books, 1982), 457.
[25]Ibid., 488.
[26]Ibid., 485–486.
[27]Daymon A. Johnson, *Francis A. Schaeffer: An Analysis of His Religious, Social, and Political Influence on the New Christian Right*, M.A. Thesis in History, California State University, 1990, 17. Here, however, he misrepresents Schaeffer's view of salvation, which is by faith alone. Schaeffer did hold centrally, however, the absolute necessity for obeying Christ's command to love in every aspect of life.

While acknowledging the complexity of Christian fundamentalism in America he concludes:

> Schaeffer was an important, perhaps the most important, intellectual and spiritual [force] behind evangelical social and political activism during the 1970s and 1980s. Whereas conservative Christians once separated from American culture, in the 70s and 80s they made their religious, social, and political presence known.[28]

According to Johnson, among influencers on the Right who claimed Schaeffer as inspiration over co-belligerency were Cal Thomas, Jerry Falwell, and Randall Terry of the controversial Operation Rescue, which had support from rabbis and Roman Catholics. Falwell through his media network distributed over 62,000 copies of *A Christian Manifesto*.

Johnson's assessment is in accord with a general perception of Schaeffer's impact upon the Right. John W. Whitehead worked closely with Fran during the final years and founded the influential Rutherford Institute. Looking back over a quarter of a century Whitehead concludes:

> Without the influence of Francis Schaeffer, who often was prodded into action by [his son] Frank, the so-called Christian Right of today would not exist. Dr. Schaeffer's groundbreaking books *How Should We Then Live?* and *Whatever Happened to the Human Race?* set the tone and agenda for the emerging Christian Right. And without the philosophical groundwork laid by these books and *A Christian Manifesto*—for which I served as Francis Schaeffer's research assistant—it is highly unlikely that people such as Pat Robertson, Jerry Falwell, James Dobson, Tim LaHaye and others would have had the political influence they wield. This despite the fact that much of what comes out of the mouths of these people would today alarm Francis Schaeffer.[29]

Both Fran and his collaborator C. Everett Koop found the process of making the five-part series of *Whatever Happened to the*

---

[28]Ibid., 83.
[29]John W. Whitehead, "Crazy for God: An Interview with Frank Schaeffer," in *oldSpeak: an online journal devoted to intellectual freedom*, The Rutherford Institute, 2007; http://www.rutherford.org/Oldspeak/Articles/Interviews/oldspeak-frankschaeffer.html.

Human Race? a grueling, all-consuming process. Koop recalls, in his
Memoirs:

> The entire project, including writing the book, filming the five movies,
> and holding seminars demanded most of my time for a year and a half.
> I continued to carry a full load at the hospital when I was there, but I
> referred the tough cases that required close and long-term follow-up
> to my colleagues. . . .
>
>   We started filming a sequence about the frail elderly and euthanasia
> in a cemetery in Queens, only a few miles from where I had grown up,
> then moved on to sites throughout America, Europe, and the Middle
> East, wherever art, history, or dramatic sequence could enhance our
> effort. There were several episodes associated with the filming that will
> live forever in my mind. In one scene, I stood on a little island in the
> Dead Sea surrounded by a thousand dolls floating in that very buoy-
> ant salty water, each doll representing a thousand abortions of unborn
> babies. We chose the site of Sodom and Gomorrah in the Dead Sea as
> a place of destruction.[30]

Filming began in August 1978, and by September 18 they had finished a scene about the newly risen Christ beside the Sea of Galilee as
part of the last episode. Of that final part Fran remarked: "It is the best
presentation of the gospel I have ever been able to make." On the final
day of shooting the film in October, Edith noticed that Fran's coat was
much too large for him. Fran, Edith, and the film crew at that time were
back in Switzerland. His rapid weight loss had become noticeable over
recent days. A call to the Mayo Clinic in Rochester, Minnesota, resulted
in a recommendation that Fran go there within days, which meant hasty
arrangements, including renewing Fran's just-expired passport. When
Fran and Edith were met at the Rochester International Airport on
Tuesday, October 10, they found that the welcoming party included two
friends from the Clinic, Dr. Victor Wahby and Dr. Carl Morlock. Fran
was told that tests were arranged for the very next day. Fran was found
to have a tumor the size of a football, as a result of lymphoma. After he
heard the results of the biopsy of a swollen neck gland, he phoned his
children in turn to tell them, "The gland is malignant, and the lymph

---

[30]Koop, *Memoirs*, 267.

system is involved." Chemotherapy treatment began in the nick of time, on October 17. It was necessary for them to live near the Clinic, and accommodation was found in a small apartment.

While Fran was undergoing chemotherapy, a new L'Abri property, long planned, was bought in Southborough, Massachusetts, with the intention that Dick and Mardi Keyes, a highly gifted couple, would lead it. At that time they were workers at English L'Abri, in Greatham Manor House, near Petersfield. Before long, a second L'Abri property, established as the American headquarters, was set up in Rochester, allowing Fran's presence there to be utilized while being treated. That meant that seminars in America on both film series could continue. In March 1979 Fran was given the welcome news that his cancer was in remission. He wrote to me on August 1 that year:

> I am sure you know that I have cancer of the lymph glands. When I went to Mayo in October I did not know how ill I was but have since found out! Incidentally, in a very providential way I was able to finish the very last work on the film *Whatever Happened to the Human Race?* just literally a couple [of] days before I left for Mayo Clinic. I was there in Rochester for five months with Edith, and you will be glad to know that the last two extensive tests showed no signs of malignancy in my body. How good it is to have a theology in which there is no tension between using the best medicine possible and looking directly to the Lord for answer to prayer.[31]

The remission lasted for many months, but by the end of that year he was having to take chemotherapy again, but this time by mouth, which allowed greater flexibility, even allowing Fran to continue living in Switzerland. On one occasion he participated in a large pro-life rally in Hyde Park, London, along with John Stott, and Malcolm Muggeridge, which was followed by a march to Trafalgar Square.

Less than two years after the cancer was discovered, I asked Fran about the impact of the affliction. We met near English L'Abri, based in Greatham, and were served cups of tea by Edith. As he spoke, he was suffering from an infection in his right arm. Had the knowledge

---

[31]Francis Schaeffer, unpublished letter to Colin Duriez, August 1, 1979, from Chalet le Chardonnet, Chèsieres, Switzerland.

of the lymphoma, the physical pressures, and the fact that his time was now limited very much affected the way he worked? Had he retired from the main L'Abri work? Did he prefer one-to-one contact with people of the earlier L'Abri days rather than the large seminars of the present time?

> Today it's just about two years since I knew. There's no doubt in my mind that I have been able to work as hard since I've known I had the lymphoma as I have in my whole life. I've been very fortunate. I count it a gift of God that I've not had the really terrible effects of chemotherapy that a lot of people have. I'm on chemotherapy right now, but it's certainly not cut down my productivity, and I'm thankful. I don't think it's made a huge difference. The fact that I've gone on, by the grace of the Lord, and done as much having cancer has been an encouragement, I think, to a lot of people. Many have said that they have been very much encouraged to push on in their own problems. And out of it the Lord gave Edith and myself so many open doors in Rochester, Minnesota, that we've opened a branch of L'Abri there. . . .
>
> It was rather humorous really. When I got to Mayo Clinic I was amazed at how many of the doctors had already read our books and knew something about them. The doctors would always say, "Now you're here to get well and not to work," which was inevitably followed by, "but" something. This time it was, "but will you show two episodes of *How Should We Then Live?* every Sunday night and then lead a discussion, with mics on the floor?" I didn't know if I could do it, because I was right in the middle of the most strenuous part of the chemotherapy. But we prayed about it, and I decided to. They thought there might be two or three hundred people turn up. That first night there were 1,500, at 27 below Fahrenheit and windy. At first it was mostly students who were asking questions, but at the end doctors were asking them. The door was so wide-open that a number of Christians in the town, doctors and others, came and asked, "Would you consider doing more here in Rochester?"
>
> I suggested we have a L'Abri conference there, and we did this in June [1980] or thereabouts. We had two thousand people there from all over the United States and Canada. Because it went so well L'Abri decided then to open a branch there. What we've done is close our branch in Los Gatos [California], and now we're going to use Rochester as our business office. But we're praying that the

Lord will use it also not just among people in general, but to show us if we can somehow get to patients who come there from all over the world. I have to go back there the rest of my life, of course, for examinations.

. . . they've shifted the treatment. Now I'm taking it all by mouth, so I can take it anywhere; so I took it here [in England] actually. It really does [make it easier]. But the other side is that you have to keep going back [to Rochester] to make sure your blood count is all right. (Then you do get viral infections just like this crazy thing in my arm. I'm sure I wouldn't have got that if it wasn't for the lowered resistance because of the chemotherapy.) It means that when Edith and I go back to Rochester we then can work in that branch exactly as we do when we come here to Greatham or to Holland or the other [L'Abri] places. There's something very good in all this. We're very happy about it.

I consider [Swiss L'Abri] our home. I've never retired. When I started making the films, most of the emphasis went into that and then the seminars [rather] than the day-by-day work in Switzerland. We have our own home there, and we provide leadership for the thing. Our work has changed, but [we are] in no sense retired. The fact is, if this is being retired I find it a bit amusing.

I like to talk one to one, but I found out that if you have a seminar with five thousand people, and you have mics on the floor, it is possible to have a feeling of intimacy in spite of the big crowd. I certainly don't have the feeling [that] I am simply lecturing to a faceless mass of people. When a person asks me questions from the floor in a discussion, I answer that person as intimately as I would in my living room.

When we had the first seminars in the States of *How Should We Then Live?* everybody said it can't be done, nobody's ever done it. But I didn't feel that. I had the impression that most people didn't feel that it was an abstract sort of relationship. Most of them felt pretty close—at least, I hope that is the case. Afterward I often look up a person who's a bit aggressive in his presentation. In that way you sort of bridge the gap between the one-to-one and the larger groups.

I think it's your attitude [that is crucial]. I say [this] very carefully: I think my ability to answer questions is a gift of God, I really do. When the fact bothered me that for so many years my work was basically one-to-one, conversation in my bedroom, or in some university setting, I would just say: Never take for granted my answer to a question. Now I keep praying that I continue to have this gift, either personally one-to-one or in a group, as long as the Lord wants me to continue. People feel your attitudes, and I don't think you can put this on, as a trick. I'm not saying I'm perfect in any of these things. But I think that if you're struggling for empathy, for human relationships, not acting as though you are the guru, and not standing higher than they are, I am convinced that there is such a thing as a mentality that comes across. If God gives you this then you say, "Thank you for the gift." That's all.[32]

As we parted after that interview we warmly shook hands, both forgetting his infected arm. A stab of pain twisted his face, but he instantly recovered. After the farewells I never saw him again. Shortly afterward, he commenced work on revising his books for inclusion in the five-volume *Complete Works*, completing the work in 1982. The seminars continued as Fran continued to fight the cancer. Late in 1983 he had to return from Switzerland to the Mayo Clinic, but once more he pulled through for a brief period of activity, including seminars.

As well as the activism of his last years, months, and even weeks, Schaeffer continued to be exercised about the issue of the authority and inerrancy of the Bible. This was an issue that he had never felt able to leave since the days of the great Gresham Machen's resistance to modernism in the mainstream Presbyterian denomination, including Princeton Seminary. His final statement on the unfinished battle for the Bible, composed with his dying energy, was the book *The Great Evangelical Disaster*.

Written with the help of his publisher and friend Lane Dennis and corrected as one of his last tasks, the book is a prophetic warning against evangelical accommodation to the world spirit of the time. Dennis did much of the work on the manuscript, including construction of the notes, while Fran was critically ill with a resurgence of the cancer during the last part of 1983 and early 1984, nearly two months in all. To counter any unintended element of harshness, Fran included as an appendix the text from his seminal booklet, *The Mark of the Christian*, emphasizing the priority of Christ's command to love. He concludes:

> We need a revolutionary message in the midst of today's relativistic thinking. By revolutionary, or radical, I mean standing against the all-

---

[32]Interview with Francis Schaeffer, 1980. See Appendix.

pervasive form which the world spirit has taken in our day. This is the
real meaning of radical. . . .

   As we have now come to the famed year 1984, what we need in
the light of the accommodation about us is a generation of radicals
for truth and for Christ. . . . Evangelicalism has done many things for
which we can be greatly thankful. But a mentality of accommodation
is indeed a disaster. . . .

   If there is not loving confrontation . . . and if we do not have the
courage to draw lines even when we wish we did not have to, then
history will look back at this time when certain "evangelical colleges"
went the way of Harvard and Yale, when certain "evangelical semi-
naries" went the way of Union Seminary in New York, and the time
when other "evangelical organizations" were lost to Christ's cause—
forever.[33]

It has been suggested that his activity in the "battle for the Bible,"
including his helping found the International Council on Biblical Inerrancy
(1977), was his separatism reemerging.[34] But for Schaeffer the battle lines
were not drawn around the inerrancy of Scripture as such. Such a position could be held coldly, without love. Rather, for him, the watershed
issue was *obeying* the Bible. It was directly linked to acknowledging the
lordship of Christ and to the authority of a distinctly Christian worldview,
within the boundaries of Scripture, a worldview that was relevant to our
day. Fran had seen that he could credibly present such a worldview to
cultural shapers such as Dr. Timothy Leary, who made a point of visiting
L'Abri in Switzerland, and the anguished Bishop James A. Pike, who had
tried to contact his dead son via a medium. According to Frank Schaeffer,
Jimmy Page of the Led Zeppelin rock band had been given a copy of
Escape from Reason by Eric Clapton.[35] Actors, painters, rock musicians,
scholars of many disciplines, journalists, media people were attracted to
L'Abri in a period when church and Christianity was (and still is) unat-
tractive. This does not mean, of course, that all were convinced.

---

[33]Francis A. Schaeffer, *The Great Evangelical Disaster* (Wheaton, IL: Crossway Books, 1984),
149–151.
[34]This point has been argued by Forrest Baird in Ronald Ruegsegger, *Reflections on Francis Schaeffer*
(Grand Rapids, MI: Zondervan, 1986), 64.
[35]Frank Schaeffer, *Crazy for God* (New York: Carroll & Graf, 2007), 211. Frank may be mistaken in his
memories here—he is at times in error over fact or interpretation elsewhere in his unashamedly subjective
and at times bizarre memoir. This sort of thing *could have happened,* however.

Francis Schaeffer's stance on inerrancy does not imply that we have to read the Bible in a wooden, uneducated way. It is true, he argues, that where Scripture touches on the cosmos—that is, where it puts a control on scientific investigation by imparting true knowledge about nature—there are absolute limits; but within those limits there is enormous freedom. The very honesty of his approach in *Genesis in Space and Time* frees him from the restrictions, for instance, of young-earth creationism, though he is undoubtedly a creationist.[36] It follows from his view that evangelical scientists who speculate that God may have created the physical part of our being through biological evolution (the view of B. B. Warfield of "Old" Princeton) are free at least to hypothesize and investigate. On the other hand, Schaeffer emphasizes strongly that modern science was founded on the presuppositions so clearly set forth in early Genesis. And he courageously defines the absolute limits. Without the actual sin of a real first man and woman in history, he reasons, for example, there is no ultimate explanation of the problem of evil. The existence of evil on earth is in fact a dramatic demonstration of the significance of human beings: the choices of Adam and Eve at the beginning of human time have shaped history to the present day. Without a fall of humankind our present world is morally normal rather than abnormal, and therefore God's judgment of the world is either meaningless or arbitrary. Evil is then a permanent part of the universe, as in gnosticism, rather than temporary, as in Judeo-Christianity (though it follows that its consequences continue to be real; Christ has marks of his death on his resurrected body).

The open nature of Schaeffer's inerrantist view of the Bible is demonstrated in his stance on eschatology. Though he was a thoroughgoing premillennialist, he treated this position as of secondary rather than of primary importance in his relations with fellow Christians. His interactions were unaffected by disagreements about the Millennium. In his own mind he was convinced that a proper emphasis upon Christ's total salvation of the human being—the integral, embodied person— was weakened by not holding to a premillennialist understanding,

---

[36]Francis A. Schaeffer, *Genesis in Space and Time* (Downers Grove, IL: InterVarsity Press, 1972).

according to his daughter Deborah.[37] The absolute limit in this case
would be (following Schaeffer's logic) the biblical teaching that Christ
will return on an actual day in the future and will rule in the physical
universe, though we cannot know the timing in advance. Eschatology
is not a trivial point—in the period of Schaeffer's ecclesiastical separatism, premillennialism was a defining principle of his breakaway
denomination's stance. In contrast, his later deep friendship with
Rookmaaker was unaffected by their sharply contrasting views on the
book of Revelation.

In the six years of his cancer his children took turns looking after
him, helping the ever-attentive Edith. After being out of action for seven
weeks because of the ravishes of his cancer, Fran in early spring 1984
mustered the strength to make a thirteen-city tour lecturing on the
disaster of evangelical accommodation. Sometimes he was so weak that
he was borne by stretcher to the location. There was no doubt of his
conviction and authenticity.

Throughout the closing of his life and to the very end Fran continued to display a fierce opposition to the idea of quietly accepting death.
Perhaps the poignant words of Dylan Thomas he had quoted so feel-
ingly in *The God Who Is There* resonated with him, though he would
not embrace Dylan's despair:

Do not go gentle into that good night . . .

For him as for St. Paul, death was the last enemy. The sundering
of spirit and body was for him an evil, the effect of the ancient fall. He
fought to stay alive, even wishing at the very end for his chemotherapy
to continue, conscious that he had much left to do and to say. His unac-
ceptance of death did not at all contradict his clinging to the truth of his
faith in what Christ had done on the cross. His passion for life—physical, bodily life—was part of his passion for God, who had guaranteed
the hope of resurrection as the key to fully restored relationship with
him. His struggle was not the opposite of faith.

Deborah felt at the time, as she was with him, that his attitude

---

[37]Telephone conversation between Deborah Middelmann and Colin Duriez, February 2008.

toward death actually helped those who were caring for him. His dying reflected the way that he had lived, through his early years as a pastor, then as a missionary, and then in his pastoral work with L'Abri. She attempted to summarize his whole attitude to death—and life:

> His view of death and his own death was having confidence that life matters and that the world matters, that life and existence is something real, true and eternal and is not going to just disappear into thin air. Because of that you fight to live, and because of that you need to go out and carry on the good fight. You do matter, and God does exist. So you put your hand to the plow, you work and you struggle—you do what you can in all different areas, with passion. You don't sit in a corner somewhere and wait to die. You don't embrace death. You see death as a terrible, terrible enemy. What you look forward to is not death, but the Second Coming. You are longing and working for that. Contrary to what people say—that you can't take anything with you—yes, you do take your work with you. It's a biblical teaching, that what you do matters and will continue on into eternity—building houses, walls, and hiking paths and the whole of human existence. You live with energy.[38]

In the final days he was brought from the hospital to his Rochester home to die in familiar surroundings. A bird feeder was set up by the window so he could enjoy seeing the creatures. As he went in and out of consciousness he had hallucinating dreams. Susan, his daughter, came from England, joining her sister Deborah and arriving days before his death. She remembered:

> Once he said to us, "I'm late, I'm late, I'm going to miss the plane. Where are my notes?" I said to him, "Dad." His eyes then cleared—he had beautiful brown eyes—totally focused. "Dad, you are not going to speak." He said, "I have to do it." "No," I said, "you're going to rest—you're finished with that. You've left people, you've left books, and you've left the teaching." I used to hike with him, and I felt as if I was hiking with him to a mountain pass. He was dying and [in his last days and hours when able he] kept saying a psalm, a Psalm of Ascent, where they were trusting in the Lord's grace, trusting in him. He held on to it like a person holding on to a climbing rope. When he'd come

[38]Interview with Udo and Debby Middelmann, 2007.

in and out of consciousness he would be saying that. I thought, "He's going up; I'm not going to go over the top with him." But it was very faith-strengthening. There were several [occasions] when he was much more lucid, and once I said, "Is it true?"—what a thing to say to a dying person—and he said, "It is absolutely true, absolutely sure."[39]

Concerning the day of his death on May 15, Edith wrote: "It was 4 A.M. precisely that a soft last breath was taken . . . and he was absent. That absence was so sharp and precise."[40]

Large numbers attended his memorial service in Rochester, Minnesota. Tributes came from the small and the great, including a personally written note from the President of the United States, Ronald Reagan. *Time*, which had reported his "mission to intellectuals" in 1960, recorded less than a quarter of a century later: "DIED. Francis Schaeffer, 72, Christian theologian and a leading scholar of evangelical Protestantism; of cancer; in Rochester, Minn. Schaeffer, a Philadelphia-born Presbyterian, and his wife in 1955 founded L'Abri (French for "the shelter"), a chalet in the Swiss Alps known among students and intellectuals for a reasoned rather than emotional approach to religious counseling. His 23 philosophical books include the bestseller *How Should We Then Live?* (1976)."[41]

Francis Schaeffer was perhaps best remembered, however, by a statement of Os Guinness, who had lived with the Schaeffer family in L'Abri, Switzerland, and was a close associate. Speaking at a memorial service in All Souls Church, Langham Place, London, Guinness said that the greatest thing about Francis Schaeffer was Francis Schaeffer.[42]

---

[39]Interview with Susan Macaulay, 2007.
[40]Edith Schaeffer, *Dear Family*, 388. Letter dated July 17, 1984.
[41]"Milestones," in *Time*, May 28, 1984; http://www.time.com/time/magazine/article/0,9171,951114-2,00. html.
[42]From notes I made at the occasion on July 25, 1984 and a short, unpublished account I wrote, both in my possession.

APPENDIX

The Undivided Schaeffer:
A Retrospective Interview
with Francis Schaeffer

September 30, 1980

An abridged version of this interview appeared in Third Way *in December 1980, entitled "Francis Schaeffer—Facing Up to the Central Questions." It took place on a sunny day, sitting in a garden in Liss, Hampshire, where the Schaeffers were staying, near English L'Abri. Occasionally the rural peace was broken by the drone of military aircraft flying overhead.*

ඔඔඔඔඔ

Colin Duriez [CD]: Let's take a specific thing—the inerrancy question. There's the whole debate in America, but here [in England] it seems to be a different kind of attitude. People don't seem to want to debate the issue. Does this reveal any basic difference to you?

Francis A. Schaeffer [FAS]: Yes. I would just say that in Britain it raises a question to me as to whether people are ready to take a stand for the things they do believe even if it's costly or if they tend to put a latitudinarian peace at any price above the concept of truth. I think that is the problem. It is a problem for all of us, of course—we all love to be undisturbed. But there has been a history in British evangelicalism of those who hold the historic Christian position not facing up to the central questions, while those on the other side don't hesitate at all to push their positions.

CD: In what context would you place David Winter's book *But*

This I Can Believe where he mentions you in a few places as standing for the inerrancy position? He disagrees with that. He's trying to find a middle way between fundamentalism and liberalism. Do you think he's succeeded?

FAS: No. It's very interesting that when the old rationalists—theological liberals—came to a dead end they moved into what I call the "existential methodology." That is, from Barth onward they tried to say that you could have a Bible with mistakes in it, and yet a religious word broke through. The older theological liberals pressed this; so they went from Barth to Brunner, to Niebuhr to Tillich to the "God is Dead" theology. Just when it has proven bankrupt on the side of the liberals, some evangelicals seem to think that they've found something new, which is a bit curious.

CD: Do you think this is basically a naive view rather than springing from a consistent philosophy?

FAS: I don't think that most theologians, and especially evangelical theologians, are aware to what extent we are infiltrated by the current thought forms around us, unless we take time to understand them, and reject them. This view that David Winter puts forth bears the marks on the secular side of Sartre, Camus, and Heidegger, and on the theological side the marks of Tillich and all that leads to. What would be intriguing if it wasn't so serious is the fact that the people who are putting this forth don't realize that this is not new. Unhappily, it is one more instance of theologians coming along with something a certain amount of time after the secular people have thought it through and thinking they've found something new, when in reality it's already been very commonplace in the general intellectual world.

CD: Do you think part of the problem in Britain has been a lack of philosophical apologetics? In America you've had more of a tradition of a strong apologetic with Van Til and others.

FAS: I don't think that's really the basic problem. I think the basic problem is that England has had a long history of latitudinarianism, both toward liberal theology and, in the Church of England, toward the Tractarian group, which has bred a mentality of latitudinarianism, so that the inherent reaction to any situation is a latitudinarian one rather than the question, what is truth and what isn't truth?

CD: When you wrote *The God Who Is There* you said the question of truth was the central one. Do you still feel that?

FAS: Of course. There is no reason to believe in Christianity if it isn't true. It is hard to put this into words, and yet I think it is crucial. I think there are many Christians—I mean, real Christians, real brothers and sisters in Christ, people I'm really fond of—who believe that certain things in the Christian faith are true, and yet, somehow or other, never relate this to *truth*. I don't know if it comes across, what I'm trying to say, but I believe it's truth—and not just religious truth, but the truth of what is. This gives you a different perspective.

The latitudinarian mentality here has been present a long, long time. There was a time fifteen, twenty years ago when I said frequently that there was more hope in Britain than in the United States because the theological colleges were booming. They had a lot of students; the liberals had very few. Everything seemed to be pushing on for a real evangelical resurgence. After Keele, and especially Nottingham, all this has been deflected. Today I think there is more possibility of a clear line in the United States and that the situation has been reversed in the last fifteen years. Of course, one always has to say that God can do what he will; that always has to be taken into account.

CD: Is this one of the reasons why you, in a sense, have put more effort into America than into Britain since the early seventies?

FAS: Well, partially. Maybe it wasn't that carefully thought through, though. One's finite; one can't do everything. It wasn't that I sat down and said, "I'm not going to spend as much time in Britain." It was simply that there were so many open doors in the United States that I went along in that direction. Now having said that, in regard to all that's occurred in the last years, I wish I could have put in more time in Britain, but I'm not sorry that I put in as much time as I did in the United States.

CD: I can see, from reading your wife's book on L'Abri and from my own experience of L'Abri, that there have been phases. You had a very quiet work, in a sense, as far as publicity was concerned, until the books began to appear in the late sixties; then you had a book period, and now you've chosen to go into films more. Are these deliberate choices or just the way that the Lord opened things up?

FAS: It was the way things developed. When I was working at L'Abri in the early days, I really expected to be talking one to one. In one way this was frustrating, in that I knew that I had answers that the Lord used there that I felt could be used more widely. On the other hand I had no plan for making it wider. I never intended even to make tapes, and the tape program just opened up. It's rather ironic now.

CD: Did it start by accident?

FAS: Somebody sent us a tape recorder, and I said, "I'll never use it. It'll kill the spontaneity of the conversation." The tape recorder must have been in our office for at least six months. Then, one Saturday night, down in our Les Mélèzes living room, we had a really bang-up conversation going with some Smith College girls. I think they were all Jewish, probably, but they certainly all were brilliant. One of our workers came up and said to Edith, "It's a shame this isn't being recorded; it'll be lost. If you'll just make a lot of noise serving tea, I'll hide the microphone in the flowers." I noticed some kind of confusion and wondered what was going on. When I found out later that the conversation had been recorded, I must say I was furious. I felt this was unfair to those girls; they thought it was a private conversation. Then to my amazement every one of the girls was delighted and bought copies of the tape to take home, not only for themselves but for their friends. This opened the tape program: it was as simple as that.

As I lectured in very many places, in Britain, Germany, and the USA, I gradually developed a basic lecture, "Speaking Historic Christianity into the Twentieth-century World." When I gave it at Wheaton College, Illinois, they asked if they could put it out as a small xeroxed book. I said, "Well, only for your students, because I don't want published books." When I saw that, however, and read it over, I realized I had a responsibility to publish. It became *The God Who Is There*.

As the books came out and sold so well—millions, in twenty-five languages—the next thing was that Franky came to me and said, "Dad, you're saying something that most people aren't saying. In order to give what you're saying a wide hearing, would you do a film?" This was a brand-new idea, and I was very reticent. The more I thought and prayed about it, the more I realized that, rather than being a discontinuity, a film is very much a continuity with writing books. Quite frankly, also, I had seen Kenneth Clark's *Civilisation* and felt that he was totally unfair, especially in the "Reformation" episode, so I wanted to counter that in some way. I remember one night in Carmel, California, when I was there for a week's vacation I happened to see this episode, and I said to Edith, "If I ever get a chance to hit that I want to hit it." So when this [chance to film] came along, it just naturally dropped into place.

[The move into filmmaking was] a very natural extension, because back in the earlier books I have a tremendous emphasis, as you know, upon the lordship of Christ in the whole of life. I was one of the first evangelical writers to speak of the meaning of Christianity in music and art and philosophy and these things. But as time went on, and I emphasized increasingly the lordship of Christ, it became obvious that the battlegrounds were not only the cultural ones and the intellectual ones but in the area of law. So with *How Should We Then Live?* I used the Supreme Court ruling in the United States on abortion as an illustration of arbitrary law and arbitrary medicine, and then in *Whatever Happened to the Human Race?* we really extended that. So there's never been any great decision, just each thing has followed after the other.

CD: Are you going to develop that even further and talk more about authoritarian government as the alternative to democracy? You mention how there are fewer and fewer countries that are democratic as the base is being removed.

FAS: I just don't know what I'll be doing. I've no big plans. My next big job is that we're going to the United States to republish the first nineteen books in four hardback copies parallel to the format of *How Should We Then Live?* and *The God Who Is There*. So as soon as I get home that's my next job. I'm going to re-edit the first nineteen books—I thought a lot about that before I agreed. I think that even the first books, *The God Who Is There* and *Escape from Reason*, are more contemporary today than they were twelve years ago, when they were written. So I think this [revision] has value, and then people can have them in permanent form, in six volumes. I don't have any plans after that [smiling].

CD: Has the knowledge of the lymphoma very much affected the way you work—the fact that your time is very limited and that you have these physical pressures?

FAS: Today it's just about two years since I knew. There's no doubt in my mind that I have been able to work as hard since I've known I had the lymphoma as I have in my whole life. I've been very fortunate. I count it a gift of God that I've not had the really terrible effects of chemotherapy that a lot of people have. I'm on chemotherapy right now, but it's certainly not cut down my productivity, and I'm thankful. I don't think it's made a huge difference. The fact that I've gone on, by the grace of the Lord, and done as much having cancer has been an encouragement, I think, to a lot of people. Many have said that they have been very much encouraged to push on in their own problems. And out of it the Lord gave Edith and myself so many open doors in Rochester, Minnesota, that we've opened a branch of L'Abri there.

CD: Is that where the Mayo Clinic is?

FAS: Yes. It was rather humorous really. When I got to Mayo Clinic I was amazed at how many of the doctors had already read our books and knew something about them. The doctors would always say, "Now you're here to get well and not to work," which was inevitably followed by, "but" something. This time it was, "but will you show two episodes of *How Should We Then Live?* every Sunday night and then lead a discussion, with mics on the floor?" I didn't know if I could do it, because I was right in the middle of the most strenuous part of the chemotherapy. But we prayed about it, and I decided to. They thought there might be two or three hundred people turn up. That first night there were 1,500, at 27 below Fahrenheit and windy. At first it was mostly students who were asking questions, but at the end doctors were asking them. The door was so wide-open that a number of Christians in the town, doctors and others, came and asked, "Would you consider doing more here in Rochester?"

I suggested we have a L'Abri conference there, and we did this in June [1980] or thereabouts. We had two thousand people there from all over the United States and Canada. Because it went so well L'Abri decided then to open a branch there. What we've done is close our branch in Los Gatos [California], and now we're going to use Rochester as our business office. But we're praying that the Lord will use it also not just among people in general, but to show us if we can somehow get to patients who come there from all over the world. I have to go back there the rest of my life, of course, for examinations.

CD: How frequently do you have to go?

FAS: It just depends what happens.

CD: Can you have the treatment you're on at the moment anywhere?

FAS: At first I couldn't. Then the last time I was here [in Britain], for a seminar in the spring, I had two courses at the Royal Free Hospital with the professor there, and that went all right. But now I've come to the place where they can't give me the drug any longer, as you can only take so much of this drug or it endangers your heart. My heart is great, but they say they don't want to take a chance. So they've shifted the treatment. Now I'm taking it all by mouth, so I can take it anywhere; so I took it here actually.

CD: Does this make life a lot easier?

FAS: It really does. But the other side is that you have to keep going back [to Rochester] to make sure your blood count is all right. (Then you do get viral infections just like this crazy thing in my arm. I'm sure I wouldn't have got that if it wasn't for the lowered resistance because of the chemotherapy.) It means that when Edith and I go back to Rochester we then can work in that branch exactly as we do when we come here to Greatham or to Holland or the other [L'Abri] places. There's something very good in all this. We're very happy about it.

CD: Do you spend most of your time in Switzerland now? Aren't you in a sense retired from the Swiss L'Abri work?

FAS: I consider [Swiss L'Abri] our home. I've never retired. When I started making the films most of the emphasis went into that and then the seminars [rather] than the day-by-day work in Switzerland. We have our own home there, and we provide leadership for the thing. Our work has changed, but [we are] in no sense retired. The fact is, if this is being retired I find it a bit amusing.

CD: Do you prefer the one-to-one contact? You mentioned how in the beginning of the work it was mainly that. If you had a choice (I know you have to do what the Lord is leading you to do), is that what you really prefer—to get down with somebody with their questions?

FAS: I like to talk one to one, but I found out that if you have a seminar with five thousand people and you have mics on the floor, it is possible to have a feeling of intimacy in spite of the big crowd. I certainly don't have the feeling [that] I am simply lecturing to a faceless mass of people. When a person asks me questions from the floor in a discussion, I answer that person as intimately as I would in my living room.

CD: I noticed at the seminar in London that one person asked a question and you rather pursued him afterward. I don't know whether you managed to catch him . . .

FAS: Yes. I thought that his question demanded a personal contact, especially as he was rather aggressive in his presentation. I wanted him to realize that though I differed with him, this didn't mean I didn't want a human contact with him. When we had the first seminars of *How Should We Then Live?* in the States everybody said it can't be done, nobody's ever done it. But I didn't feel that. I had the impression that most people didn't feel that it was an abstract sort of relationship. Most of them felt pretty close—at least, I hope that is the case. Afterward I often look up a person who's a bit aggressive in his presentation. In that way you sort of bridge the gap between the one-to-one and the larger groups.

CD: Certainly it's very different to actually go hear a person speaking than to see somebody appearing on television.

FAS: I think it's your attitude [that is crucial]. I say [this] very carefully: I think my ability to answer questions is a gift of God, I really do. When the fact bothered me that for so many years my work was basically one-to-one, conversation in my bedroom or in some university setting, I would just say: Never take for granted my answer to a question. Now I keep praying that I continue to have this gift, either personally one-to-one or in a group, as long as the Lord wants me to continue.

People feel your attitudes, and I don't think you can put this on, as a trick. I'm not saying I'm perfect in any of these things. But I think that if you're struggling for empathy, for human relationships, not acting as though you are the guru, and not standing higher than they are, I am convinced that there is such a thing as a mentality that comes across. If God gives you this then you say, "Thank you for the gift." That's all.

CD: You partly answered this before, but do you think looking at the sixties, when there was the counterculture developing, and looking now that things are more complicated to analyze culturally, or do you feel that the same principles are working out? Did you, for example, feel any excitement at what was happening in the late sixties, when people seemed to be seeking an alternative to a sort of Western status quo, or did you see it as yet another demonstration of the underlying concept of truth?

FAS: I feel that I'm right in *How Should We Then Live?* in making Berkeley very crucial. If Christ doesn't come back, my hope is that Christians would keep in mind the pivotal aspects of Berkeley. I don't think you can understand the seventies and eighties without understanding the sixties. Several generations had been taught by their university professors and had come across in the media a shift in the materialistic consensus into meaninglessness. In the sixties, as I see it, this came across. The difference was that the previous professors largely had taught this but not lived it, and suddenly the kids took it out into the streets. From that point on in the sixties you should see them as optimistic, either through Marcuse's New Left or through drugs. They thought that in either one of these two, or in combination, they were really going to be able to change society positively. Then by the time you get to the seventies this hope was all gone, I think. The Paris marches and all these things were optimistic.

CD: And the seventies?

FAS: The shift, as I see it, is into a basic feeling of just the need to live, after the hopes were gone. The seventies are marked by personal peace and affluence. This personal peace has nothing to do with Christian peace. It is the me generation saying, "Just let me alone," with the narcissistic aspects that various people have pointed out.

When people stopped revolting in the universities I think that a great number of people, including a great number of Christians, heaved a great sigh of relief. I did, in one way, but in another way I was very sad, because then these kids joined the system, not because they believed in it, but just because it was their own way to have personal peace and affluence. You can see it in the drug culture as an illustration. In the sixties the taking of drugs was an ideology, it really was. Beginning in the seventies, drugs became what they always were traditionally: a way of escape. In the sixties the kids wouldn't touch alcohol. They felt that it was very bourgeois, very middle-class. Drugs were the big thing. By the seventies they were both taking drugs and getting drunk. This was just an illustration.

Personal peace and affluence, I think, is really the mark of the seventies. Now what the eighties will be, is hard to tell.

CD: In an interview, Os Guinness suggested that the key idea in the eighties might be the idea of survival, survival at any cost. Certainly it is a word that's coming up a lot.

FAS: I would stress again what I stressed in *How Should We Then Live?*—that as the pressures of inflation, threat of atomic war, all these things increase, those who are facing them are people who only want personal peace and affluence. If you put it in that framework, then I think *survival* is a great word. As long as they can have these things, they will give up anything!

CD: Twenty years or so ago there was a big emphasis upon nuclear war. Then along came Vietnam. There is now a revival in the CND movement (Campaign for Nuclear Disarmament), and now END (European Nuclear Disarmament). Do you think the threat of nuclear war is any more real now than it was then?

FAS: Yes. I don't know what's ahead of us. I'm sure that Russia is more expansionist than it ever was, that they've never changed their direction, and that detente to them was only a tool for expansionism.

CD: So you take Solzhenitsyn's analysis of them?

FAS: His analysis and mine would be similar. Afghanistan is a natural direction. Europeans who think they can live at peace in Europe with Russia while watching what is happening in Afghanistan are naive. My personal opinion is (and I talk to many men in political fields about this) that, of course, we have to be wise and show a geopolitical sense. But having said that, the threat of war will become actualized at the moment in which Russia feels that it is to their advantage.

CD: So you feel they hold the cards.

FAS: There's no doubt about it. They have the power. But, of course, they have their own internal weaknesses too, and nobody knows how all that is going to come out.

CD: Are you surprised they haven't done anything about Poland? Or perhaps it's a bit soon.

FAS: I think it's a bit soon, but they would have done something about Poland, I think, if they weren't engulfed in Afghanistan. If I were in their leaders' position, I would have some uneasy nights. After all, the West let them bring over Cuban troops to Angola and do what they wanted to do in Ethiopia, and suddenly in Afghanistan they must have been very surprised at the outcry. Then to have Poland erupt just at that moment must have led to a very uneasy situation. They are in trouble in Afghanistan; in all probability they would have intervened in Poland if it had not been for that. I don't know of anybody among the people I talk to in the State Department who doesn't feel that Russia's coming to the peak of its power in balancing military power against economic problems, sometime rather soon. That is the danger to the rest of the world. Of course, if they move into Poland, the West doesn't want to do anything about it.

CD: Recently among Christians there's been an emphasis upon pacifism, and much thought about the Just War by those of us who aren't pacifists. John Stott has recently come out and said that over, say, the use of nuclear weapons the pacifist position and the just war position can coincide, because the weapons would so much involve civilians, non-combatants, as a feature of modern war. What are your views on the use of nuclear weapons?

FAS: One could wish, of course, that they had never been discovered, but it's a fact of life that they exist. I think the rather leftist Christians in the United States—and maybe in this country too, I don't know—calling for unilateral disarmament, for example, are totally naive. We live in a fallen world. Considering Russia's very clear inclinations, to call for unilateral disarmament would be, to my mind, folly in the geopolitical situation we face. I hope, of course, that we never see the use of atomic weapons. But two things must be said. As far as the individual is concerned, he's just as dead with the bow and arrow as he is with atomic weapons. The other thing is that, undoubtedly, nations without much restraint or balance are going to have nuclear weapons within, say, the next fifteen years, and then anything could happen.

CD: So then the deterrence theory just won't work anymore?

FAS: Think of some of the black African dictatorships in their irresponsibility toward their own people, and toward everything. What would have happened if they'd had the nuclear weapon? There is no way to make anything more than general projections of the situation, but I do believe that any concept of unilateral disarmament in the light of the preponderance of Russian military might and, for anyone who'll even look with one eye, their obvious intent is the height of irresponsibility and, for Christians, a denial of our own doctrine of the Fall.

CD: So you would distinguish between holding weapons as a defense and actually using them, even though holding them implies their use?

FAS: You have to ask for the alternative. What is the alternative if you're not going to hold them?

CD: Do you think something like the idea of the civilian population resisting would be too optimistic? In your analysis people would accept personal peace and affluence rather than, say, resisting an invader.

FAS: I think it would all depend on how close it came to home. There are two forms of pacifism, and they must be kept absolutely distinguished. The first is the old Christian pacifism of, say, Count Zinzendorf's people or the old historic Quakers. These people, I think, made the basic mistake of extending to the state the command to turn the other cheek, which is biblical (and none of us do it enough—you have to say that with absolute force). I don't feel that this is a proper extension. We must realize that we live in a fallen world, that, unhappily, as much as it grieves us, force is a necessary ingredient of the fallen world.

One thing that always interests me is that the pacifists don't take the locks off their front doors. But this biblical pacifism I respect very, very highly, and I honor these people, though I think they are mistaken. But this shouldn't be confused with the modern pacifism, the modern pacifism that controls, say, so much of our universities. It has no relationship to turning the other cheek; it is simply the fact that there is nothing worth fighting for. If they themselves were threatened, then I guess they would stir themselves.

This can fairly be paralleled in a different way, to humanitarianism in contrast to humanism. Christians ought to be humanitarian. I had a Jewish doctor talking to me in Switzerland, around a year ago. He wasn't a Christian, but he said, "I'll give you one thing. The only people helping the Boat People"—that was the time of the Boat People—"are the people who come from the Christian nations." I said, "Of course." This is the point of the way I would discuss all this. But I would add something. If we continue to throw away our humanness as exemplified by easy abortion, infanticide, euthanasia, etc., etc., if we are more and more taken up with our personal peace and affluence, even to the point of getting rid of my own baby before or after it's born, or my grandmother as she's a nuisance, I would make an absolute projection. There's going to be another group of boat people somewhere down the way, and the West isn't going to do anything about it. It's going to come, and it's coming with tremendous speed. I think these two things are related because I don't think the people who are the new kind of pacifist really care. I don't feel they care for anything except for what I call their personal peace and affluence, their own selfishness.

CD: Can I ask you a question about the background to your thinking? I understand that you studied under Van Til. I can see certain similarities between his emphasis upon presuppositions and yours. You are not what would be called a classical apologist. But perhaps I should go back a step further and ask if you see yourself primarily as an apologist in your work.

FAS: I'm glad you asked me this question because I personally do not consider myself a classical apologist, unless you define it in a certain way. If you merely mean developing a system that would be uniform everywhere at all places and that really means I can dwell in safety within that system, then I'm not an apologist. (Now I'm not being nasty toward anybody who has that calling—that's their business, but it isn't my interest, my calling.) I'm only interested in an apologetic that leads in two directions, and the one is to lead people to Christ, as Savior, and the other is that after they are Christians, for them to realize the lordship of Christ in the whole of life.

I don't believe there is any one apologetic that meets all the needs any more than I believe there is one form of evangelism that meets all the needs. So therefore, if I were in the Philippian jail with Paul and Silas, and the jailer says, "Sirs, what must I do to be saved?" this is no place to talk about apologetics, as it usually is conceived of. You say what Paul said: "Believe on the Lord Jesus Christ, and thou shalt be saved." On the other hand, if in your empathy and love—because now, I think, that's really the key, that you ought to approach every individual and lovingly try to find out where he is or she is—if in your empathy you find out that he or she is a person who still believes in truth, which is not the mark of our age, but there are still people who live there, and they're really troubled, let us say, about the historic evidences, the physical resurrection, then I think you ought to talk to them on that level. So this would then be what's usually called "evidences." But what I tried to show in *The God Who Is There*—and I must say when I rewrite it in these next few weeks [for the *Complete Works*], I realize I didn't make myself clear—all I tried to do and show there was not that what I was presenting was to be used with everybody, but even if people are twentieth-century people, there's still a way to talk to them, and then that's all. As I said, I don't think there's one form of apologetics for all people.

Now as far as presuppositions are concerned, I do believe they are crucial. I use the word a little differently from some British people. From my way of looking at them, presuppositions are not accepted by you unconsciously, as a prior condition to your first move of thought. For me, the proper way to get at it is that, if you are a thinking person, you decide what set of presuppositions are going to lead to the answers to the questions.

CD: Do you feel then that very often people need to have their basic presuppositions pointed out to them clearly so that they can see the logic of the position?

FAS: I think that a great number of people never think through what they're operating on, especially today. Most people, unhappily, accept their presuppositions unconsciously.

CD: Even educated people?

FAS: There is nobody so ignorant in these areas as the university graduate. The more they are caught in the system, the more they accept "what everybody thinks," the more blind they're apt to be—not thinking very simple things. You may begin with the molecule and chance. The really great thinkers realize the dilemma this presents concerning personality, significance, all these things. But masses of people who graduate from our best universities never once have thought where this mathematically leads—if I may put it that way. They have not thought where it absolutely leads. Interestingly enough, some intellectual writers are beginning to deal with the problems of the basic philosophy of outlook in these areas. In a way, this is a great moment for us. I am intrigued because what I read now a lot in some of the secular writers is what I put forth from the Christian side, way back in *The God Who Is There*.

CD: Aren't some of them involved in more philosophical astronomy?

FAS: In a way, philosophy is a folded subject at the moment. It is very intriguing that maybe the most imaginative areas of philosophy today are being dealt with in the area of particle physics and astronomy. They are really dealing with the dilemma of primal causes. For evangelicals this is a tremendous opportunity, if we only take advantage of it. But what bothers me is that just at this moment when we have a chance to deal with the wholeness of life, on the basis of biblical revelation, people such as David Winter and those he has popularized are throwing away all the areas of verification and falsification. It's very curious really but, to my mind, very sad. They don't seem to realize that we're undercutting our opportunity to speak just at the moment when I feel evangelicals have a tremendous opportunity. But you can't do it with a Bible that is divided existentially into spiritual things and what touches the wholeness of life.

CD: It's interesting that a number of years ago I interviewed

Professor Rookmaaker, and we were talking about you. He mentioned your booklet *The Mark of the Christian* and how he felt that the work of L'Abri was bringing together the intellectual and the devotional. In Britain there's been an emphasis upon the devotional, but there has been lots lacking in the intellectual. He felt that Holland had made a contribution in the intellectual field but lacked in the devotional. He felt, however, that L'Abri was bringing together these things through your work, and he cited *The Mark of the Christian* as an example of that. Do you think this bringing together the intellectual and the devotional is a major thrust of your work?

FAS: I would say if Christianity is truth, it ought to touch on the whole of life. The modern drift in some evangelical circles toward being emotionally and experientially based is really very, very weak. The other side of the coin, though, is that Christianity must never be reduced merely to an intellectual system. It too has to touch the whole of life, which means the devotional and so on. So to the extent that has been an emphasis of L'Abri, which I think it has, I'm thankful. I think it fits into the concept of the fullness of truth. After all, if God is there, [if] it isn't just an answer to an intellectual question, then he's really there. We should love him, we're called upon to adore him, to be in relationship to him, and, incidentally, to obey him.

We are in a pincer movement. On one hand you have the theological existentialists who are devaluating the Bible in making their division between the spiritual and the space-time cosmos. On the other hand you have people who claim to hold to the total authority of the Bible but who then, you find, are getting easy divorces and remarried. They go on being Christian leaders even though they have unbiblical divorces. In this pincer movement the Bible is being hit from two sides.

If God is really there, he is to be worshiped, he is to be adored, but he's also to be obeyed. Think back over the last ten years. How many sermons have you heard on "Thou shalt" and "Thou shalt not"? It is very few, curiously. If you listen with care to a great deal of the emotional Christianity that's being put forth, it is always what God can do for you. You hear nothing about what we're supposed to do for God. This is a tremendous lack. The concept of Christianity being truth and touching the fullness of life ought to contain all these elements. But then we would all have to say that none of us do it very well. We sure ought to struggle for it.

CD: Isn't this the kind of struggle you went through in the fifties which led to your book *True Spirituality*?

FAS: Yes, absolutely. Without those struggles I went through that led to *True Spirituality* I don't think L'Abri would ever have been born. I think the Lord has given us some intellectual answers. But you can't explain the way that L'Abri has spread over the face of the earth only on the intellectual answers. As poor as L'Abri is, there's been something there for which I'm thankful.

ACKNOWLEDGMENTS

In addition to those thanked in my Preface, grateful acknowledgment is made to the following:

Those specifically interviewed for this book (the interviewers are indicated as CC&PC = Christopher and Paulette Catherwood and CD = Colin Duriez) include:

Jerram and Vicki Barrs, July 1998, St. Louis, USA [CC&PC]

Everett and Jan Baumann, USA, August 8, 1998 [CC&PC]

Graham Birtwistle, May 18, 1998, PC Amsterdam, Holland [CD]

Lane and Ebeth Dennis, August 15, 1998, Wheaton, Illinois, USA [CC&PC]

Donald Drew, October 21, 1999, near Greatham, England [CD]

Phyllis Dunseth, October 30, 1998, Leicester, England [CD]

Stephen Duriez, April 22, 1998, East Budleigh, England [CD]

John Gillespie, August 8, 1998, Portrush, Northern Ireland [CD]

Os Guinness, August 29, 1998, McLean, Virginia, USA [CC&PC]

R. Laird and Ann Harris, August 6, 1998, Wilmington, Delaware, USA [CC&PC]

Marleen Hengalaar-Rookmaaker, May 16, 1998, Ommen, Holland [CD]

Dick and Mardi Keyes, August 7, 1998 [CC&PC]

Ranald Macaulay, October 31, 2006 Cambridge [CD]

Susan Macaulay, May 16, 2007 [CD]

Udo and Deborah Middelmann, March 21, 2007, Gryon, Switzerland [CD]

Wim and Greta Rietkierk, May 17, 1998, Utrecht, Holland [CD]

Anna Maria "Anky" Rookmaaker, May 15, 1998, Ommen, Holland [CD]

Hans R. Rookmaaker, November 30, 1971, Shropshire, England [CD]

John and Priscilla Sandri, March 20, 2007, Huémoz, Switzerland [CD]

Francis Schaeffer, September 30, 1980, Liss, England [CD]
Larry and Nancy Snyder, August 7, 1998 [CC&PC]
Hans Van Seventer, May 16, 1998, Aduard, Holland [CD]
Joanne Van Seventer, May 16, 1998, Aduard, Holland [CD]
John and Maria Walford, August 13, 1998, Wheaton, Illinois, USA
[CC&PC]
Richard and Jane Winter, August 11, 1998, St. Louis, USA
[CC&PC]
Hurvey and Dorothy Woodson, August 12, 1998, St. Louis, USA
[CC&PC]

Others who contributed with memories, wisdom, or encouragement
include the late David Porter, Trisha Porter, Oliver Barclay, Geraint
Fielder, the late John Marsh, Wade Bradshaw, Andrew Fellows, and
many others.

Thanks are also due to Baker Book House for permission to draw
upon and adapt my chapter "Francis Schaeffer," from *Handbook of
Evangelical Theologians*, edited by Walter Elwell (Baker Academic, a
division of Baker Publishing Group, 1993); to The Francis A. Schaeffer
Foundation on behalf of Edith Schaeffer for permission to reproduce
hitherto unpublished and out-of-print material by Francis and Edith
Schaeffer; to the same for supplying and allowing the use of the pho-
tographs in this book, and to David McCasland for his kind assistance
in making this possible; to Rev. Dieter Zellweger of the Karl Barth-
Nachlasskommission for use of the letter of Karl Barth to Francis
Schaeffer; and to Dr. Hans-Anton Drewes of the Karl Barth Archive and
Dr. Wayne Sparkman of the PCA Historical Center for assistance.

BIBLIOGRAPHY

Baird, Forrest. "Schaeffer's Intellectual Roots," in Ronald Ruegsegger, *Reflections on Francis Schaeffer*. Grand Rapids, MI: Zondervan, 1986.

Barclay, Oliver. *Evangelicalism in Britain 1935–1995: A Personal Sketch*. Leicester, UK: Inter-Varsity Press, 1997.

Bradshaw, Wade. *By Demonstration: God: Fifty Years and a Week at L'Abri*. Carlisle, UK: Piquant, 2005.

Burson, Scott R. and Jerry L. Walls, *C. S. Lewis and Francis Schaeffer: Lessons for a New Century from the Most Influential Apologists of Our Time*. Downers Grove, IL: InterVarsity Press, 1998.

Carlson, Betty. *Absolutely and the Golden Eggs*. Huémoz, Switzerland: Le Petit Muveran Publishers, n.d.

————————. *The Unhurried Chase*. Wheaton, IL: Tyndale House, 1970.

Catherwood, Christopher. *Five Evangelical Leaders*. Wheaton, IL: Harold Shaw, 1985. New edition, Fearn, Ross-shire, UK: Christian Focus Publications, 1994.

Dennis, Lane T. *Conversion in an Evangelical Context: A Study in the Micro-Sociology of Religion*. PhD dissertation, Northwestern University, 1980.

Dennis, Lane T., editor. *Francis A. Schaeffer: Portraits of the Man and His Work*. Wheaton, IL: Crossway Books, 1986.

————————. *The Letters of Francis Schaeffer*. Wheaton, IL: Crossway Books, 1986; Eastbourne, UK: Kingsway Publications, 1986.

Dooyeweerd, Herman. *A New Critique of Theoretical Thought*, 4 vols. Philadelphia: Presbyterian & Reformed, 1953–1958.

————————. *The Roots of Western Culture*. Toronto: Wedge, 1979.

_____. *In the Twilight of Western Thought*. Nutley, NJ: Craig Press, 1960.

Duriez, Colin. "Francis Schaeffer—Facing Up to the Central Questions." *Third Way*, 4.1, December 1980: 5–8.

_____. "Francis Schaeffer," in Walter A. Elwell, editor, *Handbook of Evangelical Theologians*. Grand Rapids, MI: Baker, 1993.

_____. "Interview with H. R. Rookmaaker." *Crusade*, April 1972. A fuller version is published in Marleen Hengelaar-Rookmaaker, editor, *The Complete Works of Hans Rookmaaker*, Vol. 6.

Follis, Bryan A. *Truth with Love: The Apologetics of Francis Schaeffer*. Wheaton, IL: Crossway Books, 2006.

Gasque, Laurel. *Hans Rookmaaker: An Open Life*, in Marleen Hengelaar-Rookmaaker, editor, *The Complete Works of Hans R. Rookmaaker*, Vol. 6. Carlisle, UK: Piquant, 2003.

Geehan, E. R., editor. *Jerusalem and Athens: Critical Discussions on the Philosophy and Apologetics of Cornelius Van Til*. Phillipsburg, NJ: Presbyterian & Reformed, 1980.

Geisler, Norman L. *Thomas Aquinas: An Evangelical Appraisal*. Grand Rapids, MI: Baker, 1991.

Hamilton, Michael S. "The Dissatisfaction of Francis Schaeffer," *Christianity Today*, March 3, 1997.

Hart, D. G., editor. *Dictionary of the Presbyterian and Reformed Tradition in America*. Downers Grove, IL: InterVarsity Press, 1999.

Henderson, Stewart, editor and compiler. *Adrift in the Eighties: The Strait Interviews*. Basingstoke, UK: Marshall, Morgan & Scott, 1986.

Hengelaar-Rookmaaker, Marleen, editor. *The Complete Works of Hans R. Rookmaaker*, 6 volumes. Carlisle, UK: Piquant, 2002–2003.

Inter-Varsity Christian Fellowship, *Introduction to Francis Schaeffer: Study Guide to a Trilogy*. London: Hodder and Stoughton, 1975.

Jacobs, Sylvester, with Linette Martin. *Portrait of a Shelter*. Downers Grove, IL: InterVarsity Press, 1973.

_____. *Born Black*. London: Hodder and Stoughton, 1977.

Johnson, Daymon A. *Francis A. Schaeffer: An Analysis of His Religious, Social, and Political Influence on the New Christian Right*. MA dissertation, history, California State University, 1990.

Kalsbeek, L. *Contours of a Christian Philosophy*. Toronto: Wedge, 1975.

Koop, C. Everett, M.D. *Koop: The Memoirs of America's Family Doctor*. New York: Random House, 1991.

Leigh, David R. *Two Apologists: Cornelius Van Til and Francis Schaeffer*. MA thesis, Wheaton College Graduate School, 1990.

Lewis, C. S. *The Allegory of Love*. New York: Oxford University Press, 1958.

_____. *De Descriptione Temporum*, in C. S. Lewis, *Selected Literary Essays*, Walter Hooper, editor. New York: Cambridge University Press, 1969.

_____. *The Discarded Image*. New York: Cambridge University Press, 1964.

_____. *Selected Literary Essays*. Walter Hooper, editor. New York: Cambridge University Press, 1969.

Machen, J. Gresham. *Christianity and Liberalism*. Grand Rapids, MI: Eerdmans, 1923.

Marshall, Catherine. *Something More*. Grand Rapids, MI: Chosen Books, 1974.

Martin, Linette. *Hans Rookmaaker: A Biography*. London: Hodder and Stoughton, 1979.

Morris, Thomas V. *Francis Schaeffer's Apologetics: A Critique*. Chicago: Moody, 1976.

Parkhurst, L. G. *Francis Schaeffer: The Man and His Message*. Eastbourne: Kingsway Publications, 1986.

Porter, David. *Arts and Minds: The Story of Nigel Goodwin*. London: Hodder and Stoughton, 1993.

Rookmaaker, Hans R. "A Dutch Christian's View of Philosophy," in Marleen Hengelaar-Rookmaaker, editor, *The Complete Works of Hans Rookmaaker*, Vol. 6. Carlisle, UK: Piquant, 2003.

_____. *Art and the Public Today*, second edition. Hué-moz-sur-Ollon, Switzerland: L'Abri Fellowship, 1969.

Ruegsegger, Ronald, *Reflections on Francis Schaeffer*. Grand Rapids, MI: Zondervan, 1986.

Schaeffer, Edith. *Christianity Is Jewish*. London and Eastbourne, UK: Coverdale House, 1975.

_____. *Common Sense Christian Living*. Nashville: Thomas Nelson, 1983.

_____. *Dear Family: The L'Abri Family Letters 1961–1986*. San Francisco: Harper and Row, 1989.

_____. *L'Abri*, revised edition. Wheaton, IL: Crossway Books, 1992.

_____. *The Tapestry*. Nashville: Word, 1981.

_____. *With Love, Edith: The L'Abri Family Letters 1948–1960*. San Francisco: Harper and Row, 1988.

Schaeffer, Francis A. *The Complete Works of Francis A. Schaeffer*, 5 vols. Wheaton, IL: Crossway Books, 1982.

_____. *How Should We Then Live?* Grand Rapids, MI: Revell, 1976.

_____. *The Letters of Francis A. Schaeffer*. Lane T. Dennis, editor. Wheaton, IL: Crossway Books, 1986.

_____. "The Lord's Work in the Lord's Way," in *No Little People*, in *Complete Works*, Vol. 3, second edition. Wheaton, IL: Crossway Books, 1985.

Schaeffer, Francis A. and C. Everett Koop, *Whatever Happened to the Human Race?* Grand Rapids, MI: Revell, 1979.

Schaeffer, Francis and Edith, *Everybody Can Know*. Wheaton, IL: Tyndale, 1973.

Schaeffer, Frank. *Crazy for God: How I Grew Up as One of the Elect, Helped Found the Religious Right, and Lived to Take All (or Almost All) of It Back*. New York: Carroll & Graf, 2007.

_____. *Portofino*. New York: Macmillan, 1992.

_____. *Saving Grandma*. New York: Berkley Books, 1997.

_____. *Zermatt*. New York: Carroll and Graf, 2003.

Stonehouse, Ned B. *J. Gresham Machen: A Biographical Memoir*. Edinburgh: The Banner of Truth Trust, 1987.

Stout, Harry S., Daniel G. Reid, Robert D. Linder, and Bruce L. Shelley, editors, *Dictionary of Christianity in America*. Downers Grove, IL: InterVarsity Press, 1990.

Walls, Jerry L. and Scott R. Burson. *C. S. Lewis and Francis Schaeffer: Lessons for a New Century from the Most Influential Apologists of Our Time*. Downers Grove, IL: InterVarsity Press, 1998.

Winter, David. *Winter's Tale: Living Through an Age of Change in Church and Media*. Oxford, UK: Lion Publishing, 2001.

Yancey, Philip. *Open Windows*. Wheaton, IL: Crossway Books, 1982.

INDEX

Abolition of Man, The (Lewis), 182

Abortion, 183, 189, 190, 191, 192, 209, 217 see also *Unborn children*

Abrahamson, Ruth, 137

Absolutely and the Golden Eggs (Carlson), 225

Absolutes, 168, 176
arbitrary absolutes, 189

Adam and Eve, 201

Addicted to Mediocrity (Frank Schaeffer), 117

Adrift in the Eighties: The Strait Interviews (Henderson, editor, compiler), 226

Afghanistan, 214, 215

Alexander, Hugh, 84

Allegory of Love, The (Lewis), 227

Allen, Dennison Maurice, 29

Allis, Oswald T., 34

American Council of Christian Churches, 49, 59, 61, 62, 63, 72, 75

Angola, 215

Anti-Semitism, 56, 179

Aquinas, Thomas, 40, 41, 101, 165, 168, 169, 171, 172

post-Aquinas, 169

Aristotle, 172

Arts and Minds: The Story of Nigel Goodwin (Porter), 227

Art and the Public Today (Rookmaaker), 228

Baird, Forrest, 62

Bakersfield College, 193

Baldung, Hans, 115

Barclay, Oliver, 167, 225

Barth, Karl, 40, 41, 65, 66, 67, 86, 94, 95, 96, 97, 98, 99, 100, 101, 166, 206
neo-Barthianism, 85, 95, 98

Basic Bible Studies (Francis Schaeffer), 166 also see *25 Basic Bible Studies*

Beatles, the, 165

Bell, Lidie C., 18

Bennet, James E., 96

Berkouwer, Gerrit Cornelis, 68

"Bible-believing Christian and the Jew, The" (Francis Schaeffer), 56

Bible Presbyterian Church, 43, 45, 48, 49, 51, 59, 71, 94, 122

Bible Protestant Church, 49

Bible Today, The, 87, 117

Bloom, Ed, 30, 31

Born Black (Jacobs), 227

Boxer Rebellion, 29

Bradshaw, Wade, 225

Bragdon, Janet, 64

Brainerd, David, 90

Brown, Harold O. J., 114, 160

Brunner, Emil, 166, 206

Buchfuehrer, Jim, 190

Burson, Scott R., 225, 229

Buswell, Oliver, 41, 43, 87, 96, 97, 99, 100, 101, 121, 122

But This I Can Believe (Winter), 205-206

By Demonstration: God: Fifty Years and a Week at L'Abri (Bradshaw), 225

Calvin, John, 89

Camp Richard Webber, 38

Camus, Albert, 206

Carlson, Betty, 117, 118, 119, 225

Carmichael, Amy, 181

Carnell, E. J., 87

Catherwood, Christopher, 10, 13, 225

Catherwood, Paulette, 10, 13

Chestnut, Sam, father of, 24

Chaudet, Paul, 131

Child Evangelism Fellowship, 57, 61, 62

Children for Christ, 11, 48, 58, 59, 60, 61, 62, 63, 77, 84, 85, 86, 92, 95, 112, 117, 139

China, 29, 30, 76

China Inland Mission, 29, 30, 163 also see *Overseas Missionary Fellowship*

China's Millions, 30

"Christian and Modern Art, The" (Francis Schaeffer), 114, 117

Christian Beacon, The, 39, 90

Christianity and Liberalism (Machen), 31, 33, 227

Christianity Is Jewish (Edith Schaeffer), 228

Christianity Today, 181

Christian Manifesto, A (Francis Schaeffer), 191, 193, 194

Christian Right, the, 171, 190, 193, 194 also see *Evangelical Right; Religious Right*

Church Before the Watching World, The (Francis Schaeffer), 188

Civil disobedience, 191, 193

Civilisation (Clark), 183, 185, 209

Clapton, Eric, 200

Clark, Kenneth, 183, 185, 209

Colson, Charles, 182

Common Sense Christian Living (Edith Schaeffer), 228

Complete Works of Francis A. Schaeffer, 172, 177, 178, 179, 188, 199, 218, 228

Complete Works of H. R. Rookmaaker, 77, 226, 227

Contours of a Christian Philosophy (Kalsbeek), 227

Conversion in an Evangelical Context: A Study in the Micro-Sociology of Religion (Dennis), 225

Covenant College, 122

Covenant Seminary, 52, 97, 122, 161

Crazy for God: How I Grew Up as One of the Elect, Helped Found the Religious Right, and Lived to Take All (or Almost All) of It Back (Frank Schaeffer), 12, 154, 190, 228

C. S. Lewis and Francis Schaeffer: Lessons for a New Century from the Most Influential Apologists of Our Time (Burson/Walls), 225, 229

Cuba, 215

Cunningham, Merce, 9

Davidson, Francis, 68

Dear Family: The L'Abri Family Letters 1961–1986 (Edith Schaeffer), 228

Death in the City (Francis Schaeffer), 160

Dali, Salvador, 164

da Vinci, Leonardo, 169

"De Descriptione Temporum" (Lewis), 227

Deism, 173

Delvaux, Paul, 98, 115

Dennis, Lane, 13, 106, 199, 225

Der Spiegel, 191

Descartes, Rene, 173

Dictionary of Christianity in America (Stout/Reid/Linder/ Shelley), 229

Dictionary of the Presbyterian and Reformed Tradition in America (Hart, editor), 226

Discarded Image, The (Lewis), 227

Dispensationalism, 42

"Dissatisfaction of Francis Schaeffer, The" (Hamilton), 226

Dobson, James, 194

Dooyeweerd, Herman, 40, 41, 79, 172, 173, 174, 175, 225

Drexel Institute, 23, 25

Duchamp, Marcel, 37

Ducker, Richard and Deidre, 157

"Dutch Christian's View of Philosophy," A" (Rookmaaker), 227

Dylan, Bob, 9, 154, 164, 165

Ecumenical movement, 67, 74, 84

Eighties, the, 213, 214

Elwell, Walter A., 226

Empire Builder for Boys (Francis and Edith Schaeffer), 58, 166

Empire Builder for Girls (Francis and Edith Schaeffer), 58, 166

England, Edward, 176

Enlightenment, the, 18, 79, 171

Escape from Reason (Francis Schaeffer), 160, 165, 167, 168, 170, 171, 172, 173, 174, 175, 176, 178, 179, 181, 184, 200, 209

Eschatology, 201, 202
   premillennialist, 42, 43, 51, 201, 202

Ethiopia, 215

Euthanasia, 183, 189, 190, 191, 217

Evangelicalism in Britain 1935–1995: A Personal Sketch (Barclay), 225

Evangelical Right, the, 191 also see *Christian Right; Religious Right*

Evangelische Omroep, 184

Everybody Can Know (Edith and Francis Schaeffer), 179, 228

Evidentialism, 177
Exhenry, Georges, 129, 130, 138
Existentialism, 13, 79, 171, 220

Faith Seminary, 41, 43, 44, 45, 46,
    48, 52, 72, 94, 121, 141
Falwell, Jerry, 194
Farel, William, 157
Federal Council of Churches, 49
    also see *National Council of
    Churches*
Fellini, Federico, 164
Fielder, Geraint, 167
Finished Work of Christ, The
    (Francis Schaeffer), 140
Five Evangelical Leaders (Cather-
    wood), 225
Follis, Bryan A., 35, 226
Fosdick, Harry Emerson, 66
Foucault, Michel, 155
Foundationalism, 177
*Francis A. Schaeffer: An Analysis
    of His Religious, Social, and
    Political Influence on the New
    Christian Right* (Johnson), 227
*Francis A. Schaeffer: Portraits of
    the Man and His Work* (Dennis,
    editor), 225
"Francis Schaeffer" (Duriez), 226
"Francis Schaeffer—Facing Up to
    the Central Questions" (Duriez),
    205, 226
Francis Schaeffer's Apologetics
    (Morris), 227
*Francis Schaeffer: The Man and
    His Message* (Parkhurst), 227
Franky Schaeffer V Productions,
    190

Freedom, 169, 170, 171, 172, 188,
    201
Free speech movement, 153
Free University of Amsterdam, 167
Freud, Sigmund, 171
Fundamentalism, 9, 33, 40, 49,
    66, 97, 99, 100, 108, 154, 182,
    193, 194, 206

Gasque, Laurel, 226
Geehan, E. R., 226
Geisler, Norman L., 226
Genesis in Space and Time (Francis
    Schaeffer), 201
Gilson, M., 172
Gnosticism, 201
God Who Is There, The (Francis
    Schaeffer), 12, 106, 160, 162,
    174, 175, 176, 177, 178, 179,
    181, 184, 202, 207, 208, 209,
    218, 219
Gospel Films, 184, 186, 190
Govier, Gordon, 181
Grace, 168, 169, 170, 171, 172,
    173, 174, 210
Graham, Billy, 181
Great Evangelical Disaster, The
    (Francis Schaeffer), 199
Greece, ancient, 168, 175
Greene, Walter, 30
Guinness, Os, 71, 164, 204, 214

Hallesby, Ole, 67, 68
Hamilton, Michael S., 226
Hampden-Sydney College, 24, 25,
    26, 27, 29, 30, 31, 35, 36
*Handbook of Evangelical Theolo-
    gians* (Elwell, editor), 226

Hans Rookmaaker: A Biography (Martin), 227

Hans Rookmaaker: An Open Life (Gasque), 226

Harris, Ann, 72

Harris, R. Laird, 43, 44

Hart, D. G., 226

Harvard, 200

Hegel, George Frederick, 42, 101, 170, 176

Heidegger, Martin, 9, 206

He Is There and He Is Not Silent (Francis Schaeffer), 160, 174, 178, 181

Henderson, Stewart, 226

Hengelaar, Marleen and Albert, 14 Marleen (Rookmaaker), 149, 226, 227

Henry, Carl F. H., 182

Herrell, Marte, 140

Highland College, 122

Hodder and Stoughton, 176

Hoffman, Charlie, 26

Holdcroft, J. Gordon, 73

Hooper, Walter, 227

Houghton, Frank, 68

How Should We Then Live? (Francis Schaeffer; book and film), 113, 172, 183, 184, 186, 187, 188, 189, 191, 194, 197, 198, 204, 209, 210, 212, 213, 214, 228

Huitker, Anky see *Rookmaaker, Anky*

Humanism, 168, 217

Independent Board for Presbyterian Foreign Missions, 34, 59, 62, 72, 73, 105, 117, 121, 122, 132

Infanticide, 183, 189, 190, 191, 217

International Church, the, 129, 139

International Council of Christian Churches, 73, 76, 84, 89, 94, 97

International Council on Biblical Inerrancy, 200

Inter-Varsity Fellowship/Inter-Varsity Christian Fellowship, 148, 165, 167, 181, 226

"Interview with H. R. Rookmaaker" (Duriez), 226

In the Twilight of Western Thought (Dooyeweerd), 174, 226

Introduction to Christian Apologetics, An (Carnell), 87

Introduction to Francis Schaeffer: Study Guide to a Trilogy (IVCF), 226

Jackson, Jeremy, 157

Jacobs, Sylvester, 135, 165, 166, 226, 227

Jamison, Dorothy ("Dot"), 137, 138 also see *Woodson, Dorothy*

Jerusalem and Athens: Critical Discussions on the Philosophy and Apologetics of Cornelius Van Til (Geehan, editor), 226

Jesson, Greg, 161, 162

J. Gresham Machen: A Biographical Memoir (Stonehouse), 229

Johnson, Daymon, 193, 194, 227

Joyce, Mary (Williamson), 15, 16

Joyce, William, 15

Just war, 215

Kalsbeek, L., 227

Ketchum, R. T., 61
Keyes, Dick and Mardi, 196
Kierkegaard, Søren, 101, 170, 171, 172, 176
Kok, Arie, 76
Koop, C. Everett, 74, 179, 189, 194, 195, 227, 228
Koop: The Memoirs of America's Family Doctor (Koop), 195, 227
Krause, John, 44
Kuiper, R. B., 34
Kuyper, Abraham, 79, 175

L'Abri (Edith Schaeffer), 127, 156, 228
L'Abri Fellowship, 9, 11, 12, 13, 29, 36, 37, 38, 44, 50, 57, 78, 79, 87, 89, 91, 105, 109, 112, 119, 127, 128, 129, 132, 133, 135, 137, 138, 139, 140, 141, 142, 147, 148, 149, 150, 154, 155, 156, 157, 158, 159, 166, 174, 181, 183, 185, 186, 187, 190, 193, 198, 200, 203, 204, 207, 208, 211, 220, 221
    English L'Abri, 148, 167, 196, 198, 211
    Rochester, Minnesota, 196, 197, 198, 210, 211
    Southborough, Massachusetts, 196
LaHaye, Tim, 194
Lathem, A. (Abraham) L., 48
Leary, Timothy, 200
Led Zeppelin, 200
Leigh, David R., 40, 227
Letters of Francis Schaeffer, The (Dennis, editor), 225, 228

Lewis, C. S., 10, 84, 165, 170, 172, 181, 182, 227
Liberalism, theological, 11, 18, 33, 40, 51, 62, 66, 67, 85, 86, 206
Linder, Robert D., 229
Lloyd-Jones, Martyn, 68
"Lord's Work in the Lord's Way, The" (Francis Schaeffer), 228

Macaulay, Ranald and Susan, 13, 148
    Ranald, 157
    Susan (Schaeffer), 48, 49, 53, 54, 58, 59, 81, 82, 83, 92, 93, 107, 112, 118, 120, 122, 123, 134, 140, 147, 157, 203
McClusky, Evelyn M., 48
Machen, J. Gresham, 31, 33, 34, 35, 38, 39, 43, 60, 87, 199, 227
McIntire, Carl, 35, 39, 43, 49, 54, 61, 90, 121, 122
McLuhan, Marshall, 165
MacRae, Allan A., 34, 37, 43, 87
Marcuse, Herbert, 154, 213
Mark of the Christian, The (Francis Schaeffer), 199, 220
Marsh, John, 167
Marshall, Catherine, 227
Martin, Linette, 226, 227
Mason, Charlotte, 93
Massey, J. B., 29
Mayo Clinic, 195, 196, 197, 199, 210
Mekkes, J. P. A., 175
Memoirs (Koop) see *Koop: The Memoirs of America's Family Doctor*
Middelmann, Udo and Deborah, 13

Deborah (Schaeffer), 17, 18, 54, 68, 82, 83, 95, 105, 109, 110, 118, 120, 130, 139, 147, 150, 157, 202, 203
Udo, 97, 110, 157
Middle Ages, the, 168
Milton, John, 10
Miracles (Lewis), 165
Modernism, New Modernism, 13, 33, 34, 40, 41, 51, 56, 66, 74, 95, 96, 97, 98, 99, 110, 114, 115, 117, 155, 171
Moral Majority, the, 191
Morlock, Carl, 195
Morris, Thomas V., 227
Morton, Johnny, 27
Mueller (Schaeffer), Carolina Wilhelmina, 16
Muggeridge, Malcolm, 196

National Council of Churches, 49
Nature, 168, 169, 171, 172, 173, 174
Neo-orthodoxy, 9, 13, 29, 40, 62, 66, 67, 74, 84, 86
New Critique of Theoretical Thought, A (Dooyeweerd), 40, 225
New Left, the, 213
Niebuhr, Reinhold, 66, 67, 98, 166, 206
Nietzsche, Friedrich, 171, 176
No Little People (Francis Schaeffer), 121, 228
Nuclear weapons, 215, 216

Ockenga, Harold John, 38, 39
Open Windows (Yancey), 229
Operation Mobilization, 167

Operation Rescue, 194
Orthodox Presbyterian Church, 35, 38
Osborne, Sam, 25
Otten, Dr., 130
Overseas Missionary Fellowship, 29

Pacifism, 216, 217
Page, Jimmy, 200
Pantheism, 173
Parents National Education Union (PNEU), 93
Parkhurst, L. G., 227
Particulars, 169
Paterson, John, 165
Paul, the apostle, 177, 202, 218
Pietà (Michelangelo), 184
Pike, Bishop James A., 200
Plato, 88
Poland, 215
Pollock, Jackson, 9
Pollution and the Death of Man (Francis Schaeffer), 179
Porter, David, 227
Portofino (Frank Schaeffer), 117, 228
Portrait of a Shelter (Jacobs/Martin), 226
Postmodernism, 9, 13, 155, 171
Powell, Robert Baden, 58
Prayer (Hallesby), 67
Presbyterian Board of Foreign Missions, 34
Presbyterian Church USA, 34, 51
Presbyterian Church of America (PCA), 10, 61
Presuppositionalism, 177

Presuppositions, 177, 217, 218, 219

Princeton Seminary, 34, 199, 201

Quakers, the, 216

Rationalism, 168, 169
Rationality, 170
Rayburn, Robert, 122
Reagan, President Ronald, 189, 191, 192, 204
Reflections on Francis Schaeffer (Ruegsegger), 225, 228
Reformation, Protestant, 169, 187
Reid, Daniel G., 229
Relativism, 42, 176, 191
Rembrandt, 115
Revelation, biblical, 169, 170, 219
Religious Right, the, 191 also see *Christian Right; Evangelical Right*
Right to Live, Right to Die, The (Koop), 189-190
Robertson, Pat, 194
Rolling Stones, the, 165
Roman Catholic Church, 74, 86, 113, 114, 189, 192, 194
Rome, ancient, 168, 184, 192
Rookmaaker, Anky, 14, 77, 85, 149
Rookmaaker, Hans, 11, 12, 45, 57, 76, 77, 78, 79, 80, 85, 86, 115, 146, 148, 149, 159, 165, 173, 174, 175, 184, 186, 187, 202, 220, 227, 228
Ruegsegger, Ronald, 225, 228
Russia, 214, 215, 216 also see *USSR*
Rutherford Institute, 194

Sanderson, John W. Jr., 52
Sandri, John and Prisca, 13
  John, 21, 26, 136, 137, 147
  Priscilla (Schaeffer), 44, 45, 53, 54, 60, 68, 71, 74, 75, 83, 92, 93, 95, 111, 118, 120, 123, 135, 136, 137, 138, 147
Santayana, George, 137
Sartre, Jean-Paul, 206
Saving Grandma (Frank Schaeffer), 16, 117, 228
Schaeffer, Edith, see esp. 10, 11, 13, 17, 30, 31, 33, 35, 36, 37, 42, 43, 44, 61, 63, 71, 74, 76, 82, 90, 91, 108, 124, 127, 131, 142, 144, 149, 159, 160, 163, 179, 181, 184, 185, 186, 187, 202, 204, 208, 228
Schaeffer, Francis August II (Franz), 16
Schaeffer, Francis August III (Frank), father of Francis Schaeffer, 16, 17, 23, 25, 49, 50
Schaeffer, Frank (Francis August Schaeffer V; Franky), 10, 117, 121, 124, 127, 137, 143, 147, 154, 157, 162, 183, 184, 189, 190, 194, 200, 208, 228
Science, 169, 170, 201
Scofield Reference Bible, 42
Scripture Union, 57
Selected Literary Essays (Lewis; Hooper, editor), 227
Seventies, the, 213, 214
Seville, Edith, 29 also see *Schaeffer, Edith*
Seville, George, 29, 36, 44, 138, 186

Shelley, Bruce L., 229
Shelton College, 96, 121
Shorter Westminster Confession, 89
Silas, 177, 218
Sixties, the, 9, 148, 153, 154, 213, 214
Smick, Elmer and Jane, 64
Smith, Jane Stuart, 129, 184
Solzhenitsyn, Aleksandr, 214
Something More (Marshall), 227
Spetter, Hendrika Beatrix (Riki), 56, 57, 78
Stam, Peter, 96
Stonehouse, Ned B., 34, 229
Stott, John, 196, 215
Stout, Harry S., 229
Student Christian Association, 27
Supreme Court, the, 189, 209
Surprised by Joy (Lewis), 165

Tapestry, The (Edith Schaeffer), 87, 159, 228
Taylor, Hudson, 29, 163, 181
Terry, Randall, 194
That Hideous Strength (Lewis), 182
Third Way, 205
Thomas, Cal, 194
Thomas, Dylan, 202
Thomas Aquinas: An Evangelical Appraisal (Geisler), 226
't Hooft, Visser, 65, 67, 76
Tillich, Paul, 166, 206
Time Magazine, 204
Tractarians, 206
True Spirituality (Francis Schaeffer), 89, 104, 105, 107, 108, 109, 179, 221

Truth with Love: The Apologetics of Francis Schaeffer (Follis), 226
25 Basic Bible Studies (Francis Schaeffer), 130
Two Apologists: Cornelius Van Til and Francis Schaeffer (Leigh), 227

Unborn children, rights of, 182
Unhurried Chase, The (Carlson), 225
Union Theological Seminary, 26, 200
Universals, 168, 169, 170
USSR, 193

Van Buskirk, 64
Van Gogh, 184
Van Prinsterer, Groen, 79, 175
Van Til, Cornelius, 34, 37, 40, 41, 79, 87, 173, 175, 206, 217
Vatican II, 114

Wahby, Victor, 195
Walls, Jerry L., 225, 229
Warfield, B. B., 201
West, the, Western thought, 41, 154, 159, 165, 172, 173, 174, 175, 178, 182, 184, 185, 187, 191, 192, 215, 217
Westminster Confession, 51
Westminster Seminary (Philadelphia), 31, 32, 33, 34, 37, 38, 39, 40, 41, 42, 43, 46, 87
Westmont College, 162
Whatever Happened to the Human Race? (Francis Schaeffer/Koop; book and film), 13, 74, 186,

188, 190, 191, 192, 194, 195, 196, 209, 228

Wheaton College, 41, 96, 161, 208

Whitehead, John, 194

Williamson (Schaeffer), Bessie, mother of Francis Schaeffer, 15, 16, 17, 160

Williamson, Wallace, 15

Wilmer, Val, 166

Wilson, David, 29

Wilson, Robert D., 31, 34

Winter, David, 205, 206, 219, 229

Winter's Tale: Living Through an Age of Change in Church and Media (Winter), 229

With Love, Edith: The L'Abri Family Letters 1948–1960 (Edith Schaeffer), 228

Wittgenstein, 9

Woodson, Dorothy, 140, 141, 142, 143, 144, 145

Woodson, Hurvey, 57, 61, 140, 141, 142, 143, 144, 145, 146

Woodson, Karl, 136

Woolley, Paul, 34, 36

Word of God and the Word of Man, The (Barth), 40

World Council of Churches, 49, 65, 68, 76

World War I, 56

World War II, 55, 56, 58, 59, 62, 182

Wright, J. Elwin, 39

Yale, 200

Yancey, Philip, 229

Young, G. Douglas, 96

Zeoli, Anthony, 23, 184

Zeoli, Billy, 184

Zermatt (Frank Schaeffer), 117, 228

Zinzendorf, Count, 216

Zorn, E. G., 61